THE NEW MEDIA MONOPOLY

THE NEW MEDIA
MONOPOLY

BEN H. BAGDIKIAN

BEACON PRESS
BOSTON

BEACON
150

BEACON PRESS
25 Beacon Street
Boston, Massachusetts 02108-2892
www.beacon.org

Beacon Press books
are published under the auspices of
the Unitarian Universalist Association of Congregations.

08 07 06 05 04 8 7 6 5 4 3 2

This book is printed on acid-free paper that meets the uncoated paper
ANSI/NISO specifications for permanence as revised in 1992.

Text design by Isaac Tobin
Composition by Wilsted & Taylor Publishing Services

LIBRARY OF CONGRESS CATALOGING-IN-PUBLICATION DATA

Bagdikian, Ben H.
    The new media monopoly / Ben H. Bagdikian.
    p. cm.
"A completely revised and updated edition of the best-selling classic
The media monopoly."
Includes bibliographical references and index.
    ISBN 0-8070-6187-5 (alk. paper)
    1. Mass media—Ownership.
    I. Bagdikian, Ben H. Media monopoly.
    II. Title.

P96.E25B34 2004
338.4′730223′0973—dc22   2003022381

CONTENTS

In this job, you have to ask the questions that tend toward greater fairness. Without the right questions, you'll never get the facts that will lead you to better answers.

DAVID BAZELON, Chief Justice of the United States Court of Appeals of the District of Columbia Circuit, 1964

FOREWORD

In the years since 1980, the political spectrum of the United States has shifted radically to the far right. What was once the center has been pushed to the left, and what was the far right is now the center. What was considered the eccentric right wing of American politics is now considered the normal conservative outlook. What was the left is now at the far edge, barely holding its precarious position and treated in the news as a sometimes amusing oddity. Republican conservatives dismiss in ridicule more moderate Republicans as heretical "Eastern moderates" or "Rockefeller Republicans" (after the former Republican vice president under President Gerald Ford in 1974).

Within the Democratic Party, conservatives in the Congressional Leadership Council have for decades pushed their party more toward what they call "the center." This included President William Clinton (1993–2001), who sponsored liberal programs but as former leader of the Democratic Leadership Council was committed to centrist initiatives and had to contend with a running battle against impeachment launched by a Republican House of Representatives. The result has been that over the years, the Republican and Democratic parties have continued to overlap so much that, as Democrats have moved toward the right, conservatives have moved to the far right.

This shift has had sweeping consequences. It has muffled social justice as a governing principle in government agencies. It has granted advantages to the wealthy and to large corporations at the expense of the middle and working classes. It has reversed earlier reforms by starving agencies like the Securities and Exchange Commission and tried to privatize Social Security, enacted under President Franklin Roosevelt, a Democrat, in the 1930s. It has cut back conservation and environmental laws first enacted by President Theodore Roosevelt, a Republican, at the turn of the twentieth century. These changes have presented to American voters the narrowest range of political and ideological choices among all industrial democracies in the world. The choices are increasingly disconnected from the country's most urgent social and economic problems.

Money from corporations and the most wealthy citizens provides most campaign funds. It pays for the corporate Washington law firms and lobbyists that influence what legislation will be introduced or disappear quietly in a congressional committee and never emerge for public debate or an open vote by the House and Senate. Money is still the mother's milk of American politics. It pays for the expensive television political advertisements and mass mailings, and it is in the nature of wealth and politics that most of this money comes from conservative sources. The major mass media have played a central role in this shift to the right.

The daily printed and broadcast news on which most Americans depend has always selected as its basic sources the titled leaders of the corporate and political world. These sources are legitimate elements in the news since these leaders make decisions that have a major influence on the country and on the world. But in a democracy more is needed. There is another side to national realities. It is the news and views of organizations whose serious studies document urgent needs of the middle class and the poor and of tax-supported basic institutions like the public schools.

Yet, only in minor, specialized exceptions do the major news media reflect this other half of the national realities. These appear in periodic colorful fragments, like an occasional human interest profile, but not in systematic, daily information from serious organizations that document feasible programs to meet the needs of most ordinary Americans.

Ideas, views, and proposed programs that go beyond those of established power centers are the domain of small-circulation political journals and magazines on what, in the United States, is called "the Left." These include books from small book publishers, progressive Internet essays, and publications like *The Nation, The Progressive,* and *Extra!* Their criticisms and proposals only slowly, and in fragments, move by osmosis into mainstream news. Even the names of progressive publications and think tanks do not normally appear as the original sources of the proposed ideas and programs. Progressive ideas and suggested programs slowly trickle into the major news, but anonymously and too late to affect pending actions in cities, states, and official Washington. They remain obscure in the daily printed and broadcast news and thus increase a public sense of hopelessness.

In contrast, the major printed and broadcast news frequently uses—prominently, unapologetically, and by name—conservative think tanks like The Heritage Foundation, American Enterprise Institute, and Hoover Institution. These conservative sources are not without useful data, but they are generated with far-right goals in mind and are regarded by the main media as more "respectable" sources. Rupert Murdoch created a serious organ of conservative thought, the *Weekly Standard,* edited by William Kristol, which is required reading in the White House of Republican president George W. Bush. The paper's editors are frequent guests of network programs of news and commentary, while editors and writers of left organizations are rarely invited.

This imbalance has had fundamental consequences. One

example is the radical change since 1980 of wealth distribution in the United States. Holders of great wealth, with minor exceptions, have always preferred political conservatives, who are the main proponents of lower income taxes (or none at all) and who favor reduced governmental social services for the general population. The progressive income tax, for example, has shrunk so drastically that the top rate for the most wealthy is less than half its level of 1970. During this period of drastic shrinkage, national household income has been moving toward the richest families with stunning speed. By 2001, the richest 15 percent of families possessed more of the national household income than all of the remaining 85 percent of Americans.[1]

The mass media are fundamental in creating this transformation. In the modern world, the major media are almost inescapable. Most of the population tell pollsters that they depend on the mass media for their news. It is a handful of large media conglomerates that create the daily and nightly news world for a majority of Americans.

* * *

Every person in our time lives in two worlds.

One is the natural, flesh-and-blood world that has been the environment of human beings since the origins of *Homo sapiens*. Men, women, and children grow up and mature in families, schools, neighborhoods, and community life. They interact face to face with other human beings in endless complex variations. They create social patterns, laws, systems of education, and codes of ethics and are influenced by instincts accumulated from immeasurable human encounters. They comprehend sights, sounds, and smells, whether in the outer reaches of Siberia or in midtown Manhattan. Instincts formed through the millennia are so embedded in human senses that even infants react to expressions of others.

The other world in which most human beings live today is the mass media world. In terms of human history, it is new and sudden. Its origins may go back to signs and symbols in prehistoric times or to Gutenberg's movable type five hundred fifty years ago. Those earlier changes ultimately undercut the traditional monarchical and religious social orders in their own time.

Today's modern mass media transcend global differences in language, culture, social class, and even penetrate illiteracy. When measured on the scale of human experience, change has come upon us swiftly, a world contrived by human beings in our own time. At its creation, it was the work of curious and ingenious individuals. But their creations have been adopted by corporations and governments with a variety of goals — some of genuine benefit for science, education, and personal gratification; some for profit, social conditioning, self-censorship, and control. Compared to the long history of face-to-face human contact, there has been too short a period for universal perception of what in the media is benevolent and what is harmful, what is designed for the privileged and what for the common good.

Today, the rapidly evolving digital world is added to the traditional media. Modern mass media in the industrial nations have transformed social relations, politics, and economic and legal structures. Most inhabitants of industrialized nations spend an extraordinary portion of their daily life within this new world. We continue to argue how individuals can find a humanistic balance between their flesh-and-blood environment and the contrived power of the new media. Nevertheless, only a handful of powerful, monopolistic corporations inundate the population day and night with news, images, publications, and sounds. It is a world into which every child is now born.

This book is an attempt to describe the nature, the impact, and the actors in this new world and how it seems to be evolving with such bewildering speed and mixed blessings in our own time.

PREFACE TO THE FIRST EDITION

As a young reporter in Providence, R.I., I used to drop by for tea in the back room of a secondhand bookstore run by Mary and Douglas Dana. Douglas, a rosy-cheeked Scot, would pull out his latest find in first editions and Mary would predict that he would keep the book and never sell it. One Saturday afternoon, Douglas showed me a first edition that made a difference in my reportorial life. It was *The Letters of Sacco and Vanzetti*, edited by Marion Denman Frankfurter and Gardner Jackson.

I knew that there had been a "Sacco and Vanzetti Case." I was seven years old when the two men were electrocuted at Charlestown Prison in Boston. I never heard anything except certitude that the two Italians were murderers and that when the switch was thrown on their electric chair there was such a powerful flow of electricity that in my hometown of Stoneham, fifteen miles away, and in all of eastern Massachusetts, the electric lights blinked. I had no childhood reason to doubt their guilt and I remember no seven-year-old's reservations about the death penalty. But I was awed by the phenomenon of thousands of homes where a flicker of darkness recorded the deaths of two criminals.

That was all I knew about Sacco and Vanzetti when I first saw Douglas Dana's book, with its good, clear type and solid binding. As I flipped through the pages my eye caught the recurring name of Alice Stone Blackwell. A feminist editor and writer, daughter of Lucy Stone, Alice Stone Blackwell, it was clear from the book, had befriended the two prisoners. I remembered seeing a poem my mother wrote and dedicated to her friend Alice Stone Blackwell. I was interested in Alice Stone Blackwell, so Douglas Dana reluctantly sold me the book.

Reading the letters of Sacco and Vanzetti started a reportorial pursuit that took much of my spare time for the next several years. It led me to a tantalizing brush with a definitive solution to the crime for which Sacco and Vanzetti were falsely convicted and killed. I learned that it was untrue that the lights blinked anywhere when the men were electrocuted. But from endless readings of the trial transcript, posttrial affidavits and appeals, official reports, interviews with principals still living, and the books that even now, sixty years later, are still being written about the case, I also learned something about the social role of newspapers.

Sacco, a shoe repairman, and Vanzetti, a fish peddler, were arrested for the killing of a paymaster and his assistant in South Braintree, Mass., in 1920. It was a cold-blooded murder on a sidewalk in daylight by five men who drove off in a car. Sacco and Vanzetti were Italian immigrants and anarchists. Their arrest came during a national hysteria, whipped by fear of the Russian Revolution a few years earlier, by an endemic bias against all "foreigners," by an uninformed public notion about anarchists, and by A. Mitchell Palmer, attorney general of the United States, who used the Department of Justice to attack all radicals in mass arrests known as "the Palmer Raids," which had become almost a national sport.

At the time of the arrests, most newspapers supported the Palmer Raids and, despite the overwhelming evidence of gross improprieties of justice, were enthusiastic about convicting Sacco and Vanzetti. The press is a mirror of sorts, which might account for its reflection and promotion of the hysteria. But in its great numbers and variety, it is also supposed to be a kind of balance wheel, bringing reason and diversity of opinion to its reporting and commentary. The balance wheel had failed.

By the time Sacco and Vanzetti were to be electrocuted in 1927, most of the serious press had changed its mind. Reporters confirmed that the state had been dishonest and suppressed evidence. Editors had become convinced that there had been a grave miscarriage of justice. It was too late. By that time the pride of the Commonwealth of Massachusetts had become attached to the need to electrocute the two defendants. The state, frozen in its attitude, resisted a commutation because, in the words of Herbert Ehrmann, an admirable lawyer in the case, it would have "signaled a weakness within our social order."

In the United States we depend on our mass media to signal, among other things, "weakness in our social order." In 1921, when Sacco and Vanzetti were tried, the newspapers failed to send that signal, though there was ample evidence to support one. By 1927, when the men were electrocuted, a significant portion of the press had changed its mind. The change did not save the two men, but it said something about the media.

The lesson repeated itself during my subsequent work as a reporter. The news media are not monolithic. They are not frozen in a permanent set of standards. But they suffer from built-in biases that protect corporate power and consequently weaken the public's ability to understand forces that create the American scene. These biases in favor of the status quo, like the ones operating during the Sacco-Vanzetti case, do not seem to change materially over time. When Senator Joseph McCarthy gained demagogic power, he did it, as did A. Mitchell Palmer thirty years earlier, with the enthusiastic support of most newspapers. The newspapers had to abandon disciplines of documentation and critical judgment in order to promote McCarthy, but they did it.

During the emergence of the civil rights movement in the 1950s, most of the best regional papers, in the North and the South, would tell me when I dropped in for the traditional "fill-in" for outside journalists, that there was no serious problem in their "colored districts." Yet in city after city there came racial explosions that surprised even the local media.

When I was reporting on structural poverty in the early 1960s, once again in the newsrooms of some of the best papers I was told that there was no significant problem. But a few years later it was clear that not only was there a problem, but it had existed for a long time.

Yet if I asked these same papers about welfare cheaters, low-level political chicanery, or failings of almost any public agency, their libraries were full of clippings.

There was, it appeared, a double standard: sensitive to failures in public bodies, but insensitive to equally important failures in the private sector, particularly in what affects the corporate world. This institutional bias does more than merely protect the corporate system. It robs the public of a chance to understand the real world.

Our picture of reality does not burst upon us in one splendid revelation. It accumulates day by day and year by year in mostly unspectacular fragments from the world scene, produced mainly by the mass media. Our view of the real world is dynamic, cumulative, and self-correcting as long as there is a pattern of evenhandedness in deciding which fragments are important. But when one important category of the fragments is filtered out, or included only vaguely, our view of the social-political world is deficient. The ultimate human intelligence—discernment of cause and effect—becomes damaged because it depends on knowledge of events in the order and significance in which they occur. When part of the linkage between cause and effect becomes obscure, the sources of our weakness and of our strength become uncertain. Errors are repeated decade after decade because something is missing in the perceptions by which we guide our social actions.

My personal associations, professional experience, and research tell me that journalists, writers, artists, and producers are, as a body, capable of producing a picture of reality that, among other things, will signal "weakness in the social order." But to express this varied picture they must work through mainstream institutions and these institutions must be diverse. As the most important institutions in the production of our view of the real social world—newspapers, magazines, radio, television, books, and movies—increasingly become the property of the most persistent beneficiaries of mass media biases, it seems important to me to write about it.

*Power corrupts; absolute
power corrupts absolutely.*
LORD ACTON, 1887

CHAPTER ONE

COMMON MEDIA FOR AN UNCOMMON NATION

New York Times, February 20, 2003 . . . Senator Byron Dorgan, Democrat of North Dakota, had a potential disaster in his district when a freight train carrying anhydrous ammonia derailed, releasing a deadly cloud over the city of Minot. When the emergency alert system failed, the police called the town radio stations, six of which are owned by the corporate giant, Clear Channel. According to news accounts, no one answered the phone at the stations for more than an hour and a half. Three hundred people were hospitalized, some partially blinded by the ammonia. Pets and livestock were killed.

Anhydrous ammonia is a popular fertilizer that also creates a noxious gas, irritating the respiratory system and burning exposed skin. It fuses clothing to the body and sucks moisture from the eyes. To date, one person has died and 400 have been hospitalized.
— HTTP://WWW.UCC.ORG/UCNEWS/MAY02/TRAIN.HTM

Clear Channel is the largest radio chain in the United States. It owns 1,240 radio stations with only 200 employees. Most of its stations, including the six in Minot, N. Dak., are operated nationwide by remote control with the same pre-recorded material.[1]

*   *   *

The United States, as said so often at home with pride and abroad with envy or hostility, is the richest country in the world. A nation of nineteen thousand cities and towns is spread across an entire continent, with the globe's most diverse population in ethnicity, race, and country of origin. Its people live in regional cultures as different as Amherst is from Amarillo. In contrast to other major nations whose origins go back millennia, the United States is a new country, less than three hundred years old. Consequently, it has not inherited the baggage of centuries of monarchs, czars, and religious potentates who held other populations powerless with absolute authority. From its birth, the United States' most sacred principle has been government by consent of the governed.

But the United States has always been in a state of constant change. Today it is living through one of the most sweeping technological innovations in its history. The speed with which the digital revolution has penetrated an entire society has been breathtaking. The computer and Internet, added to one of the world's largest quantity of mass media outlets, have altered the way millions live their daily lives. The new technology has almost miraculous functions that at their best have led to the betterment of numberless aspects of life, like science, scholarship, and medicine.

The country is unique in yet another way. It has left to each community control of its own schools, its own land use, its own fire and police, and much else, functions that in other developed countries are left solely to nationwide agencies. Given the United States' unique dependence on local civic decision making and its extraordinary multiplicity of local self-governing units and hundreds of media outlets, a rational system for a nation with such a vast diversity of people and places would be hundreds of individual local media owners, each familiar with the particular needs of his or her own community. It would be a reasonable assumption that only then would an American community receive the media programming it needs.

It would be a reasonable assumption. But it would be wrong.

Five global-dimension firms, operating with many of the characteristics of a cartel, own most of the newspapers, magazines, book publishers, motion picture studios, and radio and television stations in the United States. Each medium they own, whether magazines or broadcast stations, covers the entire country, and the owners prefer stories and programs that can be used everywhere and anywhere. Their media products reflect this. The programs broadcast in the six empty stations in Minot, N. Dak., were simultaneously being broadcast in New York City.

These five conglomerates are Time Warner, by 2003 the largest media firm in the world; The Walt Disney Company; Murdoch's News Corporation, based in Australia; Viacom; and Bertelsmann, based in Germany. Today, none of the dominant media companies bother with dominance merely in a single medium. Their strategy has been to have major holdings in all the media, from newspapers to movie studios. This gives each of the five corporations and their leaders more communications power than was exercised by any despot or dictatorship in history.

(In the manic-depressive cycle of corporate mergers that has transpired throughout the various editions of this book, the names of the Time and Warner media conglomerates have changed four times. *Time* magazine was created in 1923 by Henry Luce and his Yale classmate Briton Hadden. Luce bought out Hadden, created Time, Incorporated, and went on to issue additional magazines like *Life*. In the first edition of this book in 1983, the firm was simply Time, Incorporated. In 1990—the fourth edition—Time merged with Warner Communications to form Time Warner. In 2000—the sixth edition—America Online, the Internet server, bought it all for $182 billion in the largest merger in history and renamed the firm AOL Time Warner. In 2003, the Securities and Exchange Commission announced that it would investigate AOL's accounting methods in the prelude to AOL's purchase of Time Warner, an investigation with embarrassing implications. In October 2003, the Board of Directors voted to drop "AOL" from the firm's U.S. title. Nevertheless, "AOL Time Warner" continues to have a separate corporate life overseas, as does AOL as a separate entity. In this—the seventh edition—the company, as leader of the Big Five, returns to its former name, Time Warner, except where the business context and the date make sense to use AOL Time Warner. Whatever its title, it is still the largest media firm in the world.[2])

No imperial ruler in past history had multiple media channels that included television and satellite channels that can permeate entire societies with controlled sights and sounds. The leaders of the Big Five are not Hitlers and Stalins. They are American and foreign entrepreneurs whose corporate empires control every means by which the population learns of its society. And like any close-knit hierarchy, they find ways to cooperate so that all five can work together to expand their power, a power that has become a major force in shaping contemporary American life. The Big Five have similar boards of directors, they jointly invest in the same ventures, and they even go through motions that, in effect, lend each other money and swap properties when it is mutually advantageous.

It is not necessary for a single corporation to own everything in order to have monopoly power. Nor is it necessary to avoid certain kinds of competition. Technically, the dominant media firms are an oligopoly, the rule of a few in which any one of those few, acting alone, can alter market conditions. The most famous global cartel, the Organization of Petroleum Exporting Countries (OPEC), has had brutal shooting wars between some of its members, and there are mutual jealousies among others. But when it comes to the purpose of their cartel—oil—they speak with one voice.

Thus, Time Warner, the largest media firm in the group, competes against another member of the Big Five, Bertelsmann, the largest publisher of English-language books in the world. But in Europe, AOL Time Warner is a partner with both Bertelsmann and News Corporation in the European cable operation, Channel V. According to the Securities and Exchange Commission (SEC), in 2001 AOL Time Warner needed to inflate AOL ad sales figures quickly for stock market reasons. So, in a complex set of transactions, Bertelsmann agreed to buy $400 million worth of advertising in its "competitor," AOL Time Warner, in return for AOL Time Warner transferring to Bertelsmann additional shares in a European firm in which they were already partners. Thus, Bertelsmann, according to the SEC, helped its "competitor" look healthier than it really was.

The Big Five "competitors" engage in numerous such cartel-like relations. News Corporation, for example, has a joint venture with the European operations of Paramount Pictures, which belongs to Viacom, another of its "competitors" in the Big Five. According to French and American securities agencies, Vivendi, the disintegrating French media conglomerate, had agreed to place $25 million worth of advertising in AOL media in return for AOL giving the French firm a share of one of its operations in France.[3]

Some competition is never totally absent among the Big Five media conglomerates. The desire to be the first among many is as true for linked corporations as it is for politicians and nations. It was true two decades ago when most big media companies aspired to command market control in only one medium, for example, Gannett in newspapers; Time, Incorporated in magazines; Simon & Schuster in books; the three TV networks in radio; CBS in television; Paramount in motion pictures. But completion of that process fed an appetite for expansion toward a new and more powerful goal, a small group of interlocked corporations that now have effective control over all the media on which the American public says it depends.

Free Markets or Free Lunches?

Corporate life and capitalist philosophy are almost synonymous, and at the heart of capitalism is competition, or the contemporary incantation, "the free market." If the dominant media corporations behaved in accordance with classical capitalist dogma, each would experiment to create its own unique product. In the media world, *product* means news, entertainment, and political programs. It would mean offering differing kinds of programs that reflect the widely different tastes, backgrounds, and activities of the American population. To compete outright would mean unique products and the goal of a winner-take-all victory. Instead, the Big Five indulge in mutual aid and share investments in the same media products. They jointly conform to the periodic ratings that presume to show what kinds of programs have fractionally larger audiences, after which "the competitors" then imitate the winners and take slightly varying shares of the total profits.

One result of this constricted competition is that the thousands of media outlets carry highly duplicative content.

Another result is that an innovative newcomer can hope to become a significant participant in the industry only as one of the many subsidiaries of the billion-dollar established giants. It is only in legends that David beats Goliath. In the history of modern media, if two experimenters in a garage create an ingenious invention that could revolutionize their industry, ultimately they have limited choices: either sell their device for millions or billions to a dominant firm or risk a hostile takeover or being crushed by the vast promotion and financial resources of a threatened Goliath. In the end, Goliath wins.

Practitioners of current American capitalism do not reflect Adam Smith's eighteenth-century image of an all-out rivalry in which merchants compete by keeping prices lower and quality higher than their fellow merchants. That classical mythology would create a final battlefield with one victor and four companies reduced to leftovers or worse. No dominant media firm, given its size and wealth, wishes to risk such a loss. The Ford Motor Company and General Motors do not compete to the death because each has too much to lose in an all-or-nothing rivalry. Similarly, the major media maintain their cartel-like relationships with only marginal differences among them, a relationship that leaves all of them alive and well—but leaves the majority of Americans with artificially narrowed choices in their media. It is the small neighborhood stores and restaurants that truly compete in products, price, and quality and are willing to risk failure in the process.

The narrow choices the dominant firms offer the country are not the result of a conspiracy. Dominant media members do not sit around a table parceling out market shares, prices, and products, as is done literally by OPEC. The five dominant media firms don't need to. They share too many of the same methods and goals. But if a new firm will

7

strengthen their ability to promote the companies they already own, they will compete with each other to add it to their collections.

The possibilities for mutual promotion among all their various media is the basic reason the Big Five have become major owners of all kinds of media. For example, actors and actresses in a conglomerate's wholly owned movie studio can appear on the same company's television and cable networks, photographs of the newly minted celebrities can dominate the covers of the firm's wholly owned magazines, and those celebrities can be interviewed on the firm's wholly owned radio and television talk shows. The conglomerate can commission an author from its wholly owned book publishing firm to write a biography or purported autobiography of the new stars, which in turn is promoted on the firms' other media.

In addition to jousting for fractional points in broadcast ratings, each of the Big Five wants its shares on the stock market higher than the others (which also increases the value of shares and stock options owned by top executives). Although, if one conglomerate is momentarily ahead, it is tolerable for the others because being a momentary "loser" still allows prodigious profits. Television stations, for example, regard 30 percent profit a year as "low" (being a "loser") because the more successful TV stations that may be Number One at the moment can make 60 percent profit a year. As one of the executives in their trade, Barry Diller, once said of TV stations, "This is a business where if you are a birdbrain you have a thirty-five percent margin. Many good broadcasters have a forty-to-sixty-percent margin."[4]

Though not a literal cartel like OPEC, the Big Five, in addition to cooperation with each other when it serves a mutual purpose, have interlocking members on their boards of directors. An interlock exists when the same board member sits on the board of more than one corporation (this is illegal only if the interlocked firms would form a monopoly if they merged). According to a study by Aaron Moore in the March/April 2003 *Columbia Journalism Review,* News Corporation, Disney, Viacom, and Time Warner have forty-five interlocking directors.

It is a more significant cooperation that closely intertwines all five into a mutual aid combine. The dominant five media conglomerates have a total of 141 joint ventures, which makes them business partners with each other. To cite only one example, News Corporation shares a financial interest with its "competitors" in 63 cable systems, magazines, recording companies, and satellite channels in the United States and abroad. All five join forces in one of Washington's most powerful lobbies, the National Association of Broadcasters, to achieve the laws and regulations that increase their collective power over consumers. In 2000, for example, the National Association of Broadcasters spent $2.5 million lobbying on communications issues, using 24 of its own lobbyists plus four independent lobbying firms, and that year made 64 percent of its campaign contributions to Republicans and 36 percent to Democrats. This is in addition to the lobbying and campaign money spent by the major media corporations on their own.[5]

The media conglomerates are not the only industry whose owners have become monopolistic in the American economy. But media products are unique in one vital respect. They do not manufacture nuts and bolts: they manufacture a social and political world.

New technology has expanded the commercial mass media's unprecedented power over the knowledge and values of the country. In less than a generation, the five intertwined media corporations have enlarged their influence in the home, school, and work lives of every citizen. Their concentrated influence exercises political and cultural forces reminiscent of the royal decrees of monarchs rejected by the revolutionists of 1776.

The Big Five have become major players in altering the politics of the country. They have been able to promote new laws that increase their corporate domination and that permit them to abolish regulations that inhibit their control. Their major accomplishment is the 1996 Telecommunications Act. In the process, power of media firms, along with all corporate power in general, has diminished the place of individual citizens. In the history of the United States and in its Constitution, citizens are presumed to have the sole right to determine the shape of their democracy. But concentrated media power in news and commentary, together with corporate political contributions in general, have diminished the influence of voters over which issues and candidates will be offered on Election Day.

Conservative policies have traditionally been preferred by all large corporations, including the large media conglomerates. The country's five dominant media corporations are now among the five hundred largest corporations in the world.[6] These five corporations dominate one of the two worlds in which every modern person is destined to live.

It is still true, of course, that the face-to-face, flesh-and-blood environment continues to be the daily reality for human beings. It is part of human evolution and if it has any order and social principles it is the result of the millennia of insights, conventions, and experiences of the human race.

In contrast, the mass media world began in earnest only two hundred fifty years ago. Many of its most dramatic and influential elements have emerged within the lifetimes of the present generation. The media world—newspapers, magazines, books, radio, television, movies, and now the Internet—occupies a major role in the commerce and private life of the entire population.

New Media in a New World

Media corporations have always possessed the power to affect politics. That is not new in history. But the five dominant corporations—Time Warner, Disney, News Corporation, Viacom, and Bertelsmann—have power that media in past history did not, power created by new technology and the near uniformity of their political goals. The political and social content projected by these media to the country's population has had real consequences: the United States has the most politically constricted voter choices among the world's developed democracies. That raises fundamental questions about how and by whom the nature of democracy shall be determined.

The magnitude of the change may be more readily understood by looking back from today's twenty-first century. In retrospect, the awesome power of the contemporary mass media has in one generation been a major factor in reversing the country's progressive political, social, and economic momentum of the twentieth century. As a result, in the United States, the twenty-first century inherited a new, more extreme brand of conservative policies.

Twentieth-century politics began with a Republican president, Theodore Roosevelt (1901–1909), at a time when every city of any size had five or more competing newspapers with a broad range of politics, right, center, and left.

With the support of a number of influential periodicals and a portion of its newspapers, Theodore Roosevelt initiated historic conservation of natural resources and dismantled huge interlocked corporate conglomerates, then called *trusts.* The control of trusts in writing laws, bribing officials, and damaging the social welfare had been exposed month after month by some of the country's leading writers in its most influential periodicals—Lincoln Steffens, Owen Wister, Ida Tarbell, Louis Brandeis (sixteen years before he became a member of the U.S. Supreme Court), Upton Sinclair, and many others. Their investigative articles appeared in major media—newspapers published by Joseph Pulitzer, E.W. Scripps, and the early Hearst. Articles asking for reform were centerpieces of influential national magazines like *Harper's, Atlantic, Cosmopolitan, McClure's,* and *Century.*

That fundamental period of confronting the urgent new needs of industrial democracy ended when J. P. Morgan and John D. Rockefeller decided to buy *Harper's* and *Atlantic* and other angry financiers paid high salaries to the most skilled editors to take positions more compatible with the vision of Wall Street banking houses. That, along with World War I, ended the period of reform.[7]

A similar period of reform repaired the chaos created by the wildly uninhibited free markets of the 1920s. Franklin Roosevelt's New Deal (1932–1945) established new social and regulatory agencies after the Great Depression's corporate breakdowns. The New Deal also established immediate jobs and agencies for housing and feeding the country's poor and middle-class families. While Franklin Roosevelt, unlike his cousin Theodore, had no overwhelming media support before his election, the newspapers, which were the only medium that really counted at the time, had lost much of their credibility. They had glorified the failed policies that produced the shambles of the Wall Street Crash of 1929 and the Great Depression that followed. By the time that Franklin Roosevelt ran for president in 1932, desperate unemployment and murmurings of popular revolt were ominous. Fear led many of the once-conservative or neutral newspapers and magazines to moderate their opposition to the election of Roosevelt.

Roosevelt created what were, for that period, radical reforms, like the Securities and Exchange Commission to monitor corporations that sold shares to the public; Social Security to create old age pensions for much of the population; and laws that prevented banks from speculating in the stock market with their depositors' money. The uninhibited free market had created the wild euphoria of every-man-a-millionaire in the 1920s, which then led to the chaos. This had a temporary chastening effect on the main media's normal philosophy of "leave business alone."

In contrast, the presidencies of Ronald Reagan (1981–1988) and of the Bushes—George H. W. Bush (1989–1993), the forty-first president, and his son, George W. Bush, the forty-third president, who took office in 2000—again created an abrupt reversal. After his ascendancy to the presidency in 2000, the younger Bush engaged in a systematic reversal or cancellation of earlier natural resource conservation plans, reduced welfare, and adopted economic policies that hastened the flow of wealth to the most wealthy. The theory espoused by President Reagan had been that the wealth at the top would trickle down to create jobs for middle-class and poor workers. It was a long-discredited theory characterized by John Kenneth Galbraith: "If you feed the horse with enough oats, sooner or later it will leave something behind for the sparrows."

Any dynamic democracy inevitably changes political direction as conditions and public desires evolve. The radical changes of the late twentieth century obviously reflected universal alterations in technology, world economics, and other underlying tides. But the contemporary power of mass media imagery controlled by a small number of like-minded giant corporations played a powerful role. The media of that period, particularly broadcasters, were compliant with requests of the Reagan White House, for example, to limit access of reporters to the president himself.[8] The former actor's folksy personality distracted much of the public's attention from the disastrous consequences that followed an expanded national debt. What happened after the 1990s in the American economy was an eerie echo of the wild storms of the 1920s that brought the crash of 1929.

There are multiple reasons for the politics of any country to change, but with growing force the major media play a central role in the United States. In the years after 1980, conservatives began the chant of "get the government off our backs" that accelerated the steady elimination of a genuinely progressive income tax. They adopted the goal of uninhibited corporate power. Political slogans advocating a shrinking government and arguments involving that idea filled the reportorial and commentary agendas of most of the country's major news outlets. It was the beginning of the end of government-as-protector-of-the-consumer and the start of government-as-the-protector-of-big-business. And the news industry, now a part of the five dominant corporations, reflected this new direction.

By the time Bush the Younger had become president, the most influential media were no longer the powerful *Harper's, Century,* and other influential national organs of one hundred years earlier that had helped to expose abuses and campaigned to limit the power of massive corporations. In sharp contrast to the major media that led to Theodore Roosevelt's reforms, the most adversarial media in 2000, both in size of audience and political influence, were the right-wing talk shows and a major broadcast network, the Murdoch News Corporation's Fox network, with its overt conservatism. Murdoch went further and personally created the *Weekly Standard,* the intellectual Bible of contemporary American conservatism and of the administration of Bush the Younger. Murdoch's magazine is delivered each week to top-level White House figures. The office of Vice President Cheney alone receives a special delivery of thirty copies.[9]

It is not simply a random artifact in media politics that three of the largest broadcast outlets insistently promote bombastic far-right political positions. Murdoch's Fox radio and television have almost unwavering right-wing commentators. The two largest radio groups, Clear Channel and Cumulus, whose holdings dwarf the rest of radio, are committed to a daily flood of far-right propagandistic programming along with their automated music. Twenty-two percent of Americans polled say their main source of news is radio talk shows.[10] In a little more than a decade, American radio has become a powerful organ of right-wing propaganda. The most widely distributed afternoon talk show is Rush Limbaugh's, whose opinions are not only right-wing but frequently based on untruths.[11]

Dominant media owners have highly conservative politics and choose their talk show hosts accordingly. Editor Ron Rodriques of the trade magazine *Radio & Records* said, "I can't think of a single card-carrying liberal talk show syndicated nationwide."[12] The one clearly liberal talk show performer, Jim Hightower of ABC, was fired in 1995 by the head of Disney, Michael Eisner, the week after Eisner bought the Disney company, which owns ABC.

The political content of the remaining four of the Big Five is hardly a counter to Fox and the ultraconservatism and bad reporting of dominant talk shows. American television viewers have a choice of NBC (now owned by General Electric), CBS (now owned by one of the Big Five, Viacom), and ABC, now owned by another of the Big Five, Disney. Diversity among the tens of thousands of United States media outlets is no longer a government goal. In 2002, the chairman of the Federal Communications Commission, Michael Powell, expressed the opinion that it would not be so bad if one broadcast giant owned every station in an entire metropolitan area.[13]

The machinery of contemporary media is not a minor mechanism. The 280 million Americans are served, along with assorted other small local and national media, by 1,468 daily newspapers, 6,000 different magazines, 10,000 radio stations, 2,700 television and cable stations, and 2,600 book publishers.[14] The Internet gave birth to a new and still unpredictable force, as later portions of this book will describe. Though today's media reach more Americans than ever before, they are controlled by the smallest number of owners than ever before. In 1983 there were fifty dominant media corporations; today there are five. These five corporations decide what most citizens will — or will not — learn.[15]

It may not be coincidental that during these years of consolidation of mass media ownership the country's political spectrum, as reflected in its news, shifted. As noted, what was once liberal is now depicted as radical and even unpatriotic. The shift does not reflect the political and social values of the American public as a whole. A recent Harris poll showed that 42 percent of Americans say they are politically moderate, middle-of-the-road, slightly liberal, liberal, or extremely liberal, compared to 33 percent for the same categories of conservatives, with 25 percent saying "Don't know or haven't thought about it."[16]

Dollars versus Votes

One force creating the spectrum change has been, to put it simply, money—the quantities of cash used to gain office. Spontaneous national and world events and the accidents of new personalities inevitably play a part in determining a country's legislation and policies. But in American politics, beyond any other single force, money has determined which issues and candidates will dominate the national discourse that, in turn, selects the issues and choices available to voters on Election Day.

The largest source of political money has come from corporations eager to protect their expanded power and treasure. The country's massive media conglomerates are no different—with the crucial exception that they are directly related to voting patterns because their product happens to be a social-political one. It is, tragically, a self-feeding process: the larger the media corporation, the greater its political influence, which produces a still larger media corporation with still greater political power.

The cost of running for office has risen in parallel with the enlarged size of American industries and the size of their political contributions to preferred candidates and parties.

In 1952, the money spent by all candidates and parties for all federal election campaigns—House, Senate, and presidency—was $140 million (sic). In 2000, the races spent in excess of $5 billion. Spending in the 2000 presidential campaign alone was $1 billion.[17]

The growth of money in politics is multiplied by what it

pays for—the growth of consultants skilled in, among other things, the arts of guile and deception that have been enhanced by use of new technology in discovering the tastes and income of the public.

Television political ads are the most common and expensive campaign instrument and the largest single expenditure in American political campaigns. Typically, the commercials are brief, from a few seconds to five minutes, during which most of the content consists of slogans and symbols (waving Americans flags are almost obligatory), useless as sources of relevant information. Television stations and networks are, of course, the recipients of most of the money that buys air time. This is why the country's political spectrum is heavily influenced by which candidate has the most money.

Incumbents always have an advantage in attracting money from all sources because even conservative business leaders want influence with whoever happens to vote for legislation, even if it is a liberal. Nevertheless, if one eliminates incumbents, the big spenders have almost always been the winners. Beginning in 1976, candidates who spent more than $500,000 were increasingly Republicans.[18] Conservatives perpetually accuse Democrats of bowing to *special interests*. In the conservative lexicon, these are code words for labor unions. And, indeed, labor unions in 2000, for example, gave Democrats $90 million and Republicans only $5 million. But in the 1990s, corporate and trade association political action committees gave Republicans twice as much money as they gave to Democrats and in quantities many multiples larger than labor union political contributions.[19] In the crucial midterm 2002 elections, when control of the Senate depended on a few votes, Democrats spent $44 million and Republicans $80 million. Republicans gained control of

Congress, undoubtedly helped by President Bush, who, two months before the election, suddenly declared that the country would go to war against Iraq and that opponents would be seen as supporters of Saddam Hussein's tyranny. That alone took domestic economic troubles off the front pages and out of TV news programs.

Increasingly, House and Senate candidates have spent their own money on campaigns, a choice available only to multimillionaires. Thus, the money both of the wealthy and of corporate interests has come to dominate American politics in the single generation during which the country's political spectrum has shifted far to the right.

The View from the Top

The major news media overwhelmingly quote the men and women who lead hierarchies of power. Powerful officials are a legitimate element in news because the public needs to know what leaders in public and private life are saying and doing. But official pronouncements are only a fraction of the realities within the population. Complete news requires more. Leaders, whether in public or private life and whatever their personal ethical standards, like most human beings, seldom wish to publicize information that discloses their mistakes or issues they wish to keep in the background or with which they disagree. Officials do not always say the whole truth.

Citizen groups issuing serious contrary studies and proposals for mending gaps in the social fabric get only sporadic and minimal attention in the major media. Consequently, some of the country's most pressing problems remain muted. Unless powerful official voices press for attention and remedies for those missing issues, the pressing problems remain unresolved.

It is not rare for speakers and large organizations to complain publicly that it is shameful for the richest and most powerful country in the world to have increasing numbers of citizens homeless, that the United States is the only industrial country in the world without universal health care, or that its rhetorical support of education seems to believe that this requires no additional money from the federal government—even though it is the federal government that requires local schools to meet higher standards. Or that the country withdrew unilaterally from previous treaties to protect the planetary environment. Or that, despite agreement to restrict existing stocks of Russian and American nuclear weapons, President Bush the Younger announced that he would consider military action against countries initiating nuclear weapons research while simultaneously announcing that the United States would restart its own nuclear weapons research.

These issues are not absent from major news media. They are reported but then they are dropped, though national stories about a distant kidnapped child can continue on front pages and television news for weeks. There is nothing harmful and often some good in persistent stories about individual human tragedies. But in the national news agenda, there is no such media persistence with problems that afflict millions. It is an unrelenting tragedy that more than 41 million Americans remain without health care, that millions of young people are jammed into inadequate classrooms with inadequate teaching staffs, that deterioration threatens Planet Earth as a human habitat, or that a similar threat is growth of nuclear weaponry in the United States and the rest of the world. Or that preemptive war as a permanent policy is the law of the jungle.

News executives claim periodically that no one's really interested in unmet domestic needs, or people are tired of bad news, or we had a story on that. This is the same industry that is proud of its ability to be artful and ingenious in making any kind of story interesting, in which many of the same editors pursue the "lost child story" that, in fact, interests only part of the audience and is ignored by the rest. Every reader of a newspaper or viewer of television will pay close attention and absorb copious detail on an issue that affects that reader personally, whether it is a jobless bookkeeper or the national prospects for the unemployed or a family member desperate for possible treatments for Alzheimer's disease.

The major news media fail to deal systematically with the variety of compelling social needs of the entire population. Those needs remain hidden crises, obscured in the daily flood of other kinds of news. Yet the weight of most reputable surveys shows that, in the late twentieth and early twenty-first century, most Americans were deeply concerned with systematic lack of funds for their children's education, access to health care, the growing crises in unemployment, homelessness, and steady deterioration of city and state finances.

But these issues are not high priorities among the most lavish contributors to political candidates and parties. Corporations have other high-priority issues. There is a world of wealth, stratospheric in its imperial heights, which is so beyond the life of most Americans that it is barely imaginable.

When There Are No Limits

Though not typical of the average profitable corporation, disclosures in recent years show excesses that can be achieved by "getting the government off our backs." It was only through divorce paper filings that shareholders of General Electric (GE) and the public learned about the lack of limits on compensation that some large corporate leaders quietly grant themselves while keeping their stockholders and the public unaware of their almost obscene money and perquisites.

The most striking disclosure was the compensation and pension benefits for Jack Welch, the much-celebrated leader of General Electric, learned only when his wife's divorce filings became public. Mr. Welch, while still CEO of GE, received $16.7 million a year; access to the corporate aircraft; use of an $80,000-a-month Manhattan apartment, with its expenses (including wine, food, laundry, toiletries, and newspapers) paid for by the company; along with floor-level seats to New York Knicks basketball games, VIP seating at Wimbledon tennis games, a box at Yankee Stadium and Boston Red Sox games, four country club fees, security and limousine service at all times, satellite TV in his four homes, and dining bills at a favorite restaurant.

In retirement, Welch's pension continues most of the perquisites for life, plus $86,535 for the first thirty days of each year's consultancy, plus $17,307 for each additional day. These otherworldly heights of excess not only were hidden from the average American but also were vague to shareholders, thanks to obscure or undecipherable footnotes in annual reports.[20]

Tyco, one of the Enron-like fiascos, forgave a $19 million loan to executive Dennis Koslowski, who needed it to pay for an additional home in Florida. Kozlowski and his partners were later charged with looting $600 million from their company.[21]

Vain Ambition Produced No "Big Six"

When Vivendi, the house of cards concocted by French corporate adventurer Jean-Marie Messier, came apart, his dream of a media empire gave GE a chance to join the Big Five that now dominate American media.[22] Under Messier, Vivendi's buying spree had included the United States' last major independent publishing house, Houghton Mifflin, based in Boston, which was then sold to an investment group that operated it with changes in the company's mix of printed and online services.

Messier's hard-headed successor, Jean-Renee Fourtou, salvaged Vivendi by GE's $3.8 billion purchase and assumption of $1.6 billion in debt, giving GE 80 percent ownership of Vivendi-Universal, which includes Universal studios. This purchase also gave GE's new chairman, Jeffrey Immelt, the foundation to convert GE from a large collection of older industrial assets (weaponry, jet engines, etc.) to the new hot industry, the media. Immelt has said that the old industries were paying one-digit profits while the media pay 25–60 percent.[23]

Immelt foresees an enlarged GE as a vertically integrated media firm overshadowing its older products. GE already owned the NBC TV network and cable networks including the USA Network, Sci-Fi, CNBC, MSNBC, Bravo, and Trio. The deal added Universal Pictures, Universal Television (producer of the high-profit program *Law & Order*), shares in five theme parks, and Telemundo, the big Spanish-language network. Barry Diller owns 7 percent of Vivendi. Despite Immelt's vision of GE as a major media conglomerate, GE was also planning to acquire the London-based medical firm Amersham for $9.5 billion and still promotes sales of GE gas turbines and wind energy, high-tech ovens, and medical devices like magnetic resonance imaging (MRI).

Immelt still has to escape what Hollywood calls "the Curse of Universal," a threat based on a long line of business and other failures of former owners of the studio, from its founder Carl Laemmle in 1912 to the unfortunate Messier.[24]

New names, systems, and services inevitably will, like GE, emerge; they add an increment to the media scene but do not approach the magnitude and power of the truly giant all-media conglomerates described in this book.

"Humble" Domination

The phrase "humble beginning" is almost obligatory in many corporate histories. Often it has been even more humble than displayed in the company's history. In the case of all parties to the $107 billion in Messier's deals, they were, indeed, if not humble at least not magisterial. Messier's former company name had been a water company and became a major builder of such systems worldwide. But it really began humbly as sewage. The original Vivendi firm inherited the bumbling Louis Napoleon's attempt to regain stature by constructing the Paris sewers. Vivendi's target, Seagram, for which Messier paid $34 million in stock, [25] had the reputation of humbly shipping impressive quantities of liquor from Canada into the United States during Prohibition via groups the tabloids insisted on calling "gangs," using the word "smuggling," although neither word appeared in Seagram official company literature. Seagram was started as a humble Canadian saloon by the Bronfman family.[26]

There has also been genuine public service by the senior Bronfman, who helped rescue European Jews from persecution or worse and was instrumental in exposing the Nazi collaboration of Kurt Waldheim, former secretary-general of the United Nations. He also helped track down Swiss bankers who profited from money once deposited by Jews murdered in the Holocaust.[27]

A Built-in Imbalance

Most of the more conventionally wealthy families are able to buy private services that ordinary families cannot obtain in a publicly funded school or other community and national facilities that suffer from budget cuts made, among other reasons, to provide tax cuts for the wealthy.

The many decades of only passing consideration of the major needs of most people have produced hopelessness about the possibility for change. Consequently, masses of potential voters have become resigned to the assumption that what the major media tell them is the norm and now unchangeable. In the first edition of this book, twenty years ago, I observed "media power is political power." The five dominant media firms, now among the largest in the world, have that power and use it to enhance the values preferred by the corporate world of which they are a part.

The imbalance between issues important to corporate hierarchies and those most urgent to the population at large is obscured by the neutralist tone of modern news. The rightward impact of modern news is not in the celebrated inflamed language that once characterized nineteenth-century sensationalist headlines and language. Today the imbalance is in what is chosen—or not chosen—for print or broadcast. Media politics are reflected in the selection of commentators and talk show hosts. It is exercised powerfully in what their corporations privately lobby for in legislation and regulations, and in the contributions they and their leaders make to political parties and candidates. It is the inevitable desire of most large corporations to have a political environment that is friendly to weakening minimum standards for public service and safety in order to produce maximum corporate profit levels and lower the corporate share of city, state, and federal taxes. But these seldom provide comparable benefits for the common good, like health care, safe environments, and properly funded public education.

In the last twenty-five years, the media world has experienced accelerated inventions and with them conflicts and uncertainties about which media will survive and which will die off. Yet again, newspeople agonize whether a new method of communication that distracts the country's youths might condemn the daily newspaper to an early death. Similar questions have arisen about other traditional media, like magazines and books, to be dealt with later.

As Gutenberg's movable type was in his day, the new electronic media as a social force remain in a still-uncertain balance. Today, massive demonstrations protesting a government policy have been gathered solely by marshaling sympathizers by Internet. At the same time, the digital revolution has made ambiguous the privacy within one's home because a government official, or anyone else with enough skill, can enter the citizen's computer from a remote location and thereby end the historic assumption that "my home is my castle."

That question hovers over the extraordinary but unpredictable innovations of the electronic media and the transformations that are continuing in our time.

Men, such as they are, very naturally seek money or power; and power because it is as good as money.
RALPH WALDO EMERSON, 1837

CHAPTER TWO

THE BIG FIVE

In 1983, the men and women who headed the fifty mass media corporations that dominated American audiences could have fit comfortably in a modest hotel ballroom. The people heading the twenty dominant newspaper chains probably would form one conversational cluster to complain about newsprint prices; twenty magazine moguls in a different circle denounce postal rates; the broadcast network people in another corner, not being in the newspaper or magazine business, exchange indignations about government radio and television regulations; the book people compete in outrage over greed of writers' agents; and movie people gossip about sexual achievements of their stars.

By 2003, five men controlled all these media once run by the fifty corporations of twenty years earlier. These five, owners of additional digital corporations, could fit in a generous phone booth. Granted, it would be a tight fit, and it would be filled with some tensions.

In this imaginary phone booth would be Richard Parsons, chairman and chief executive officer (CEO) of Time Warner, who would be cautious about his job, because he was now chief of the world's largest media firm only because his former co-chiefs, Steve Case and Carl Levin, had been dethroned. Michael Eisner, chief of Disney, would demand his own space the way he had after he and his old friend Michael Ovitz engineered capture of the vast Mickey Mouse empire by promising co-leadership, whereupon Eisner dumped his old friend on the principle of One Empire, One Emperor. The notoriously irascible Sumner Redstone, ruler of Viacom, formerly CBS, would be all elbows because News Corp's Rupert Murdoch had bought Hughes Electronics' satellite-transmitted DirecTV, which gives Murdoch financial and technical power surpassing Viacom. Finally, the fifth occupant would be Reinhard Mohn, patriarch of the 168-year-old German firm Bertelsmann, as aloof as one can be in a crowded phone booth because he is head of, among other things, the world's largest publisher of English-language books, but not long before had been caught lying about his firm's Nazi-era history.

Admittedly, it may be difficult to imagine five of the world's most influential executives standing in one phone booth, an act usually reserved for college students competing for a place in the *Guinness Book of World Records* (which says the record is twenty-five young men at St. Mary's College in Moraga, California).[1] It takes a stretch of imagination to think of five corporate executives doing the same thing. On the other hand, it would have been difficult to imagine in 1983 that the corporations that owned all the country's dominant mass media would, in less than twenty years, shrink from fifty separate companies to five.

If, however, one looks at the properties of the dominant five, it provides some insight into how it could have happened. Their steady accumulation of power in the world of news, radio, television, magazines, books, and movies gave them a steady accumulation of power in politics. Political leaders and parties know that the news media control how those politicians are depicted to the voting public; the more powerful the leading media, the more powerful their influence over politicians and national policy. Prudent politicians treat the desires of all large corporations with care. But politicians treat the country's most powerful media corporations with something approaching reverence.

That political awe has permitted the five dominant media firms to ignore or make laws that let them absorb the lion's share of the 37,000 different media outlets in the United States. (The number jumps to 54,000 if one counts all weeklies, semiweeklies, and advertising weeklies and all "periodicals," including strictly local ones. The number becomes 178,000 if one counts all "information industries.")[2] Some writers' commercial guides claim they can find 7,700 local book publishers for authors. Whatever the number, U.S. communications systems are formidable. This book deals with the media—daily newspapers, nationally distributed magazines, broadcasting, and motion pictures—used by the majority of Americans and their influence on the country's politics and policies.

Political leaders hunger for continuous favorable treatment in the big media. The Big Five hunger for the $236 billion spent every year for advertising in the mass media and the approximately $800 billion that Americans spend on media products themselves.[3] In 2002, for example, the average consumer spent $212 for basic cable, $100 for books, $110 for home videos, $71 for music recordings, $58 for daily newspapers, $45 for magazines, $45 for online Internet services, and $36 on movies.[4] It is not surprising that a country with 280 million people living in more than 100 million households is a marketplace that has led ambitious entrepreneurs, no longer inhibited by former government rules, to congeal into a small handful of corporations. The fewer the owning corporations, the larger each one's share of the annual harvest of the billions of consumer dollars.

Who and what are these dominant five media corporations?

Time Warner, The Largest

On January 10, 2000, the American television audience was invited to the most expensive marriage ceremony in history. It was a corporate wedding, so the loving couple were two men, and it was not uncouth to mention money. In the Wall Street Book of Common Stock, it is mandatory to mention the wealth of newly joined couples. That is why the news mentioned that the ritual combined one party worth $163 billion with its soul mate worth $120 billion.

The merger joined America Online, headed by Steven Case, and Time Warner, headed by Gerald Levin (in corporate weddings it is not always easy to distinguish which is the groom and which the bride). Case, forty-two years old, had built a firm with the most common acronym, aol, for the servers that lead to sites in the vast universe of the Internet. Earlier, AOL had already merged with competitors Netscape and CompuServe. Levin's Time Warner had been the empire Henry Luce had built seventy-seven years earlier when Luce had co-founded *Time* magazine. Long before the marriage, Luce and his successors at Time, Inc. had spawned a growing family of magazines that included *Life, Fortune, Holiday, Sports Illustrated,* and *People;* Time, Inc. later merged with Warner Brothers, which itself had gathered other firms in music, movies, television, and newer media.

In addition to its other headline-making news, the merger became the most spectacular celebration of what was, at the time, the ultimate holy word on Wall Street, *synergy*. Synergy, borrowed from physiology, describes how the combination of two separate entities produces a power greater than the simple addition of the two. The word became a mantra with merger specialists, investment bankers, and entrepreneurs. It seemed inevitable that combining the two corporations would more than double their separate powers in the marketplace.

AOL Time Warner was seen as synergy perfected: Time Warner had by this time a large quantity of media products from magazines to movies (an undifferentiated commodity known on Wall Street as "content"), and AOL had the best pipeline through which to send this "content" instantly to customers' computers.

A list of the properties controlled by AOL Time Warner takes ten typed pages listing 292 separate companies and subsidiaries. Of these, twenty-two are joint ventures with other major corporations involved in varying degrees with media operations. These partners include 3Com, eBay, Hewlett-Packard, Citigroup, Ticketmaster, American Express, Homestore, Sony, Viva, Bertelsmann, Polygram, and Amazon.com. Some of the more familiar fully owned properties of Time Warner include Book-of-the-Month Club; Little, Brown publishers; HBO, with its seven channels; CNN; seven specialized and foreign-language channels; Road Runner; Warner Brothers Studios; Weight Watchers; Popular Science; and fifty-two different record labels.[5]

The marriage ran into difficulties over, as usual, money. The couple's wedding required massive debt, but it was a time when debt was considered unimportant. In 2000, the marketplace was flooded by investors in the digital world eager for magical pieces of paper called *stock options* that had made some people millionaires overnight. Major banks with fine old nineteenth-century names lent billions without looking too closely at the arithmetic in the borrowers' balance sheets (or at their own, it later became clear). The public was told that this was the "new economy." Dismissed as hopelessly obsolete were notions like judging a company on the basis of whether there was some relationship between income and outgo or between assets and liabilities.

The new economy developed, at the very least, birth pains. By 2003, Time Warner had a metaphoric yard sale on its front lawn. It was trying to sell its book divisions, the fifth largest in the country, worth more than $30 million. Steven Case and Gerald Levin had been unseated by unhappy board members, and by 2002 the Securities and Exchange Commission and the Department of Justice had announced that they wished to examine how AOL had kept its books before the merger.[6]

But it was still the biggest media firm in the world.

Disney, the Mouse That Roared

The loveable rodent with big ears, the one called Mickey, with the squeaky, babylike voice and the innocent charm, is really more than seventy-five years old and makes more than $25 billion a year.[7] To be more precise, he and his playmates really make that money for his corporate parent, the Walt Disney Company. The firm now controls more subsidiaries than Walt himself had added, like his first Disneyland. The innocence of Mickey and his friends Goofy, Dumbo, and the Seven Dwarfs enchanted generations of children around the world. David Low, the British political cartoonist, called Walt "the most significant figure in graphic arts since Leonardo."[8]

It is true that Walt Disney, the father of the mouse

empire, was a country boy who became an international phenomenon. His creations are everywhere in the world — "Topolino" in Italy, "Mi Lao Shu" in China, and "Mikki Maus" in Russia. His *Fantasia,* a series of color movie episodes set to music played by the Philadelphia Symphony Orchestra, is still presented periodically in theaters all over the world.[9]

Walt's touch with the tastes of children was genuine. He grew up on a Missouri farm, and after his Uncle Mike, a locomotive engineer on the Atchison, Topeka, and Santa Fe, bought him a box of crayons, Walt drew pictures of tiny animals on everything, including the side of the farm truck. When the farm failed, the family moved to Chicago, where, after his daytime high school classes, Walt went to night classes at the Academy of Fine Arts. After he had become a Hollywood success, a legend grew that he had no ability in art, but it was not true (although, when his artists went on strike shortly after World War II, their picket signs read, "Walt Can't Draw").[10] When Walt Disney died in 1966 of lung cancer (he had chain-smoked French Gitane cigarettes), radio-television commentator Eric Severeid said, "We'll never see his like again."[11]

Severeid was right, but the Disney company grew in ways Walt might not have imagined. It would become the seventy-third largest industry in the United States under a leader whose roots could not be more different. Michael Eisner, chairman and CEO of the Walt Disney Company, grew up in a fashionable Park Avenue apartment in New York City, the son of an affluent lawyer. His parents required him to do two hours of homework for every hour he watched television. Michael began as a premedical student at Dennison University (A.B., Class of 1964) but switched to English literature and theater. He then got a job as a clerk in the Federal Communications Commission. But in six weeks he went to CBS children's programming, where his job was picking the right spot in which to drop commercials.

Eisner was not charmed with the routine, and instantly he sent out hundreds of résumés. He received only one response, but that one was crucial. It was from Barry Diller, head of programming at ABC. Diller, who by 1967 had produced his own TV special, "Feelin' Groovy at Marine World," became Eisner's mentor. When Diller became chairman of the board, he made Eisner president and CEO. Eisner soon cut costs at Paramount Pictures to $8.5 million per picture at a time when the industry average was 30 percent higher.

Eisner had caught the merger and acquisition fever of the 1980s and 1990s. In 1984 he was named ABC's chairman and CEO, and ten years later acquired the newspaper-broadcast chain ABC/Cap Cities. It became the Walt Disney Company. When Eisner hired Michael Ovitz, "the most powerful man in Hollywood" and head of the dominant Creative Artists Agency, *Time* magazine ran a full-color portrait of Ovitz in royal robes and a crown.[12]

The national media coronation of Ovitz may have been a tactical pitfall. The Walt Disney Company was now a global empire, and empires seldom remain peaceful with co-emperors. In a short time, Ovitz "the most powerful man" was out. The *Los Angeles Times* published a satirical "My Dinner with Ovitz," in which Ovitz blames his fate on Hollywood's "gay mafia," in which he seemed to include other big names like David Geffen, Michael Eisner, Barry Diller, and many others.[13]

Eisner, who has a talent for promoting his own enterprises, had a reputation for wanting nothing about his personal life publicized. If he heard of some possibility, he made rigorous efforts to suppress it. But inevitably there were moves for the usual tell-it-all books about any powerful national figure, and that began a battle. Broadway Books commissioned an Eisner biography, *Keys to the Kingdom*, by Kim Masters, a contributor to *Vanity Fair*, with a $700,000 advance. The publisher's spring catalog listed it as "brilliantly reported." But the head of Broadway Books suddenly decided that the "brilliantly reported" manuscript was "unacceptable." Another publisher, Morrow Books, found it fine and picked it up. The suspicion was that Eisner, increasingly powerful, had the original contract killed.

In the nature of many celebrity biographies, this became a mud fight. The book was said to include Eisner's quarrel with his former protégé Jeffrey Katzenberg. Author Masters said her original editor had received a Disney demand to cancel the book. There were Hollywood rumors that Broadways Book's parent firm, Bertelsmann, was planning to buy some German television stations from Eisner's Disney company and did not wish to displease Eisner.[14]

Despite the ingredients of a stereotypical Hollywood publicity war, a more immediate problem arose. Board members, including Walt's nephew Roy Disney, questioned the Disney company's falling revenues and shareholder value. There were pointed queries about Disney accounting and about Eisner personally. The usual rumors questioned whether the directors were about to take back Eisner's "keys to the kingdom."

Disney ownership of a hockey team called The Mighty Ducks of Anaheim does not begin to describe the vastness of the kingdom. Hollywood is still its symbolic heart, with eight movie production studios and distributors: Walt Disney Pictures, Touchstone Pictures, Miramax, Buena Vista Home Video, Buena Vista Home Entertainment, Buena Vista International, Hollywood Pictures, and Caravan Pictures.

The Walt Disney Company controls eight book house imprints under Walt Disney Company Book Publishing and ABC Publishing Group; seventeen magazines; the ABC Television Network, with ten owned and operated stations of its own including in the five top markets; thirty radio stations, including all the major markets; eleven cable channels, including Disney, ESPN (jointly), A&E, and the History Channel; thirteen international broadcast channels stretching from Australia to Brazil; seven production and sports units around the world; and seventeen Internet sites, including the ABC group, ESPN.sportszone, NFL.com, NBAZ.com, and NASCAR.com. Its five music groups include the Buena Vista, Lyric Street, and Walt Disney labels, and live theater productions growing out of the movies *The Lion King, Beauty and the Beast,* and *King David.*

The company has a quarter interest in the Anaheim Angels baseball team and owns fifteen theme parks and its cruise line. It has its own interactive subsidiaries, with CD-ROMs for video games, and computer software. Its more than one hundred retail stores sell Disney-related products. Almost as an afterthought, it has a part interest in Bass oil and gas production.

Like all other dominant media corporations, Disney takes on cartel-like character through twenty-six joint ventures with other corporations, most of them media companies that constitute Disney's main "competitors." Some of the joint ventures are with General Electric (whose NBC competes head to head with ABC, Hearst, ESPN, Comcast, and Liberty Media).

By late 2003, Eisner's leadership of the Disney empire was seriously threatened. Disney stock was falling in value and Roy Disney, nephew of Walt Disney and vice chairman of the board, resigned along with another board member. He issued a highly publicized demand that Eisner resign as well.

The "magic kingdom" apparently had lost some of its magic, especially in financial performance of its ABC network and one of its most profitable divisions, the Disney cruises.[15] This encouraged big cable's Comcast to move toward merger or purchase.

Murdoch's News Corp: Hearst Reborn?

When Murdoch's News Corporation acquired Hughes's DirecTV satellite system, it not only added $9 billion a year in annual income but also gave his Fox programs a new medium for reaching millions of homes through small rooftop satellite dishes. Though fiberoptic channel, with its huge transmission capacity, has a better foothold, Murdoch's new acquisition gave him the power to intimidate bigger systems like Time Warner and cable systems, by offering home gadgets to record his programs via DirecTV without commercials. The possibility of eliminating commercials is a perpetual nightmare for media industries and their advertisers. Consequently, promises of adless commercial television and cable programs have a short half-life: once adless cable programs have accumulated a large enough audience, grateful for the absence of commercial interruptions, the program owners seem unable to resist selling their audiences to eager advertisers.

Furthermore, Murdoch realized he could use DirecTV to put himself on both sides of bargaining tables. He is a tough and patient negotiator and can use earlier acquisitions of his cluster of Fox sports channels plus DirecTV to get his own price for carrying schedules of big sports teams and special events. Other network outlets, like Disney's ESPN, ESPN2, and ESPNRegional (some held jointly with Hearst) may have to deal with DirecTV, as will cable companies for households desiring Fox-originated sports. Professional teams use broadcast rights as a major source of their income, but Murdoch can make them sell him their broadcast rights for less because his acquisitions have further reduced the number of bidders.

In bargaining between owners of sports teams selling broadcast rights and the broadcasters bidding for them, Murdoch found a way to be both buyer and seller. Like other media companies, he wanted broadcast rights for popular sports events. So he bought the teams. At one time he owned the Los Angeles Dodgers, New York Knicks, and part interest in four others, plus Fox Sports Radio Network. Gene Kimmelman of Consumers Union said, "Hold on to your wallets. Prices will go through the roof." The rising prices will, of course, result in higher payments by the public.

Those who possess that kind of power seldom permit it to remain idle. The mass media, especially the news media, have used their power to obtain special governmental favors for themselves and their properties. Rupert Murdoch, brazen in his methods, makes clear what other major media owners achieve by more conventional methods, like campaign contributions and lobbying in Washington.

Brazen or not, two impulses seem to drive Murdoch's business life—the accumulation of as much media power as possible and the use of that power to promote his deep-seated conservative politics.

Born Keith Rupert Murdoch in 1931, he soon dropped the Keith and, at the age of twenty-three, was given control of a faltering paper in Adelaide, a tiny part of his father's Australian news empire (an echo of the original William Randolph Hearst, whose rich father gave him a present of his first paper, the *San Francisco Examiner*). At Oxford, Murdoch had been a wild Marxist, nicknamed "Red Rupert," a youthful fling with leftism that settled into ultraconservatism (again, a parallel with the transformation of young socialist Hearst, who soon became the adult reactionary Hearst).

Murdoch became an unrelenting builder of international media empires. He left his Australian papers for England, where he soon owned two of Great Britain's largest papers, an afternoon sleazy tabloid and a Sunday paper full of overflowing female bodies and sensational gossip.

Wanting direct political power beyond his sensationalist moneymakers, he moved to acquire two more newspapers that happened to be among the world's most influential, the *Sunday Times* and the (daily) *Times*. Because he already had acquired two national newspapers with circulations in the millions, his acquisition of the Sunday and daily *Times* was forbidden by England's Monopoly Commission. But he obtained stock pending official approval and used his media to help Conservative candidate Margaret Thatcher win election as prime minister. With Thatcher's cooperation, Murdoch broke the Minority Commission rules and acquired both *Times* newspapers.[16] *The Economist* magazine reported that Murdoch's British holdings in 2000 had $2.1 billion in profits, but by creative bookkeeping and political influence he did not pay a shilling in British taxes. This would not be the first time Murdoch would use his media power to evade laws and regulations that might interfere with his acquiring still more media power.

If Murdoch wants something sufficiently valuable, he can momentarily suspend his personal politics. When China disapproved of Murdoch's satellite news carrying British Broadcasting Company (BBC) items critical of Communist China, he immediately dropped the BBC from his Asian satellite programs. When he decided to establish a U.S. empire, he bought the once-liberal tabloid, the *New York Post*, and with the support of New York's Democratic mayor (whom he had wooed with pleasing stories in the *Post*), he gained approval. When he decided to create his own U.S. radio and television network, Fox, he was confronted by an American law no broadcaster had ever circumvented, though many had tried. The law requires that no foreign entity may own more than 24.9 percent of a U.S. radio or television station. Murdoch changed his citizenship from Australian to United States, but that gesture was not enough. He still failed to comply with the broadcast law that requires the broadcaster's parent corporation to be based within the United States.

Murdoch refused to move the company because he had special tax advantages in Australia. Instead, he used his new American power base of four newspapers and two magazines as levers for his legendary political behind-the-scenes navigating to obtain special favors. It was a shock to other foreign firms, which had attempted but never succeeded in entering U.S. broadcasting, when Murdoch was granted the first waiver of that United States–only ownership law that had ever been granted. It still has never been granted to anyone else.

Still dedicated to his right-wing politics but willing to make temporary suspensions for corporate advantages, in 1980 he applied for a taxpayer-subsidized loan from the Export-Import Bank of the United States. The bank staff rejected the application. Murdoch had lunch in the White House with President Jimmy Carter, a Democrat, and with the president of the Export-Import Bank. Two days later Murdoch's *New York Post* endorsed Carter in a bitterly fought New York presidential primary. Six days later the Export-Import Bank gave Murdoch his loan for $290 million for his airline, a loan underwritten by American taxpayers for a foreign airline.

After Newt Gingrich (whose ultraconservative politics

were also Murdoch's) led the 1994 Republican sweep of Congress, he was considered the most powerful politician in the United States. Murdoch, through his wholly owned book house, HarperCollins, offered Gingrich $4.5 million for an as-yet-unwritten book.[17]

Murdoch now has the Fox television network, the most violent and conservative in U.S. broadcasting. Beyond that, he has created a vast global network of properties and complex media partnerships. As he ages, he remains in command of the huge operations. His two sons could inherit leadership if they can avoid ruinous sibling rivalries that have afflicted other media empires whose children, like King Lear's, quarreled over their inheritance with disastrous results.[18]

Murdoch's empire is one to whet the appetite of a possible heir. In book publishing alone, the parent firm, News Corporation, owns HarperCollins Publishers, with twenty-six imprints that include HarperCollins (once Harper and Row), William Morrow, and Avon, with $1 billion annual revenues.[19]

In due course, one station at a time, small group by small group, Murdoch's Fox Network has emerged as the fourth TV network, joining what had been the old-line triumvirate of ABC, CBS, and NBC. Fox has twenty-three wholly owned or affiliated network stations in the United States; is the prime broadcaster of sports, with twenty different sports-broadcasting franchises around the country; and has a reputation for the network with the most violent shows on TV, a superlative that in U.S. television requires a truly prodigious flow of blood on the screen.

The man famous for the most open display of supporting only far-right commentators, many of them shouters of insults about broadcasters considered insufficiently conservative, seems to have a certain lack of self-awareness. When satirical author Al Franken issued a book called *Lies, and the Lying Liars Who Tell Them: A Fair and Balanced Look at the Right*, lawyers for Murdoch filed a lawsuit claiming the theft of a trademark, namely, the title of Murdoch's news coverage, "Fair and Balanced," which an outside observer might consider cleverly self-satirical except that Murdoch uses it in dead, literal earnest. His lawyers told the court that Mr. Franken's book would "blur and tarnish" Murdoch's news.[20]

Bibles, Bottoms and Bosoms

With Murdoch's acquisition of DirecTV, the number of television and data channels he owns runs into the hundreds. He has thirty cable and satellite properties, including a half-interest in the National Geographic cable channel, in which he shares ownership with not only National Geographic but also his broadcast "competitor," General Electric, which owns NBC. Outside the United States, Murdoch owns twenty-eight broadcast channels in the United Kingdom, eight of them shared ownership with Paramount, Nickelodeon, and other British broadcasters. He owns two services in Germany, sixteen in Australia, one in Canada, six in India, a minority stake in an Italian station, two in Indonesia, two in Japan, and eight in Latin America.

Murdoch owns eight magazines in the United States, one of which is a conservative weekly edited by William Kristol and is the political primer for George W. Bush's White House policymakers.[21]

Motion pictures are also in the collection of the News Corporation, with eight subsidiaries, including Twentieth Century Fox. The total empire includes media in North and South America, Asia, and Australia. Murdoch owns thirty-one newspapers in Australia, three in Fiji—one in English, one in Fijian, and one in Hindi—and a half-interest in a New

Zealand newspaper chain. He is the largest broadcaster in Asia, with forty channels in eight languages, covering fifty-three countries.

His partnerships include major competitors in the United States, such as General Electric (NBC) and Paramount (Viacom).

Mr. Murdoch is a man of many parts. He still publishes the sex-and-sensation *News of the World,* which has the largest circulation in the United Kingdom, and, as noted by Rod and Alma Holmgren in *Outrageous Fortune,*[22] Murdoch has been called "buccaneer, tycoon, octopus, gambler, union scourge, and pirate." But he is also the owner of Vondervan, the company that publishes the largest number of commercially printed Bibles in America. One wonders whether somewhere a publishing deity grants Murdoch absolution because his "bottoms-and-breasts" *News of the World* has 4 million circulation, but his Vondervan sells 7 million Bibles a year.[23]

Viacom

What is now the fourth largest media conglomerate in the country began in the back room of a house in Chicago, where family members of a Russian immigrant spent their days rolling cigars. An uncle took each day's production to find smoke shops that would sell them. The business prospered, and Sam Paley, the cigar maker, opened first a small plant and then a dozen factories; finally he created a prize brand, La Palina, as in "Paley." Sam took his young son, William, into the business and sent him to the University of Chicago and the Wharton School of Business, by which time the family had moved to Philadelphia. Today's giant, Viacom, might not exist if young William had not taken advantage of a wild idea when he was left in charge while the rest of the family took a European vacation. He spent fifty dollars a week of company money to buy air time to put on what he called "The La Palina Hour" (it ran only thirty minutes).

A family friend bought a group of scattered radio stations that he called the Columbia Broadcasting System (CBS), though they were separate operations and not a system or network. In any case, they were dwarfed by the giant NBC. Soon, the CBS stations approached bankruptcy. Purely out of friendship, Sam Paley bought out his debt-loaded friend and, as much to be rid of a friendly burden as anything else, turned the stations over to his son William. Sam told a friend, "I just bought the Columbia Broadcasting System for my son. I paid a quarter of a million for it." Sam added that he doubted that it would amount to much.

CBS had no affiliates like those of NBC, which were required to take some programs from network headquarters on condition that they paid NBC, gave some time from their local schedules, and let NBC keep the money from its commercials. A real network was the only way the scattered CBS stations could hope to become a real system with a chance to compete with NBC. But CBS affiliates weren't willing to sacrifice any of their own moneymaking time for an unproven upstart. So William told his distant stations that he would produce shows himself and, unlike NBC, let the affiliates have them free of charge if they would give him spots during their schedule for a few of his CBS-made programs and commercials. CBS thus became a real network.[24]

With the start of World War II in Europe, CBS knew it needed correspondents in what was becoming the Battle of Britain against German air bombardments. In London, a tall, lean man from North Carolina was assigned to the job. For American listeners, his deep, resonant voice became a link to the sound of German bombs falling in London. As the war spread and America's role expanded, so did CBS reporting, and soon the tall, lean man from North Carolina, Edward R. Murrow, had gathered around him the reporters called "Murrow's Boys." For decades thereafter, they were the voices of CBS News—voices like those of Walter Cronkite, Howard K. Smith, Charles Collingwood, Marvin Kalb, and Charles Kuralt. Murrow's producer was a man born Ferdinand Friendly Wachheimer in Providence, R.I. A local Providence station hired him, and the first day his boss announced bluntly, "From now on your name is 'Fred Friendly.'"

The Murrow-Friendly team lasted until Murrow, whose chain-smoking was almost his trademark, died of cancer in 1965.[25]

For fifty years CBS was the gold standard of American radio and television news. It had the best documentary unit and the best news staff in American radio and television. When something big happened in the world, sophisticated Americans turned to CBS because when they suddenly heard, "We interrupt this program . . ." they knew that, if it was truly important, CBS would put it on the air at once and do it with trusted reporters. (CNN's twenty-four-hour news was not created until 1980 by Ted Turner.)

If the 1990s was the decade of the dot.com boom and bust, the 1980s was the decade of the hostile takeover. Investors looking for a killing would watch balance sheets of big corporations to see if they were putting some of their comfortable profits into more quality, giving some to shareholders, and putting some into reserves for a rainy day. Spotting that kind of prudent financial management, the takeover specialists would begin buying blocks of stock, thus raising profits to push share prices even higher. This would entice shareholders to sell their stock while prices were rising. Then, at the right moment, the hostile takeover operator would sell it all off to make instant millions and billions. Often, these operators left behind weakened or wrecked companies.

In 1986, CBS knew it was a target. General Electric had just paid $96 billion for RCA with its subsidiary, NBC.[26] CBS feared a similar fate and, like some other traditional corporations facing hostile takeovers, they looked for a "white knight," a sympathetic firm they could trust to buy enough controlling stock to rebuff the marauders. The Paleys believed they had found one in Lawrence Tisch, whose Leow's Investment Company owned billions in Manhattan real estate. Tisch agreed to be the white knight who would save CBS. In 1995, "White Knight" Tisch sold CBS to Westinghouse, which began selling off CBS subsidiaries for fabulous profits; Sony, for example, paid Tisch $2 billion for CBS Music Group alone.[27] In 1999, Viacom, headed by Sumner Redstone, who had become rich as the head of a film distribution firm, bought CBS for $50 billion. The CBS network came with its boss, Mel Karmazin. Three years earlier Karmazin had sold his radio group, Infinity Broadcasting, to Westinghouse Electric.[28] Karmazin had hoped to buy CBS himself. It was inevitable that Karmazin, with a tough and hard-driving personality, and Redstone would clash. Redstone won by conceding that Karmazin would have a three-year contract, to 2003, and that whenever Redstone, then eighty years old, ceased to be CEO, Karmazin would get the job.[29]

The two sparring leaders of the fourth largest media conglomerate in the country and one of the two hundred largest in the world are an odd couple: Redstone, a New Englander, Boston Latin, Harvard '44, Harvard Law School '47, and a familiar among high federal court judges, the Masons and the Harvard Club; Karmazin, born in a Long Island City housing project, his father a cab driver, his mother a factory worker. Starting as a smalltime worker in an ad agency, Karmazin worked with demonic zeal selling ads and became a phenomenon. He took a job at the new Infinity station group on condition that he get 1 percent of ownership, $125,000 starting salary, and a red Mercedes. After NBC fired "shock jock" Howard Stern and raunchy talk radio star Don Imus, Karmazin hired them for CBS on condition that their broadcast rants would never mention the name Mel Karmazin. His old boss, John Kluge of Metromedia, says that Karmazin's stake in CBS is worth $400 million, but in his ambitious and frugal way (except for the red Mercedes) "he acts like it's $40,000."

Redstone and Karmazin may be an odd couple, but after a period of public battle over the negotiations, they renewed the partnership in 2003, making peace only in a subtly worded press release. Together, feuding or not, they rule one of the largest media conglomerates in the world.

Bertelsmann and Its Ghost

If one drives southwest from Hanover, Germany, and is careful to remain on Berliner Strasse for about 125 kilometers, one will come to Gutersloh, a pleasant town of sculptured tulip gardens, high-spired churches, and tree-lined streams and lakes. It is a town of thirty-six thousand that lists as an honorary citizen, among others, Reinhard Mohn. This is the ancestral home of the Mohn family, who happen to own the privately owned firm of Bertelsmann A.G., the fifth largest media corporation in the United States and, among other things, the largest printer of English-language books in the world. Yet, Gutersloh is so obscure that it isn't even mentioned in American travel guide books on Germany, including the ones Bertelsmann owns, Fodor's Travel Guides.

The picturesque town gives little hint that Bertelsmann is one of the world's largest broadcasters, magazine publishers, and record companies, as well as a massive book publishing business. Like the other members of the Big Five that dominate the American media world, Bertelsmann's list of media companies is lengthy. It requires nine typed pages. Thirty percent of its holdings are in the United States, bringing from this source alone $63 billion annually.

Most of Bertelsmann's eighty-two book subsidiaries were once freestanding, independent publishing houses, some of them household words not so many years ago — Alfred Knopf, Pantheon, Random House, Ballantine, Bantam, Crown, Doubleday, and Modern Library. Its magazine groups include familiar names like *Family Circle* and *Parents* (joint ventures). The twenty different record labels issued by Bertelsmann include RCA, RCA Victor, and Windham Hill. Like others in the Big Five, Bertelsmann has shared enterprises with its "competitors," including a 50-50 ownership with Disney of a German TV operation, Super RTL.[30]

With all its power, Bertelsmann is haunted by a ghost.

Of all the new corporations that dominate the American scene, none can trace uninterrupted lineage as far back as Bertelsmann. In 1835, Carl Bertelsmann set up a print shop in Gutersloh to publish Lutheran hymn books. The company printed German-language editions of Lord Byron and the fairy tales of the Brothers Grimm. By the early 1900s, the company was a major publishing house with growing international subsidiaries.

With the advent of Hitler and Nazism in the 1930s and the aftermath horrors of the Holocaust in World War II, questions were asked how the company had emerged from the war ready to resume its growth around the world. To queries like "What did you do under Hitler?" the Bertelsmann official answer was, in effect, "We suffered for our anti-Nazism." Postwar records seemed to confirm this because in 1944 there was a temporary closure of the Bertelsmann plant in Gutersloh. But as postwar German archives became available, German sociologist Hersch Fischler discovered that, during the war, Bertelsmann had, in fact, been the largest publisher under Hitler. Among its 19 million books, it had large contracts from the Nazi Propaganda Ministry, including anti-Semitic tracts supporting Hitler's insistence that Germans needed to take over central and western Europe. One book echoed Hitler's propaganda claim. Bertelsmann's anti-Semitic tracts were standard literature for Hitler's Brown Shirts.

In Germany, as everywhere else, media power is political power, so even in postwar anti-Nazi Germany, Professor Fischler's findings were not printed in any German newspapers or magazines. They appeared first only in Switzerland and later in *The Nation* in the United States. Bertelsmann apologized and appointed a commission of four historians to study the entire wartime history of the company. As it had said, the company did stop publishing during the war but not because of its alleged anti-Nazism. The deteriorating Nazi regime had simply run out of paper. Presumably, by now the Nazi-era ghost has been exorcized, and the Bertelsmann empire continues to expand.[31]

In late 2003, Bertelsmann experienced the *Lear*-like question of family-run empires that was also true when Rupert Murdoch was forced to decide which of two sons would someday become the new leader. In the case of Bertelsmann, the leader was Reinhard Mohn, at eighty-six, an age that inevitably creates a sense of urgency over succession. His much younger wife, Elisabeth, sixty-six, is head of the trust that controls a majority of Bertelsmann stock and sits on the four-member committee within the board of directors that selects top executives. Some board members and executives have been restive over Mrs. Mohn's increasing power in replacing three executives and her appointing two of her three sons to operating influence within the giant firm. The German magazine *Der Spiegel* quoted one unhappy Bertelsmann executive as fearing "a matriarchal dynasty."[32]

Though unrelated to family members, the chieftains of the other three of the Big Five had their own leadership stresses. Case and Levin were unseated at Time Warner; Eisner was in trouble at Disney; and Redstone and Karmazin eyed each other warily on succession to the Viacom throne. Despite skirmishes over top leadership, the Big Five media conglomerates possess such commanding size and power in the marketplace that boardroom rivalries leave untouched their corporate domination of the country's mass media. Rivalries for top titles are merely part of personal intrigues typical of all hierarchies, described by Shakespeare, "Uneasy lies the head that wears a crown."[33]

* * *

As mentioned earlier, there might have been a sixth giant firm, Vivendi, of France, if its leader, Jean-Marie Messier, had not been too eager to join the club.[34]

Directors without Direction

The dominant media conglomerates are theoretically led by boards of directors who select the executives who run their enterprises. The theory in capitalist history and U.S. corporate law is that the boards are solely obligated to the stockholders of their company, who are owners of the firm. Stockholders by law elect the board of directors, who theoretically use their expertise to oversee the executives they appoint to do their duty to stockholders. In actuality, something else usually exists. It is not unusual for strong executives to select the directors who are supposed to monitor them, which guarantees sympathy and permissiveness. In most cases, the directors are identical as a class: they are, themselves, top executives of other large firms and conform to the culture typical of men and women who run large multinational corporations. Some are top men and women from the largest banks, directors who can facilitate credit and money for benefit of both their borrowing firm and their lending bank.

Though the Big Five are multinational corporations with complex financial and operational structures, family members of each firm's president sit on the board. Or the directors are friends who are also corporate executives. In a marginal public relations gesture, from time to time the board includes someone whose name is associated with a popularly known philanthropy.

It is illegal to have directors who interlock directorates with competing firms, but most board members have such complex interrelations that the law is seldom applied.

The News Corporation is headed by Rupert Murdoch, who became a U.S. citizen because he wanted to build a broadcast network and his American citizenship might finesse the law that no foreign entity may own more than 24.9 percent of a U.S. broadcast license. It was a transparent finesse because he kept his parent firm based in Australia for tax purposes. His board members include eleven interlocking directors, though ostensibly not in competitive firms. They include directors of British Airways, Compaq Computers, Rothschild Investment Trust, a media company, and YankeeNets, a professional hockey team. Murdoch family members sit on the News Corporation board: Rupert is chairman and chief executive, son Lachlan is deputy chief operating officer, and his younger brother, James, is chairman and CEO of the firm's major subsidiary, BskyB.[35]

Disney's board is heavy with executives from familiar big firms, and the "public" member is the internationally known, former U.S. senator George Mitchell (who has six other big firm directorships). It also includes three officers of the company, chairman and CEO Michael Eisner, president and chief operating officer Robert Iger, and vice chairman Roy Disney. Other directors include those from Boeing, City National Bank, Hospital Corporation of American (Columbia/HCA Healthcare Corp.), Edison International, two from FedEx, Northwest Airlines, Sotheby's, Starwood Hotels, Sun Microsystems, Xerox, and the media firm Yahoo. Ten of the sixteen directors have interlocks.[36]

Viacom's sixteen board members are from Avon Products, ChevronTexaco, Coca-Cola, Federal Reserve Bank of New York, Grupo Television, Home Depot, Kellogg, Knight-Ridder news company, Marriott, New York Stock Exchange, Ogilvy & Mather, TIAA-CREF, and Sun Microsystems (whose director also sits on the Disney board). Also among the directors are members of the family: Sumner Redstone, chairman and CEO; Brent Redstone; and Shari Redstone.[37]

Time Warner includes former Philip Morris CEO Michael Miles, who holds seven other directorships, and American Express, Cendant, ChevronTexaco, Citigroup, Dell Computer, Estee Lauder Companies, Fannie Mae, FedEx, Hilton Hotels, Morgan Stanley, Pearson plc (a major media firm), PepsiCola, and Sun Microsystems.[38]

Bertelsmann has a variety of boards and members, some honorary and titled, others members of the Mohn owning family and the Bertelsmann Foundation. Directors who sit on boards of firms familiar to Americans are those sitting on directorships of Mobilcom, Ernst & Young, Deutsche Bank, Lufthansa, Siemens, the newspaper *Neue Züricher Zeitung,*

Bombardier, GlaxoSmithKline, Petrofina, Princeton Review, Random House Mondadori, BMW, and Hapag-Lloyd. A separate supervisory board includes Reinhard Mohn, chairman emeritus of the firm; Gerd Schulte-Hillen, chairman; Rolf-E Breuer, chairman of Deutsche Bank; Liz Mohn, another family member; and an officer from IBM, plus others.[39]

It became clear during the boom, bust, and thievery by high officers during the 1990s and the early twenty-first century that boards of directors of some of the largest corporations in the United States had little knowledge of or influence over their top executives. A high degree of incuriosity and indifference permitted officers to make basic decisions without discussion or even notification of their directors. Balance sheets with unorthodox, illegal, or even nonexistent categories of assets and liabilities not only led to the Enron type of illegalities and total breakdown but also illuminated the distance so many boards of directors kept from what should have been their responsibilities. As a result, new regulations called for directors to sign off personally on public financial reports of the firms, causing dismay in more than one board member who had little real knowledge of what he or she was supposed to "direct" and "approve."

It is ironic that some of the greatest American corporations seem periodically to confirm the unhappy insight of Karl Marx that, left to its own devices, capitalism held within it the seeds of its own destruction.[40]

More immediately, the epidemic of greed and fraud grew out of the new doctrine of "the free market," which was taken as freedom from all responsibility, a misreading of a truly free market, in which firms with sufficient size and independence can truly compete among themselves.

There has been a high human cost to the failure of rigorous governmental oversight and antitrust suits in cases of market domination by major corporations with links to each other. By the turn of the twenty-first century, hundreds of thousands of employees had lost their jobs and pensions, and ordinary stockholders had been shocked by the sudden losses of large corporations whose executives operated fast and loose without independent, informed, and responsible boards of directors.

Beyond that, there is a basic lack of logic in a free market without serious governmental regulation. Every business in the world, whether it is a corner mom-and-pop candy store or a multinational conglomerate, is eager to dominate its market. The mom-and-pop store wants more of the community candy business than the store a block away. The global corporation, like the small corner store, wants the biggest available market share. Unfortunately, the perfect market share that all so eagerly aim for is 100 percent, which is a monopoly. That is why the not-so-hidden meaning behind the slogan "get government off our backs" eventually is "let us have either a monopoly or cooperative arrangements with a small number of our companies in the same business."

Adam Smith, the Scottish philosopher-prophet of capitalism so often cited as justification for monopolists, said his brilliant idea of capitalism instead of feudalism would fail if there were monopolies. He also wrote, in his historic treatise *An Inquiry into the Nature and Causes of the Wealth of Nations,* that he did not trust businessmen.[41] For whatever significance one wishes to invest in the coincidence, Smith published his book in 1776, a date of more than minor significance in the history of the United States.

What hath God wrought?
SAMUEL F. B. MORSE on his
invention of telegraphy

CHAPTER THREE

THE INTERNET

Millions of computer users around the world may feel empathy—or even mean satisfaction—to learn that the first recorded victims of a computer crash on October 20, 1969, were two of the most sophisticated computer people in the world. A small group of the scientists at the University of California at Los Angeles (UCLA) were excitedly trying a novel notion with a novel machine. They were attempting to get their computer to talk to another computer three hundred miles away, at the Stanford Research Institute in Palo Alto, California.

"We had a guy sitting at the computer console at UCLA wearing a telephone headset and a microphone, talking to another guy at Stanford," Professor Leonard Kleinrock told an interviewer from the *Toronto Star*. "When everything was set up he was going to type the 'L-O-G' and the Stanford computer would automatically add 'IN' to complete the word, 'LOGIN.' So our guy typed the 'L' and asked his counterpart at Stanford, 'Did you get the 'L?' Then they did the same thing for 'O' and the whole system crashed."[1]

Today millions of computers crash periodically, usually with more provocation than someone typing the letter "O." But in 1969, most people did not know the meaning of "computer crash." First, they would have to be told that there is an electronic machine called the computer that creates and transmits words, images, music, and data and from time to time, this experimental device has a nervous breakdown. It goes into a catatonic fit, becoming motionless and sullenly unresponsive, making no sounds. The only symptom is the too-familiar image of a nonfunctioning hourglass or arrow meaning, "I'm in a coma."

The Internet remains ambiguous as a "mass" medium because of its multiple functions and individualistic usage. On one hand, it does not fit the usual definition of a mass medium because it has no centralized control deciding what shall be disseminated to the general public. On the other hand, it is a medium that has demonstrated its mass effects in news, in general information, and in its growing impact on a large portion of the population.

The Internet is important in this book because it has had a significant influence on the traditional mass media. Samuel Morse's telegraph shrank geography as a factor in communications. For all practical purposes, when he sent his historic message by an actual wire to Congress to demonstrate the invention, Baltimore and Washington might have been as close as two people talking on the sidewalk. Among other things, the telegraph also changed the nature of news and newspapers. The Internet holds still greater capacities for shrinking not only distance in the communication of messages, but it has also eliminated the wire connection, thus spreading instant transmission to all parts of the world. It has made available an almost unimaginable mass of the world's information. Like the telegraph, it has changed the operations of all the mass media and in addition has invented original forms of news and other media.

The Internet has already become both a competitor against the printed news industry and also an adjunct to it.

Few newspapers of normal size, for example, lack a web site with briefs of their most important or popular stories. In some cases, with a subscription one can receive not only Internet copies of the newspaper's entire printed story but additional information on the same subject beyond what was printed.

Magazines have their Internet versions in the form of "zines." Magazine-like articles and advertisements appear on their own web sites. Books appear in digital form, which has raised questions about the future viability of centrally produced books printed on paper, as we have known them for centuries.

Consequently, the history and subsequent emergence of the computer into the modern media scene is as significant as the invention of high-speed presses was to the history and social effects of newspapers and magazines.

Professor Kleinrock's experience with computer-to-computer communication, despite its crash, was infinitely more sophisticated than the original computer at the University of Pennsylvania in 1944. That was an electronic monster called Eniac (Electronic Numerical Integrator and Computer) that weighed thirty tons, was the size of a modest house, contained nineteen thousand vacuum tubes, and, when it was finally working, could multiply 9 by 9.[2]

It all began in 1939, when it became clear that there would be war in Europe. President Franklin Roosevelt realized that if Britain and France fell, Hitler planned to isolate the United States. He also knew that the United States, its military still traumatized by the carnage of World War I's land battles and by the Great Depression, had only skeletal military technology to face the formidable, advanced Nazi air force and its state-of-the-art land weapons. Roosevelt, faced with a strong antiwar movement at home, was privately convinced that a European-Asian general war would inevitably involve the United States. He took euphemistic measures like aid "to our British cousins," and at home, he initiated what was then arcane technology of no interest to the general public.

Military experts told Roosevelt that our ground weapons were hopelessly obsolete, including nineteenth-century methods of aiming shells and air bombs. In both cases it was, "That one went too far, let's adjust—oops! That was too short, so let's try something in between." In the meantime, enemy high-tech weaponry could wipe out the American cannon and aircraft. The need was for calculating machines that would instantly calculate and correct artillery and aerial bomb trajectories.

The Army commissioned a laboratory at the University of Pennsylvania to come up with an electronic method. The technology was intimidating. It was not successful until 1945, the last year of the war. By then Eniac could go from simple multiplication to square roots and complex trigonometric calculations.[3]

Eniac's successors eventually developed billions of times more speed, and only then could the Internet be created. Fifty years later, the thirty-ton monster at the University of Pennsylvania had become a popular, hand-held device small enough to be slipped into a pocket or purse and with a billion times greater capacity and speed.[4]

The Internet: Liberator or Big Brother?

In a stunningly short time, the computer's Internet has become a moving force that has transformed the world of communications and the mass media. It has raised conflicts with existing laws, created legal struggles with the media oligopoly, become an instrument for mobilizing mass protests, accelerated the rate of social change around the globe, and introduced a new political battleground over a range of issues from obscenity to copyright law.

Within thirty-two years, in the United States alone, 2 million more people a month would be using the Internet for the first time, and more than 90 percent of children between the ages of five and seventeen would already use computers at home or in school. By 2003, more than 160 million Americans were using the Internet. The advance was so rapid that young people have grown up with almost instinctual familiarity with the machine and its complex programs, while many older men and women still take courses in basic computer skills. More than one parent has had to ask an adolescent child how to solve a computer problem.[5]

By 2003, an Internet shop was established at the 17,400-foot level of Mount Everest, at 25 degrees below zero. The chilled entrepreneurs assumed that the twenty thousand people a year who get to at least that level of the world's tallest mountain would not resist sending an instant e-mail announcement of their feat to friends in other parts of the world.[6]

A Machine with Its Own Language

The Internet has its own language and grammar, also as familiar to millions as addressing an envelope to be sent by the post office. Like postal mail, whose zip codes are used without necessarily understanding mechanisms within the zip code system, the Internet has exotic addresses with terms used every day by people who neither know nor care to know their literal meanings. Computer users see "http://www," for example, read it or type it without concern for its literal meaning. The beginning, "http," is "HyperText

Markup Language" that permits displays of material possibly related or relevant to the precise item for which the user asked, while "www" is "World Wide Web," which extends any computer to any other computer in the world. A common part of an e-mail address is "dot.com," the "com" indicating an address for a business or corporation. Other common address terms are "dot.gov" for governmental units and "dot.edu" for colleges and universities.[7]

Like the system itself, the growth of Internet and computer languages has been phenomenal, and many Internet citations are used in this book and its notes. In 2003, one Internet publisher claimed a 33,000-word glossary. By that year, there were already 350 dictionaries of computer terms published in the United States.[8]

World use of the Internet for e-mail is now a major competitor with governmental postal systems, including in the United States. The first postal service in the country was started one hundred years before there was an independent United States. Although the U.S. Post Office continues to be an effective and massive system, since the computer and Internet e-mail entered the scene, the historic service has been given the humiliating Internet term *snail mail*. From 1980, before the computer was a common household device, to 1990, the postal service enjoyed a 57 percent increase in pieces of mail handled, but during the 1990s, it had slowed to a 26 percent increase.[9]

As the Internet grew in size and versatility, a wide variety of users grew in parallel—individuals; commercial firms; advertisers; governments of cities, counties, and states; national executives and their clerks; ad agencies; political parties; protest movements; and philanthropic organizations. The Internet is widely used to play games on the monitor screen or to look for possible mates or dates. Many company trucks and vans that once carried large numerals of their street and city addresses and phone numbers, more frequently now show only their Internet dot.com address.

Like Gutenberg's movable type and printing, the Internet has introduced social and legal complications. It has altered many parent-child patterns. Parents who think their children are playing computer games may ask, "Are you doing your homework?" and the child may turn to the homework—using the same computer. The traditional "separation" that late adolescents normally experience as they enter early adulthood in distant colleges is altered, typically by daily or weekly "chats" with parents by way of portable laptop computers that maintain the earlier household parent-child familiarity.[10]

During the growth of the economy and of computer use in the 1990s, the "dot-com boom," it became possible to play the stock market by home computer. There was always a stock market open somewhere in the world. Thousands of newcomers to the stock market spent days or nights in e-trading. As in any casino, some made fortunes and most went broke when they discovered that stocks do not endlessly and universally rise in value.

Nevertheless, in 2003, a Pew Foundation study found that among family members and close friends of those who used the Internet, 42 percent of adults chose not to. They preferred handwritten letters or feared the computer's notorious seductive ability to make users forget the passage of time. These deliberate nonusers did not want to reduce their normal face-to-face activities.[11] (The hours of unnoticed time one can spend on the Internet has its own jargon, a *time swamp*.)

Personal and organizational e-mail grows at a sometimes appalling rate, much of it welcomed but much of it unwanted. More than one commercial or personal user has turned on the Internet to find fifty or one hundred new incoming messages to be answered or quickly canceled (*zapped* in computer slang).[12]

Despite the spectacular rise of Internet use, a 2002 Harris Poll on the use of leisure time found that reading headed the list, with 28 percent of those polled. Next came TV watching, with 20 percent. Gallup and Pew polls showed similar results—in the last twenty years reading has remained the most common use of leisure time.[13]

At the same time, the Pew Internet and American Life Project reports that nonusers of the Internet include disproportionate numbers of minority, rural, and low-income families with members who did not attend college. When the desire is great enough, many of those without home computers go to public libraries, in which computers are now standard fixtures, or to homes of friends who do have computers so they can communicate with distant sons or daughters; this was particularly noticeable during the U.S. war in Iraq in 2003.[14]

Privacy, a constitutional protection under the Fourth Amendment, has become more complex with widespread use of computers and the Internet. Every computer in the world has a unique, usually unseen, identification number. Because the computer is sensitive to outside signals, secret intrusions can implant a destructive "virus" or "worm" with a message to destroy the computer's contents. Antivirus programs are a substantial commercial product.

The intrusion can come from sophisticated individuals, usually under the age of thirty, variously known as hackers, crackers, sneakers, cyberpunks, and phreaks. They learn how to discover computer addresses and decode passwords and coded messages. Some do it for the sheer egotistical demonstration of computer skill, others out of malice and mischief. Secret electronic intrusion can also be for theft or examination of private correspondence, "break-ins" of particular concern to commercial firms, whose correspondence and work often constitute a major part of their enterprise. Many industrial and financial firms routinely encode much of their communication.

Computer hacking has given birth to new categories of laws and penalties, especially if the hacker steals credit card numbers, valuable computer files, or software designs, or if he uses the new knowledge to engage a computer user in a fraudulent financial scheme. Penalties for malicious computer intrusion range from a $500 fine to fifteen years in prison or, if criminal activity crosses state lines, a $250,000 fine and a year in prison for each offense.[15]

Historic civil liberties have been altered because the same secret intrusion can now be accomplished by government agencies. A major change in privacy occurred after the attacks against the United States on September 11, 2001. In the shock of the devastating catastrophe that destroyed the two World Trade Center buildings and part of the Pentagon, President Bush proposed and Congress acquiesced in the USA Patriot Act, which gave the federal government sweeping powers to override the Fourth Amendment and, among other things, make unannounced and secret intrusions into private homes and computers without obtaining a warrant from the normal court system. That was not legal prior to 9/11 (national shorthand for the date of the al Qaeda attacks and its many consequences). The Patriot Act expires in 2005, but there is no expiration date for the "sneak and peek" provisions that permit the FBI and CIA to make secret visits to homes and offices without informing their owners.[16] The new government power is a major contradiction of central provisions of the Bill of Rights.

Private and commercial computers have proliferated as free or fee-based. Close to universal in public libraries, they have become a common device in commercial centers and computer shops and are often a twin enterprise with a coffee café. They followed the earlier path of copying centers created by the predecessor technology of high-quality, fast copying machines. It is now common to find a copying machine as an adjunct to small town's supermarket or drugstore. Here, for varying fees, the public can copy printed texts or items like illustrated wedding and birth announcements. Despite common placards warning that some copied material may be subject to copyright restrictions, quantities of privately duplicated documents are, knowingly or not, copyrighted material. Duplicators of copyrighted documents may do so legally without paying a fee under an exception. The exception, called *fair use*, is to use only a brief portion of the document—typically a paragraph or two—that does not substitute for a paid purchase of the whole copyrighted work.

The Ownership of Words

The Internet has added to the complexities of copyright. Copyright, historically, was enacted to protect the creators of literature, art, and other personal works and their publishers. But as creative work has quickly become the property of the dominant media conglomerates, copyright has become a public and legislative battle. On one side the media industry has used its considerable political power to gain unprecedented extension of copyright protection of their media products. On the other side are scholars, scientists, and civil libertarians who fear "perpetual copyright," in which more and more of national and world culture disappears from the free public domain and becomes available only after paying a license or usage fee to one of the dominant media corporations.

Media conglomerates control so much information and

their media products bring in such high revenues that they fight the use of home computers to reproduce commercial recordings and other copyrighted digital material. Media firms' copyrighted properties include music in various forms, and they have created a continuing battle centered on music compact disks (CDs). As computer sound improved, a generation adept at computer skills and devoted to popular music found itself in the center of legal battles.

Compact disks represent a substantial commercial enterprise that some time ago replaced the older phonograph records (although they are sold in what are still called *record stores*). Phonograph records required banks of expensive materials: recording equipment, studios, and manufacturing plants. But most personal computers allow the user to insert inexpensive blank compact disks that cost a dollar or less, and record ("download") musical numbers. Commercial music CDs in the familiar jewel box cases cost an average of seventeen dollars and contain the manufacturer's own selection of performers and songs, but a CD can be copied from the Internet for $9.99.[17]

Younger users found that they could select their own favorite individual musical numbers, often with the best-known performers and the most popular songs, put them all on one CD of their own, and do it for the cost of the blank CD. They could also send it by computer to friends. Often that informal network is in homes and on campuses across the country. In the usual geometric progression, where each number is multiplied by the preceding number, as in 1-3-9-27-81-243 . . . , as one student sent a self-made CD recording to six friends and each of the six friends sent it to six other friends, and so on, it was not long before the number of privately reproduced CDs could reach a million. One firm, Napster, even provided a large collection of popular numbers free to computer users. Napster, like most of the free computer services, made its profits from advertisers whose product promotions ran alongside the computer message. Almost all the copied songs were copyrighted.

The recording industry, faced with tracking down and suing a seemingly infinite number of young people, brought suit against Napster and won. Though Napster in its old form disappeared, other firms like KaZaA took its place, and they too became involved in industry lawsuits. The record industry, most of them subsidiaries of the Big Five media giants, has been resigned to easy copying and reacted by permitting downloading legally if one paid a monthly fee or purchased special computer programs from record companies. The music industry permits listeners to have access to a pool of about 150,000 songs online for nine or ten dollars a month and ninety-nine cents per download of one copy on one CD that can serve no more than two computers and is not sent outside the home or office.[18]

Illegal recording of copyrighted material is hardly limited to college students in the United States. It is a worldwide phenomenon. In Peru, for example, 98 percent of CDs are said to be pirated in this way, the highest rate in the world but indicative of unlicensed copying globally.[19] Since 1999, the sales of recording firms have dropped 14 percent. These firms place much of the blame on pirated disks. What is offered tourists and pedestrians on city street corners by nervous men keeping an eye out for the police are usually pirated CDs. They are the digital counterparts of cheap imitations of high-priced branded items, like "genuine" Gucci handbags and Rolex watches sold by the same kind of furtive sidewalk vendors.

Pirated CDs have been joined by privately and usually secretly made copies of motion pictures. These involve optical disks, digital (DVD) blank disks, and videocassettes. By 2002, DVD players, quickly superceding videocassettes, were in 50 million homes. Though downloading an entire motion picture is more complex and far more time consuming (requiring several hours), the Motion Picture Association claims that as many as 600,000 films are copied a day. The association has worked with manufacturers to create devices that will manufacture DVDs that cannot be copied, has sent agents with night-vision glasses into theaters to catch individuals with recording equipment in their laps, and plans theater previews with notices warning that the movies about to be shown are copyrighted, with criminal penalties for unauthorized copying. One firm experiments with DVDs that will self-destruct after being used twice. The industry has succeeded in amending laws in some states to make it a crime to copy cable and TV output.[20]

Another action by the largest media corporations has alarmed scholarly users of journals and books. This is a campaign to extend even further the years of copyright control.

Spam—Digital Telemarketing and e-Bank Robbery

Yet another problem created by the rapid penetration of the Internet has been *spam,* the unwanted intrusion into personal computers using e-mail of commercial advertisements, some of which have bombastic graphic explosions and other eye-catching advertising (named for the brand name of a canned *spiced ham,* for which World War II soldiers had a less reverent term). The attraction for advertisers is obvious: a captive audience at the lowest price per capita of any medium, five hundred dollars to intrude on a million e-mail messages. Some members of Congress have asked for legislation that would require spam advertisers to list valid e-mail addresses, which would make it easy for irritated computer users to demand that their computers be removed from the spammer's list. A 2003 law created a national do-not-call list that forbids commercial telephone telemarketers to call those numbers. The law imposes heavy dollar penalties for firms that ignore each request to cease their unwanted calls. (Telemarketers for philanthropic organizations and political campaigns are exempted from the new law.)

Nevertheless, by 2002, AOL, one of the most popular Internet service providers, with 35 million customers, said that 70 percent of its nearly 2 billion messages were spam. It is still a low-cost, legal way to reach customers, costing $500 to $2,000 dollars to reach a million e-mail recipients, compared to a minimum of $230,000 to do it by the post office's bulk mail.[21] Another popular Internet access provider, Earthlink, had to deal with one illegal spammer who sent 825 million e-mails using 343 credit cards and bank accounts the culprit had gained by breaching the usual safeguards in the system.[22] Eventually, after a lengthy and costly investigation, the spammer was caught.

It is a measure of the speed and efficiency of Internet communication that it overshadows a printed and mailed version of spam—the daily delivery to personal mailboxes by the U.S. Postal Service.

While Internet spam and postal delivery of spam are clearly different in sheer numbers, they both display a measure of the endurance of a historic pattern of technology. A new technology widely adopted by society seldom causes its older competitor to disappear at once. The usual result is that both continue for significant periods, sometimes for decades and even centuries. Books and scrolls were in simultaneous use for thirteen centuries (scrolls still exist as honorific documents, like graduation certificates and awards). Horses and automobiles, for example, remained in use together for decades.

Consequently, Internet and postal spam have continued to exist together. Mass marketers of printed material select zip codes covering neighborhoods shown by census data to have affluent residents, and many homes find that their daily mail delivery is mostly printed spam—unasked-for catalogues and supermarket and wholesale outlet flyers, many of them addressed merely to "Resident." Like Internet spammers, printed spammers, whether philanthropic organizations sending continual appeals for funds or commercial firms inviting new business, have learned to use misleading envelopes marked "URGENT" or "time-sensitive material inside." Their mass addressing machines frequently use what appears to be handwritten personal addresses and vague return addresses. Even though most weary householders whose mail is more spam than personal messages have learned the telltale signs of printed spam and send it unopened from mailbox to waste basket, enough gets opened and read—as little as 3 or 4 percent—that it is still profitable for print spammers.

If Internet spam has any redeeming social value, it does not require denuding the landscape of materials from which to make paper for print spammers. Internet spam is an electronic pattern on a computer screen and denudes only the patience of the home or office user having to navigate the inundation of electronic junk mail among genuine personal Internet e-mail and information services.

The magnitude of spam, nevertheless, is massive. Microsoft, the largest provider of Internet mail accounts, in 2003 brought a series of lawsuits against a known group of spammers who, according to Microsoft, sent e-mail users more than 20 billion e-mail messages that were commercial promotions not requested by the computer user. Microsoft's e-mail server is "hotmail," and in its lawsuit Microsoft claims that it has 140 million users of hotmail who receive a total of 2.5 billion e-mail messages a day, 80 percent of which is spam. Other major Internet e-mail providers say they have similar problems with spam. Microsoft and other firms offer filters to weed out spam, but it remains uncertain whether filters can alter the massive spreading of spam. Sending out spam messages is so inexpensive per one thousand recipients that, even if most of it is zapped out unread, enough will pique a receiver's curiosity to result in profitable sales. With every mailbox, computer e-mail service, or message, the odds are that the visitor is a sales pitch.[23]

Lost in the universal new culture of the Internet is the fact that the canned meat from which the Internet term *spam* descended is still alive and angry. The *San Francisco Chronicle* reported on July 3, 2003, that the Hormel Meat Company had brought suit against a firm selling antispam computer software, alleging that it was damaging the reputation of the meat product that is still sold in markets.

Mickey Mouse Meets Barbie Doll

Copyright complexities created by computers have extended far beyond collegians or Peruvians exchanging song collections. Media firms now own most of the money-making media of all kinds, and copyright law is essential to their large annual revenues. Ordinarily, copyrighted material has a definite half-life. When the copyright runs out, the material goes into the public domain, free for use by anyone; if the product is sold, the price is not automatically higher because a license fee charged by the copyright holder has no longer been added to the retail price. Thus, copyright is a monopoly for whoever owns the copyright.

Copyright law is in the U.S. Constitution. "The Congress shall have Power. . . . To promote the progress of science and useful arts, by securing for limited times to Authorized Inventors the exclusive Right to their own Writings and Discoveries."[24]

The first copyright lasted 14–14, or fourteen years from creation plus one renewal for another fourteen years. In 1909 the term increased to 28–28. A 1976 revision expanded the copyright term to the life of the author plus fifty years. In 1990 it was expanded to include computer software and in 1992 to include audio and video recordings. The Digital Millennium Copyright Act of 1998 was optimistically thought to solve any problems created by the digital revolution. It did not.

The massive collection of media material by a few powerful conglomerates in the last thirty years created a historic shift from the original focus on individual authors and the large number of independent publishers to the modern drive by large national and international media conglomerates to protect masses of material and their billions of revenues under their control for as long as possible.

The most publicized (and lobbied) reopening and extending of copyright law was the terrifying prospect for the Disney Company that the copyright on Mickey Mouse would expire in 2003. This expiration endangered not only the fortunes of the movie rodent but profits from sales of millions of T-shirts, toys, and other emblems of the mouse. This, with the help of other media corporate lobbying, led to the Sonny Bono Copyright Extension Act (the full and legal name of the law, named for the late singer and member of Congress). It extended copyright by twenty years, to the life of the author or creator plus seventy years. Thus, control of Mickey Mouse is expanded to 2023, Pluto to 2025, Goofy to 2029, and Donald Duck to 2029—ninety-five years after the duck first appeared in a film. The new law provides a term of life of the author plus seventy years for work for hire and for anonymous works taken over by some entity to a total of 120 years.[25]

Symbolic of the new interest in copyright, which once was an arcane corner of law limited to specialists, is the realization that the homely song "Happy Birthday" is copyrighted. The song was written in 1893 by a kindergarten teacher in Louisville, Ky., as "Good Morning to You" for greeting the teacher. When Western Union telegraph delivered telegrams by uniformed young men riding bicycles, among the messages that could be purchased at a premium rate was "Happy Birthday" sung by the bicycle messenger at the recipient's front door.

The copyright to "Happy Birthday" now belongs to Time Warner, which earns about $2 million a year from the song's license fees. There is no attempt to prevent the song being sung in private homes or hole-in-the-wall restaurants, but a copyright fee is applied to large, highly frequented restaurants and other public places. Some fashionable restaurants have stopped their staffs from singing it for birthday-celebrating patrons and instead use improvised tunes and words of their own. University film-making classes are warned not to have scenes where people sing "Happy Birthday." But broadcasters and other users in public places with paying audiences are supposed to pay a royalty each time the song is used.

There are limits on what violates copyright. A Danish group recorded a satirical song including the lyrics "I'm a blonde bimbo in a fantasy world / Dress me up, make it tight, I'm your doll." Mattel, toymakers who own the copyright on the Barbie doll, sued the song group because the lyrics could be interpreted to refer to Barbie. (Apparently, Mattel was willing to assume in court that "Barbie," the quintessence of cute dolls for little girls, could be a "bimbo.") The Supreme Court rejected the suit, saying that satire of a commonly known object is not violation of copyright.[26]

Despite the new laws, computer web sites still offer copyright-dodging computer programs for a price. These may or may not be legal and may or not work, but they typify the still-growing place of the computer in the media world and the growing conflict between private ownership and uninhibited public access.

Were it left up to me to decide whether we should have a government without newspapers or newspapers without government, I should not hesitate a moment to prefer the latter.
THOMAS JEFFERSON, 1787, before he became president

Nothing can now be believed which is seen in a newspaper.
THOMAS JEFFERSON, 1807, while he was president

CHAPTER FOUR

(NOT) ALL THE NEWS THAT'S FIT TO PRINT

In the autumn of 2002, the major news media faced a historic test of their place in American democracy. The crucial test has always been that, when faced with government coercion or distortion of reality, the news media, protected by the First Amendment of the Constitution, would tell the American people the closest approach to the truth that is possible for a human institution.

In 2002, the main body of the American news media failed that test.

*   *   *

In January 1998, New Line Pictures of Hollywood released a Barry Levinson movie with a moderately interesting plot. A U.S. president is facing problems in his hopes for re-election. He calls in a noted political propagandist to cover up the presidential vulnerability. The spin doctor, played by Robert DeNiro, has a bold idea: divert public attention from the president's domestic problems by starting a war. The movie was called *Wag the Dog*.[1]

In real life, as midterm elections approached in September 2002, the Bush White House had mounting problems. The headlines meant troubles for the Republicans, who controlled the presidency and both houses of Congress but the Senate only barely, within two votes. National trends favored Democrats. Front pages of major papers and TV network news almost daily reported rising unemployment and more mass layoffs,[2] the national economy was in trouble, the stock market was sinking, and new scandals of corporate fraud and theft were reported day after day.[3] Executives and other corporate insiders, knowing that their companies would soon suffer losses or face fraud investigations, were further destabilizing the economy by dumping their own stocks at mammoth profits before warning other shareholders that their shares might be worthless, possibly by bankruptcy.

President Bush and Vice President Richard Cheney had entered office having just sold personal stocks in companies they controlled under circumstances similar enough to raise eyebrows.[4] The powerful Senate Republican majority leader, Trent Lott, had to resign after revelations that he had delivered a racist-tainted speech and maintained racist membership in a Mississippi group.[5] If Democrats took the Senate, there would be bruising queries into Republican embarrassments involving both the White House and the Congress.

But it was not to be. After Labor Day, when serious election campaigns were building, President Bush, speaking in front of the Statue of Liberty, announced that he would go to war against Iraq and its dictator Saddam Hussein. Hussein, the president said, possessed "weapons of mass destruction" that created an imminent threat to the United States. When some dubious Democrats asked for details before going to war, President Bush accused them of unconcern for the security of their country. That silenced the Democratic leadership, and American troops gathered on Iraq's borders as war fever escalated.

Later, in his State of the Union speech, President Bush announced that "intelligence sources" had found that Iraq had 30,000 munitions capable of delivering chemical agents, 500 tons of chemical weapons, 25,000 liters of anthrax, and 38,000 liters of botulism toxin. Iraq, he said, harbored major al Qaeda cells determined to destroy the United States and was importing uranium for nuclear bombs.[6]

The president said the danger was such an imminent threat to the United States that he would not wait for results from inspectors from the United Nations and the International Atomic Energy Commission, who already were combing Iraq. He said he had "lost patience" with the United Nations. With 260,000 U.S. troops waiting on the Kuwait border of Iraq, the president made clear that he would invade Iraq at once.

From that moment on, the domestic issues of the United States disappeared off front pages and network prime news. Despite worsening domestic problems, what dominated the news was the country's preparation for war with flags flying, photographs of Marines preparing for the invasion, and video scenes of fighter planes catapulting from decks of aircraft carriers. Though the economy at home sank even deeper, it was now relegated to minor news as the White House intensified its pronouncements of imminent war. Wars and approaching wars always benefit incumbents in high office, and the Republicans swept the midterm elections, winning control of both House and Senate.

The sudden turn of events had a remarkable similarity to the four-year-old movie *Wag the Dog*. If the president had "wagged the dog," unfortunately, the bulk of the country's news media wagged its tail in happy agreement.

The Obedient Tail That Wagged

It has been the proud boast of the U.S. news media that, unlike the puppet press of dictatorial governments, the American news takes particular pleasure in finding high officials who are lying or straying from the truth by exaggeration. But in plans for the 2002 war in Iraq, they had failed their duty.

Months later, with Iraq in rubble after heavy U.S. air bombardment and tank attacks, American troops took control of the shattered country. But no one could find the weapons of mass destruction President Bush had said were an imminent threat to the United States. Several thousand people, presumably civilian Iraqis, had been killed. American casualties, while far smaller, mounted with each day of occupation, as did massive sabotage of American military equipment.

One Iraqi battle episode dramatized the penalty when journalists become uncritical partners of government. Once President Bush's invasion had swept into Iraq with little or no organized resistance, there emerged the case of Private Jessica Lynch, an American woman soldier whose convoy took a wrong turn into an ambush. Private Lynch was injured when her vehicle collided with a truck. She was found by Iraqi doctors, who took her to what remained of a nearby Iraqi hospital.

That night, at U.S. Army headquarters, American corre-spondents were awakened for what was assumed to be a "hot story." Thinking that the unusual call in the middle of the night for an urgent press release meant that perhaps Hus-sein had been captured, the sleepy correspondents gathered and were told "the Jessica Lynch story."

Correspondents were told that Lynch had emptied her rifle fighting off attackers. Left without ammunition, she had been captured, sustained bullet and stab wounds, and been taken to an Iraqi hospital where Iraqi doctors slapped and interrogated her as she lay in bed with broken legs and arms and body burns. Shortly after midnight, a special U.S. unit with night vision glasses stormed the hospital with guns firing and special video cameras to record it all. Private Lynch was rescued from her Iraqi doctors, taken to a nearby helicopter, and flown to safekeeping for treatment by Amer-ican physicians. Later, the army announced that she could not be interviewed because she had suffered total loss of memory. The official video record and army story of her res-cue was shown on U.S. television, rousing horror and fury among viewers at the brutal Iraqi treatment of a wounded American woman soldier.

The story was false. The "rescuing" units did charge into the Iraqi hospital and retrieve Lynch, and she was part of the convoy that had lost its way and been ambushed. But Private Lynch had no bullet wounds or knife stabs; she had needed the usual treatment for broken bones and other injuries, which the Iraqi medical staff handled with kindness and pro-priety. They were attempting to find U.S. troops to whom they could return Private Lynch when the special units of the U.S. Army stormed into the hospital. Later, her father was indignant at the claim that she had any loss of memory. He said she had a clear mind about it all.[7]

The U.S. Army, of course, knew their original story was

false as soon as Iraqi doctors returned Private Lynch to her "rescuers." After the false story had gone through a complete news cycle as a sadistic horror, the army eventually corrected its fairy story. But only after the known falsity was permitted to spread throughout the world.

The significance is not that an incorrect initial story had been told. In the confusion of war these can occur innocently. But the incident demonstrated two significant consequences of the entire invasion. What the president's critics eventually called "a big lie" was his assertion of imminent danger to the United States from Iraq's readiness to use its huge stocks of weapons of mass destruction and its preparations for nuclear bombs aimed at the United States. That "big lie" preordained the almost inevitable, namely, the little "lies" to support it.

After the false version of the Jessica Lynch story was vividly displayed on world television, it is possible that many viewers believe to this day the legend of sadistic Iraqi doctors abusing a wounded American woman soldier, who was saved only by a heroic rescue by American special forces.

More than a year after President Bush's call to war, despite total control of Iraq and the seizure and interrogation of Iraqi nuclear, biological, and toxic gas experts, none of the massive weapons of mass destruction had been found. No al Qaeda cells were unearthed. The charge that Hussein was importing uranium had been known to be based on a forged document exposed months earlier by the CIA and a former U.S. ambassador as a forgery.[8]

Three months after President Bush declared the invasion "Mission Accomplished," angry Iraqi crowds, now without water, electricity, or food in the ruined cities, yelled angrily at American patrols, and American troops were killed and wounded by shadowy Iraqi and other Islamic guerrilla forces working to undermine U.S. control.

The Middle East had been destabilized, and many foreign populations and governments saw the invasion as a pretext for U.S. control of Iraqi oil and Persian Gulf petroleum channels. A substantial portion of the world's billion Muslims regarded the United States with fear, suspicion, or active hatred. Two of the country's important allies, France and Germany, felt they had been misled and referred to with contempt when they declined to join in President Bush's dismissal of U.N. inspectors and invasion of Iraq. Thereafter, both countries dealt with visiting high American officials with coolness and gestures that in diplomatic protocol are recognized as deliberately insulting (like having a foreign official of obviously lower rank officially greet a high American official).

One of the peculiarities of the Gulf War was an innovation of the Bush Pentagon. More than five hundred American journalists were "embedded" with particular fighting units of the military. This implied unimpeded access to the actuality of fighting, uninhibited by the restrictions and censorship of the first Iraq war under Bush the Elder in 1981. In actuality, it produced much firsthand video and reporting of individual movements in the invasion, but it was also a technique that produced less than a full view of the war.

Most of the embedded journalists were inexperienced and forbidden access to the commanders who had the full picture. George Wilson, one of the country's most experienced and respected military correspondents, reported in issues of the *National Journal* that the television images of ferocious and bitter fighting in the invasion were misleading. By his own observation during the invasion, the coalition forces found almost none of the standard minimum defenses of a country expecting an invasion—no tank traps, no earthen protective embankments, no serious minefields, and scarcely any evidence of uniformed military opposition. U.S.

troops, a minimal force so they could move fast, as insisted upon by Secretary of Defense Rumsfeld, met no organized resistance. Embedded television crews did transmit to the American television audience that the only real difficulty was the weather, with footage of masked special forces pushing through swirling sandstorms.[9]

Although President Bush could strut across the deck of the carrier *Abraham Lincoln* to proclaim, on national television, "Mission Accomplished," apparently neither he nor the American public was prepared for the postinvasion period of total chaos, guerrilla attacks by Iraqi groups in civilian dress, and crowds of Iraqis screaming "Go home" to American troops. The full impact of the postwar situation emerged from Iraq only slowly and painfully, an impact worsened by the avoidable flaws in the major news media.

The Legend of Private Lynch in microcosm reflects the more lasting corrosive effects of widespread deceptions about powerful events. Fundamental deceptions damage the public's ability to maintain a rational view of the real world. Once a basic untruth is rooted, it blurs a society's perception of reality and, consequently, the intelligence with which society reacts to events.

"Later" Is Too Late

Six months later, on June 22, 2003, by which time the basic grounds used for the preemptive invasion of Iraq were shown to be clearly untrue, the *New York Times* Sunday Week in Review ran a remarkably sweeping display that occupied the entire top half of the section's cover page. Over a color photograph of President Bush, a bold headline in large letters read: "Bush May Have Exaggerated but Did He Lie?" Surrounding the presidential photograph in familiar pose before microphones were boxed quotations of the president since found to be either exaggerations or lies.

It was, at long last, a clear examination of what President Bush had said and what appeared to be the contrary reality.

It was also a melodramatic statement for the most influential newspaper in the country to contribute to the history of the entire war. But it was too late to prevent the damage. That information had been known but not used at the time the president had announced he would go to war. That was when the country's news audience had been glued to the unfolding news.

In October 2002, five months before the preinvasion bombing of Iraq, Senator Robert Byrd, a Democrat from West Virginia, had publicized this past history of the "weapons of mass destruction" and placed the full details into that day's *Congressional Record*.[10] These details were never reported by the main print or broadcast media. Instead, there were snippets of Senator Byrd uttering brief, melancholic phrases, the video news giving the impression merely of an aging and somewhat pitiable old orator doing his sixty-second turn in the well of the Senate.

Independent documented information is most needed at the time when officialdom announces a crucial decision. That is when the audience is paying full and anxious attention to conflicting views being debated in Congress. In the prelude to the Iraqi invasion, the grounds used by President Bush to justify an immediate invasion were not new. They had been known for years in voluminous detail.

In the 1980s and afterward, the United States underwrote twenty-four American corporations so they could sell to Saddam Hussein weapons of mass destruction, which he used against Iran, at that time the prime Middle Eastern enemy of the United States. Hussein used U.S.-supplied poison gas against the Iranis and his Kurdish minorities while the United States looked the other way. This was the same Saddam Hussein who then, as in 2000, was a tyrant subjecting dissenters in his regime to unspeakable tortures and committing genocide against his Kurdish minorities.

In some ways even more disturbing was the failure of the major media to make clear to the public the meaning of crucial news reported by the news media themselves but treated as an interesting but ordinary news item. It was admitted by White House aides that the timing of the war announcement was calculated for maximum political effect on the approaching midterm elections. Andrew H. Card Jr., the White House chief of staff coordinating the effort, was asked why, if the White House knew during the summer that it would go to war in the fall, it had waited until the September election campaign season. Card replied, "You don't introduce new products in August."[11]

Sooner or later, important contrary news may be printed and broadcast, but in this and in too many other cases, "later" is "too late" to serve the country.

Hussein's dictatorship had committed horrors against dissenters among his own people, but he had been doing this for years with Washington's knowledge. Iraq, however, was unrelated to the September 11 attacks on the United States. All the attackers had been Saudis, and their mastermind, Osama bin Laden, was a Saudi multimillionaire Islamic fundamentalist who despised Hussein's secularism.

The Iraqi invasion left the country in shambles. The American occupying troops found no weapons of mass destruction, no nuclear bombs, no biological or poison gas supplies, and only a few missiles incapable of reaching beyond Iraq's immediate neighbors. Apparently, the catch phrase "weapons of mass destruction" was merely an excuse, and an invalid one, at that. Later, a chief architect of the war plans, Deputy Secretary of Defense Paul Wolfowitz, told an interviewer for the magazine *Vanity Fair:* "For bureaucratic reasons, we settled on one issue, 'weapons of mass destruction,' because it was the one everyone could agree on."[12] The immediate real reason, Wolfowitz told the interviewer, was to make it easier to remove U.S. troops from Saudi Arabia because the Saudi ruling family feared internal danger from Osama bin Laden's al Qaeda. Bin Laden is, or was (he had not been accounted for by late 2003), from a rich Saudi family.

The most important media were unusually accepting of official briefings at face value. There is little record of correspondents of major news organizations asking the authorities publicly to explain the record disclosed by Senator Byrd or to answer questions raised by *Slate* (a Microsoft Internet magazine) and by a Seymour Hersh article in *The New Yorker.* In the major news on which most Americans depend, such questions were, at best, a minor footnote overwhelmed by war drums in the headlines and on major TV network news.

The First Casualty

The main news media once again had succumbed to what many had hoped was a relic of the past. In a democracy, it should no longer be the case that "when war comes the first casualty is truth."[13] It is even worse that, when war is proposed but not yet begun, the news media fail to clarify the known facts and limit their main information source to the government, which is not, of course, going to display information and argue publicly against what it wishes to do.

If the country had taken the time to learn the details of Senator Byrd's full statement and if the main news media had examined their own files about the earlier Iraqi war of Bush the Elder and made the facts clear to the country, that might have given pause to the hand of Bush the Younger in ordering the reduction of Iraq to rubble.

But most of the country's major media, constitutionally and popularly expected to be the nation's primary truth tellers, became the first casualty. And while the proposed war was not yet a military engagement, the main media demonstrated that they could still be coerced, even at that crucial stage, into abandonment of their democratic duty and journalistic integrity when high officials challenge their patriotism and wave the American flag at them.

There have been too many past failures. They suggest not so much the inevitable imperfections of any human endeavor but a systemic flaw. The major news media present the public with unnecessarily incomplete news because, with rare exceptions, they take their news from governmental and private power centers and shun important contrary information because it is considered "too liberal" or "left."

Fifty years ago, the most crucial media, with the exception of only a handful of newspapers, failed to examine the available truth during Senator Joseph McCarthy's six years of national hysteria that destroyed individuals and damaged institutions and important agencies of government. His bombastic accusations of communist spies in government agencies exposed not one subversive who had not already been identified and dealt with by government agencies.

An end to the McCarthyist rampage came with the help of a historic incident in American journalistic history. In 1953, Edward R. Murrow broadcast another brutal televised destruction of an innocent. Murrow ended his damning review by confronting the entire American population with Shakespeare's line, "The fault, dear Brutus, is not in our stars, but in ourselves."[14] In the aftermath, CBS cancelled Murrow's program and from then on had him do relatively uncontroversial interviews with celebrities.

For more that a decade, from 1954 to the early 1960s, the main media failed to report the futile tragedy of the Vietnam War; the war news seen by most of the public was based almost entirely on official military and governmental briefings. Not until thirteen years after the United States officially entered the war in Vietnam did the truth about that tragic war come to most Americans when *The New Yorker* began publishing articles by independent American observers, a striking new voice among its best-known peers. *The New Yorker* continued to report the truth about the war even though the magazine, for the first time in its history, lost its place among the top publications in advertising revenue. Angered or frightened corporations stopped buying ads in what had once been the most profitable and most elite of popular magazines.[15] *The New Yorker* stories were a dash of cold water on years of official illusion and the refusal of presidents to accept the political penalty risked by admitting that they knew that the entire Indochinese military campaign was a tragic mistake. The mistake caused 212,000 U.S. casualties and the deaths of more than 2 million Indochinese.

War: Inevitable Lies, Deceptions, and Amnesia

The Iraqi invasion was not the first war in history, including U.S. history, to be started as a matter of official convenience or vanity of power rather than the necessity of repulsing invaders or ending cruel occupation. Wars are particularly vulnerable to one-sided reporting because war and approaching war arouse patriotism and support of the country's armed forces. Governments know this and use it to maintain a war fever that supports the authorities and intimidates opponents. That is why it is even more important for the news media in a democracy to provide the balance that best serves rational decision making among the population at large.

The inherent stupidity of war is peculiar to the human race. Some wars have started because enemies have thrust this pathology upon each other or have lusted for it on their own. Throughout the 800,000 words of his *War and Peace*, Tolstoy keeps asking why 10 million men would march toward the west to meet 10 million men marching toward the east for the sole purpose of slaughtering as many perfect strangers as possible. He concludes that the quest for power is unquenchable.[16]

The American Revolution began thanks to the stupidity of the British Crown, heedless that the colonists valued being English subjects and simply wanted to be treated like English citizens. The British underestimated the great riches in the North American continent and preferred to fight France, an old obsession, so they could continue to make money from East Indian spices.[17] It helped that they underestimated George Washington's stature and his deliberate avoidance of every possible engagement between the highly visible red-coated troops of the king and his own army of near-naked, starving men on the constant edge of mutiny. Washington knew the British were slow learners about not marching in rigid formation. He could hide the wretched condition of his army because the news media of the period were more interested in politics and the splendid British balls in Philadelphia than in accompanying Washington's army and reporting the miserable conditions it endured.

There was opposition in the English Parliament and some of the press. But there, too, opposition was overwhelmed by those friendly with the Crown and its foreign trade.

If real people and places had not been hurt, the War of 1812 against Britain would have made a comic movie with Peter Sellers. It was a classic case of the double-edged sword of speed or lack of it in communication. It also reflected the split between the North and its antiwar press and the South with its pro-war press. President Madison was a southerner and could not resist declaring war against the more powerful British, who had been seizing American vessels and crews. (Madison had a tiny navy of six ships, and the British had more than one hundred.) In London, the British had announced that they would no longer seize American ships, but by the time the sailing vessel carried that news across the Atlantic, the war had begun—the British had burned the White House, the Capitol, and other public buildings and had bombarded Baltimore and its harbor's Fort McHenry. British and Americans meeting in Ghent, Belgium, signed a peace treaty, ending the war on December 24, but, again, the sailing ship carrying the news reached the United States too late.

The biggest engagement of the war, the Battle of New Orleans, was fought a week later, on January 1, with the American army under Stonewall Jackson shooting from behind bales of cotton at the splendidly red-coated English troops. Jackson won a great victory that made him famous enough to become the seventh president of the United States.[18] During that war, the Americans lost their government buildings, but a young Maryland poet named Francis Scott Key composed a poem inspired by seeing the tattered U.S. flag still flying over Fort McHenry in the glare of bombs bursting in air. Key's poem was set to the tune of an English drinking song, and the new country got its national anthem, "The Star-Spangled Banner."

The clearest case of a media-inspired war—the 1898 Spanish-American War to get the Spanish out of Cuba—was pretty much an invention of William Randolph Hearst, aided and abetted by Joseph Pulitzer. Spain considered Cuba part of her Latin American possessions. Periodic rebellions by natives had been put down, some with savagery that was covered vividly by American daily papers, particularly the expansionist Hearst paper the *Journal* and the paper of Hearst's rival, Joseph Pulitzer's *World*. Any real brutality was embroidered by florid details added by the Hearst and Pulitzer writers.

The newspapers had a free hand for two reasons. The multiple rebellions on the island endangered heavy American corporate investments there, and President Theodore Roosevelt had an interest in keeping Spain out of the hemisphere and was under pressure to protect endangered American firms in Cuba. The island was in such turmoil that it was difficult to obtain clear, systematic information. In the void, Hearst and Pulitzer became the U.S. source of real and imagined events, specializing in gory and sexual details of real and imagined atrocities. Hearst had what he called "commissioners" on the island, a stable of artists and writers sending back what they guessed might be happening. Hearst finally decided to get the better of Pulitzer and send some big-name "commissioners" to Cuba. Richard Harding Davis was the best-known correspondent in the United States and was sent to Cuba at three thousand dollars a month (at the time a fortune for reporters anywhere). He wrote stories like one about Spanish officials taking all the clothes off three Cuban girls preparing to board an American steamer for New York. The Spanish said they were simply looking for smuggled documents under the girls' clothing. The Hearst front page headline was "DOES OUR FLAG PROTECT WOMEN?"

Raising the level of vivid stories led to Hearst adding one of the best-known artists of the time, Frederic Remington, to join Davis. For the "three naked girls" story, Remington drew an imagined scene of the three girls being undressed by men. Davis felt it necessary to state that he had never said that men undressed the young women. Female Spanish inspectors did the search.

Hearst asked for more pictures of the war from Remington. By this time, Remington seemed to have had enough and sent Hearst a cable: "Everything is quiet. There is no trouble here. There will be no war. I wish to return."

Hearst immediately cabled back: "Please remain. You furnish the pictures and I'll furnish the war."[19]

Few publishers today would allow the Spanish-American War antics of Hearst and Pulitzer. That kind of journalism survives only in a few tabloids with little respect. Instead, the distortions and omissions are less crude, but they are far from absent. They come instead from the standard operations of the most widely absorbed, serious print and broadcast news outlets, which are still wedded to the declarations of authority figures for their news.

President Bush was not the first president to say, as he did about Iraq, that "those who are not with us are against us." The best performance of the news has often been when it sees that "us" at all times means the people of the country. It is the ordinary citizens who depend on credible information in their news. Whenever the news media have forgotten that the "us" is not just the leadership of government, it has been the "us" of the citizenry who have suffered the consequences of official deception or errors.

Fellow citizens, we cannot escape history.
ABRAHAM LINCOLN, 1862

CHAPTER FIVE

ALL THE NEWS THAT FITS?

The horrors committed by the Saudi al Qaeda hijackers against the United States on September 11, 2001, changed the history of our era. Those acts shook the American view of itself as a laudable democracy safe in its power, protected by two oceans eastward and westward and friendly neighbors on its borders north and south. After that day, for the first time since the American Civil War, there was no longer security from a devastating attack that shed the blood of thousands on their own American soil.

The attack shook something else in the national mentality: a stunned American population slowly became aware that many of the masses of the world, especially within the Islamic world, viewed the United States with cynicism or hatred. The Muslim masses had never loomed large in the popular American consciousness. But now national magazines ran large sections with titles like "Why do they hate us?" To this day, only dimly do most Americans see any possible reason why the United States would be the recipient of anything but gratitude or awe from foreign populations.

Why would there be anything but thanks from impoverished foreigners for decades of copious U.S. foreign aid? Most Americans do not follow the annual complexities of foreign aid budgets in the Congress and had taken for granted that "foreign aid" meant that we were providing the destitute people of the world with unending food, education, and other necessities leading to a better life.

Years after the 9/11 attack, many Americans still look for explanations of the malice and cynicism of those we had treated with unending benevolence. Explanations will be difficult for most Americans because the news media on which they have depended for decades have obscured or simply ignored the realities.

For all the genuine good the United States has done for decades, both officially and by nongovernmental organizations working to reduce global misery, there is a subtle but fundamental flaw when it comes to official behavior in the real world.

It is a psychological truism that if a powerful individual commits a crime or acts contrary to common ethical behavior, one reaction is to rationalize the act as necessary and justified. The individual assumes that since the act was necessary and therefore good, reasonable people will agree. If some do not, they are either ignorant and can be ignored or hostile and can be considered an enemy.

Every American knew that in the old Soviet Union the Communist Party controlled the press and frequently lied or looked the other way. Americans either sneered or laughed at the Soviet Press, and with good reason.

But no powerful nation is without a dark side to its history. The United States is no exception. Within the United States, the country's media are permitted by the Constitution to disagree, but too often they should have disagreed and did not. During crucial eras since World War II, the majority of the media behaved as obedient partners with their government and with marauding American corporations exploiting weaker foreign countries.

Among nations, the United States is hardly alone in concealing its unsavory acts or seeing them as an ultimate necessity for the world. During the decades of the cold war, both the Soviet Union and the United States used sabotage, spying, lying, and elimination of democratically elected governments that did not serve their purpose in the deadly rivalry of the nuclear superpowers. Earlier, the British imperial monarchy committed similar acts with self-righteous justifications during its domination of the world. From the sixteenth to the nineteenth century, every global power did so, including, at times, the Roman Catholic Church. It exerted its power to dominate by dubious means, including, in some countries, the Inquisition, and did it in the name of religious purity.

The Christian Crusades to redeem the Middle Eastern "holy places" were initiated in part because by the eleventh century Rome feared that, with Western Europe finally secure for the church, there was a dangerous combination of impoverished peasants and fully armed, unemployed knights. Pope Urban determined that a prudent solution would be to send the eager knights and the unsettled peasantry to Palestine in a series of international mass crusades to redeem control of what the Europeans called "our Holy Places" related to the birth and early life of Christ. The resulting Crusades were often fiascos. But they were depicted to the masses as the holiest of missions.[1]

Christian countries have seldom realized that the Islamic world has never forgiven the West. Most Christians still celebrate the Crusades, ignoring that the targets were also Islamic holy places and that the great Islamic leader, Saladin, had defeated the Crusaders. Typical of continuing Christian misperceptions was President George W. Bush's 2002 announcement that he would defeat America's enemies in the Middle East in a great "crusade." Informed of the immediate anger at the word from Muslims, the president eliminated the word *crusade* from his invasion announcements.[2] That the United States has not been alone in self-justifying delusions is little comfort. The superpower that still sincerely believes it is "the last best hope of earth," as Abraham Lincoln said,[3] has more to lose by evading the standard of honesty with its own people.

U.S. citizens generally are at a disadvantage in understanding foreign policy. Some is due to indifference because of its two protective oceans. Some arises from the extraordinary fact that the United States, the world's only superpower, has fewer correspondents permanently stationed in foreign capitals than any other major Western nation. The result for U.S. media is a remarkably small pool of expertise on foreign culture and politics within their own organizations. Britain, France, Germany, and Japan, for example, have far more foreign correspondents with depth of service in important global locations. Because of this, many other governments understand the impressions the United States makes on the leaders and populations of other countries far more readily than do U.S. news services and, consequently, the American general public.

Even Americans' impression of our largess to the downtrodden of the world is faulty. U.S. foreign aid is large in dollar numbers, but among all industrial democracies its foreign aid is the smallest percentage of its gross domestic product. The Council for a Livable World Education Fund reports that most U.S. aid is for the military of the recipient nations and that 90 percent of all American foreign aid has gone to the Middle East, with most of that to Israel or regimes like Egypt's, which keep their restive Islamic masses under control. When groups in foreign countries, including the Islamic countries, march in aggressive protest and are fired upon by their police and militias, most of the time it is with U.S.-supplied weapons. Whatever most Americans may think about the nature of their country's aid to other nations, most of the unhappy populations of those countries see the United States as the source of the tear gas, water cannons, and bullets that knock them down or kill them.[4]

The American population suffers another grave disadvantage. Over the years, within the United States, accurate, eyewitness, and documented accounts of dubious American involvement in the suppression of foreign leftist or anti-American protest movements have appeared almost exclusively in smaller periodicals like *The Nation, The Progressive, The New Republic, Extra!,* the late I. F. Stone's *I. F. Stone Weekly,* or the late George Seldes' *In Fact.* Broadcast news of repressive or subversive American acts abroad is seldom reported by the major networks but instead by minor outlets like Pacifica radio stations and David Barsamian's Alternative Radio. These smaller media use native nongovernmental sources within the affected countries, previously unreported testimony before congressional committees, or the research of American scholars like Noam Chomsky and other academics who are not significant sources for the main media because they are seen either as leftist or merely antiestablishment professors.

The late I. F. Stone, who was dismissed or ignored as a leftist, was famous for unearthing the government's own documents to prove when the government was either lying or in a state of denial. (Since his death, Stone has been occasionally lionized as a brave naysayer in accounts by major media that ignored his research when he was living. The *New York Times* obituary said he was "a pugnacious advocate of civil liberties, peace and truth," adding that his integrity was conceded even by his detractors.)[5] Similarly, George

Seldes' *In Fact* regularly caught the main media ignoring their own files on newly relevant past events. After his death, a documentary by Rick Goldsmith on Seldes' life received national attention. But minor voices telling anti-establishment truths cannot overcome the lack of wider recognition among average Americans.

A pernicious aftermath of any faulty or false journalistic reporting is that the flawed information remains in a news organization's memory bank—the libraries all organizations keep of their past news by subject matter. When the major U.S. news organizations commit errors of omission and commission in their original reports, these errors are perpetuated into the future.

During the cold war between the United States and the Soviet Union, major U.S. news media ignored or reported inaccurately ugly episodes perpetrated by the United States or its subsidized indigenous groups in Central and South America. In the major news, inhumane acts either were not reported at all or were depicted as necessary for the world's benefit.

For decades after the 1880s, for example, the American firm United Fruit Company behaved like a portable sovereign nation, transferring its huge Chiquita banana plantations wherever it wished. If a nation was an unwilling host, United Fruit simply overthrew it and installed its own compliant leaders (the origin of the term *banana republic*).[6]

When the United States became involved in the tangled attempts to shortcut the voyage from Atlantic to Pacific, rather than sailing around the treacherous tip of South America, it finally took over the project to build a canal in Colombia, the narrowest strip of land separating the two oceans. When Colombia declined an American offer to pay to build and operate the canal, the United States supported a rebellion that took over what would be the canal area and called it a new nation, "Panama."[7]

In the 1950s, the United States supported the overthrow of the democratically elected, pro-communist president of Guatemala, Jacabo Arbenz, when he proposed expropriation of United Fruit plantations. The United States replaced him with a compliant leader, who then killed supporters of the former regime. In 1973, when Salvador Allende was elected the socialist president of Chile and proposed nationalizing American-owned copper mines and other industries, the Central Intelligence Agency (CIA), with help from agents of American corporate executives and upper-class Chileans, deliberately destabilized the Chilean economy. In the ensuing unrest, Allende was assassinated. He was replaced by the U.S.-selected Augusto Pinochet, who proceeded to kill uncounted thousands of Chileans who simply "disappeared."[8] In Nicaragua, the United States created the "Contras" to overthrow the socialist government. In 1975, similar acts were repeated in East Timor and elsewhere.

At the time of these events, the accounts read by most Americans were the propagandistic reports issued by Washington and its foreign embassies, giving ordinary readers and viewers the impression that these moves were either spontaneous or beneficent actions by the United States to oppose communism, further social justice, or prevent threats to the security of the United States.[9]

Though the United States was not alone in committing unsavory foreign acts, it had something more precious at risk. The USSR was a communist dictatorship. The United States is a democracy. The Soviet Union ruthlessly controlled its news media. The United States takes pride in the First Amendment of the Constitution that forbids such control. In the cold war, both the Soviet Union and the United

States used lies as weapons (their intelligence agencies created the now standard euphemism, "disinformation"). But a democracy cannot lie to another nation without telling that lie to its own people. Democracies aren't supposed to lie to their citizens.

If one overlooks the damage to a nation's standards of truthfulness with its own population, what remains is the resulting inability of most citizens of the only surviving superpower to understand the attitude of suspicion and hostility with which so much of the world's unhappy populations view the United States. Even after one takes into account malicious misinformation about the United States that periodically appears in foreign countries, the intelligentsia and many foreign populations have more accurate information about undemocratic and often cruel acts by the United States than does the average American. The main U.S. news services generally have reported the official Washington version of events without independent investigations in the field, so most Americans assume that their country did not condone the use of torture or subversive revolutions in other countries. They believe that all official behavior abroad has been fighting for freedom and democracy in the world. This is a major reason for puzzlement after 9/11, when the question was asked, "Why do they hate us?"

The Sins of the Past Revisited

Many of the lapses in coverage by the main news media date from the forty years of the cold war, during which the U.S. news itself became doctrinaire in its support of U.S. official foreign policy. It did not match the control of Moscow over every item of news that failed to adhere to and promote all

Soviet domestic and foreign policies. But U.S. news agencies, reflecting the passions of the time, reported any domestic or foreign activity that was labeled "Marxist" in hostile and self-censoring news. This weakened democratic exposure to diversity in political news, and Americans would pay a penalty long after the end of the cold war.

As noted, examples include Soviet-American clashes in Guatemala, East Timor, and Chile, where there were serious atrocities. In Guatemala, the United States felt the most need to worry about the suspicions of surrounding Latin American countries regarding U.S. intervention. Guatemala had the most publicized presence of American corporations, mainly the United Fruit Company, the railroad system used to ship out American products produced in the country, and the country's largest electricity-generating system. The Guatemalan intervention was a long-drawn-out process over several years. It was in the early days of the cold war and was opposed by Jacobo Arbenz Guzman, who had Communist Party participation in his regime and open Soviet support; the USSR shipped weaponry to Arbenz. These highly publicized actions, reported prominently in American newspapers, most importantly the *New York Times,* created nervous worry among other Latin American countries containing large American corporations; these governments worried that the same big power interventions would come their way. Arbenz became president in 1951 and immediately announced the expropriation of United Fruit and the suspension of constitutional civil liberties.[10] It was 1954 before the U.S.-supported military overthrew Arbenz by supporting a general who created periodic public relations embarrassments in the United States, with his thousands of "disappearances" and murders of individual American citizens, including religious missionaries.

Almost twenty-five years later, rebels fighting for East Timorese independence were undercut by clandestine U.S. activity, and by then this was standard cold war news. The *New York Times* itself implied but did not specify the clandestine role of American agencies. For example, a December 7, 1975, page 1 story in the *New York Times* simply noted that the invasion by Indonesian troops "came little more than twelve hours after President Ford left Indonesia following a 19-hour state visit." Another story by *Times* correspondent Bill Kovach said, "President Ford has proposed military aid for fiscal 1976 of $44.9 million for Indonesia, more than double the current $20.9 million," and an increase in strictly economic aid.[11]

In the case of Chile, there was still a degree of self-consciousness in U.S. news reports of complicity in the overthrow of President Salvador Allende in 1973. One news story reported that "the White House and the State Department both sought to counter a view widely held in Latin America that the United States knew in advance the plans for Tuesday's coup, which resulted in Dr. Allende's death."[12]

That is now past history. What is relevant is how those former sins of omission and evasions frowned upon in good journalism have been visited upon the future. For example, in August 2002 the *New York Times* printed a long, heart-rending story of women excavating graves in a Guatemalan village looking for eight hundred villagers killed and buried during Guatemala's civil war. In the thirteenth paragraph, the *Times* mentioned vaguely, as it had not at the time the events occurred, that "the American government generally supported the Guatemalan government" and that the Guatemalan "military and its allies in death squads ... [had] singled out leftist guerillas." The *Times* story, a half-century after the fact, continued the painful aftermath for the members of the village without further mention of who had paid for their tragedies.[13]

As late as January 4, 2003, in a long story about the international competition for possession of the former dictator of Chile, President Pinochet, to try him for his long record of torture and crimes against thousands from 1973 to 1990, the *New York Times* referred to him only as having managed a "military coup" against President Allende. In the prolonged episode of Pinochet's resistance to extradition from England, the *Times* and other American major news media repeatedly failed to mention that Pinochet had been directed in his crimes by U.S. agents and had been supported by Washington during his long, bloody regime.

Today, the entries in standard encyclopedias on modern Chile and President Salvador Allende refer to those past events of U.S. involvement. *The Columbia Encyclopedia,* fifth edition (1993), for example, prints that Allende fell after economic disarray and violent opposition "caused in part by the U.S. economic blockade and undercover activities of the U.S. Central Intelligence Agency." If reliable reference books at the time and later record a correct history, it is even less excusable that important segments of the country's most powerful newspapers and television network news programs have chosen not to.

American citizens have been affected by the same selective amnesia about similar episodes elsewhere. In 1975, President Suharto sent his militia into East Timor when that large island on the archipelago moved for independence. Henry Kissinger, secretary of state under President Gerald Ford in 1975, sent a secret message to President Suharto that the United States would have no objection if Suharto took "rapid or drastic action" in East Timor, but "it is important that whatever you do succeeds quickly ... We understand your

problem." "Whatever you do" turned out to be the mass murder by Suharto's military of about 200,000 East Timorese. As
late as 1998, the *New York Times* Sunday Week in Review
wrote that "Suharto is no Saddam." Today, when East Timor
is in the news it is seldom mentioned outside the alternative
media that the United States supported the Suharto military
in his ethnic cleansing of the Chinese and Timorese.[14]

The average citizen depends on printed and broadcast
news and should not have to run to the reference section of
a library every time he or she reads or watches the daily
news. The amnesia of the major media on these episodes increases the cynical view of U.S. foreign policy among some
of our allies. Their leaders and most of their public have seen
or suffered from U.S. subversive undermining of their past
regimes. Most Americans have not seen the same accounts
in their own news media. Consequently, most U.S. tourists
to Latin America are puzzled when they see South American cartoonists depict what they label "The Octopus from
the North" or when foreign leaders and news services in Europe and Asia refer to incidents as "another" aggression by
the United States.

Tending to Business

Whatever their amnesia about past foreign acts by the
United States, the most persistent absence of relevant news
in the major media is what the major media know with exquisite detail: important information about the major media
themselves. Control of public information by a handful of
powerful global firms weakens democracy by omission of
news that might interfere with media's maximizing their
own profits. The same tendency makes the news media sym-

pathetic to similar profit maximization by whatever means among corporations in general. That sympathy and empathy would aid and assist in one of the most spectacular ethical blots in U.S. private enterprise.

In the late twentieth and early twenty-first centuries, the public heard seemingly endless accounts of dishonest and criminal behavior at the top levels of some of the country's largest corporations. It was the sudden appearance of names like Enron, Tyco, and WorldCom; of the country's largest accounting firms, whose supposed incorruptibility is a foundation of proper capitalism, like the auditing firm Arthur Andersen; of major brokerage firms, whose legal goal is to work for the benefit of their clients, like Merrill Lynch; and of the country's most prestigious banks, like J. P. Morgan and Citibank—all had been corrupted by committing fraud or outright theft. By early 2003, investigators were considering criminal charges of fraud against at least 130 major corporations.[15]

The chief watchdog of American corporate life on which capitalism depends for its own protection is the Securities and Exchange Commission. But it had become a toothless watchdog unable or unwilling to bark at large corporations, thanks to conservatives who had cut its budget.

Almost worse, most of the major media also were turning a blind eye to it all. Every metropolitan newspaper in the country has a daily special section specializing in business and corporate affairs. But for decades they devoted most of their space and energies to the celebration of top corporate executives as heroes or geniuses, ignoring evidence printed in what they saw as left-of-center publications and Naderite watchdog groups that took pleasure in investigating and publicizing sins of corporations. This has not been the daily stuff of most big-media business reporters.

The Flag and the Dow Jones Industrial Average

Once media conglomerates became a major enterprise in the American economy, Wall Street took an intense interest in the media industry. But Wall Street was not content to be an observant spectator. It began to dictate the policies of media companies, with a goal of ever-rising profits.

All publicly traded industries, including media conglomerates, depend on access to banking and credit to expand and to manage debt. When Wall Street analysts find a corporation's share prices rising insufficiently, they no longer recommend the company's stock as a good buy, thereby affecting easy access to their lenders and stockholders. Consequently, the indicator Wall Street takes most seriously is rising share prices because of higher profits. Wall Street thus found easy entry into the control of policies of many media organizations that had already begun to shrink their news budgets to raise share prices. Most often these economies were made at the expense of proper news.

The trend became a dramatic and destructive symbol at the *Los Angeles Times,* one of the most highly reputed daily papers in the country. A prominent professional standard journalists have tried to uphold is to maintain the "Wall of Separation between Church and State." This is universally understood within the profession to mean that the news reported by professional journalists (the Church) should in no way be influenced by the business interests of the paper's business department and advertisers (the State). The "Wall" was always porous, but the concept and implicit acceptance by management strengthened reporters' arguments for ethical news.

As described in an earlier edition of this book, in 1997

Mark Willes was hired as president and CEO by the majority shareholders to raise the stock price of the Times Company. Willes introduced what sounded like a revolutionary move: news would no longer be selected by the editors but by co-editors, one to be from the paper's business department. Willes said that whenever anyone in the news department tried to raise the "Wall of separation of Church and State," he would "get a bazooka ... to blow it down."[16] Wall Street was delighted and the paper's share prices rose.

Willes had come from General Mills, whose chief products were breakfast cereals. Whatever his expertise in merchandising Cheerios and Chex, he was yet another example of an executive taking over a newspaper and assuming that news is "just another business." It isn't. The news staff rebelled and lost some of its best reporters. A particularly gross instance of the paper pandering to an advertiser disgusted Otis Chandler, the leader of the Chandler family, which had owned the *Times* since 1892, and the man who had converted the paper from its drab conservatism to one of the most respected papers in the country. Chandler sold his stock, and the paper was sold to the Chicago Tribune Company.[17]

Most of the more reputable papers have at least publicly rejected Willes's crass form of combining news and advertising, but today most news is a subsidiary in large multimedia conglomerates that are traded on the stock market. Media conglomerates are under demands from Wall Street to show ever higher stock profits, and the pressure is welcomed by many media top executives, whose high compensation is buttressed or in the form of company shares or stock options.

To meet the profit pressures, newspapers have been cutting reportorial costs by reducing staff size and news space, and broadcast media have cut serious air time on radio and television. As a result, many newspapers have lost some of their best journalists, and the public has lost daily access to their reporting. At least one paper lost its publisher. Jay Harris, publisher of the well-regarded *San Jose Mercury News* from 1994 to 2001, resigned when the Knight-Ridder management ordered him to increase the paper's profits by cutting his budget, which would include the budget for news and staff. He went on to form the Center for Study of Journalism and Democracy at the University of Southern California.[18]

Some of the country's best editors have left their papers for the same reason but, unlike Harris, did not publicize that they resigned rather than follow orders. When most top executives of major journalistic organizations are appointed, they must sign an agreement that their pension benefits, keyed to issues of highly profitable stock options, depend on their never making any public criticism of the news organization, even after they have left the company. This explains why the public reason given usually is something like "to spend more time with my family."

Perpetuating News Amnesia

A centuries-old hole in news media treatment is reporting on internal finances of the media themselves. The *New York Times* published many useful stories in 2002 and 2003 about Federal Communications Commission (FCC) Chairman Michael Powell's desire to lift restrictions on a broadcast station's ownership of a newspaper in the same community. But according to Jeff Chester of Democratic Media, it did not report that "on Dec. 3, 2001, the New York Times Company, along with other major newspaper and broadcasting companies, filed voluminous documents . . . [that] urged the FCC to abandon the quarter-century old safeguard that prevents a company from owning both a newspaper and a broadcast outlet in the same community."[19]

If it had not been for the Iraqi war, the biggest story of 2002 would have been the epidemic of greed and fraud that brought down some of the largest corporations in the country. It seemed almost impossible that so much cheating of this magnitude remained secret, that no one detected that so many huge corporations were quietly creating novel bookkeeping to make losses look like profits. Year in and year out, daily tonnage of newsprint has been devoted to financial and corporate news and hours of air time on network programs have focused on corporate investments and finance.

Business reporting, like real estate and automotive news, has a morbid past. For most of the twentieth century, the business pages of daily papers and the financial programs on television treated business leaders as heroic captains of industry. Business reporters of the past, for example, dealt either with press releases from the publicity departments of corporations, or, if the news medium was important enough, its reporter was periodically permitted to enter the inner sanctum of "the man himself," the head of the company, about whom the reporter would write a story. This tended to produce either sycophants or the illusion of having been admitted to the most accurate possible news that existed.

In the aftermath of the rude awakening of 2001, with vast fraud and theft among some of the largest corporations and banks, attention turned to the fast-growing ranks of business reporters in American journalism. Where were they when dishonesty and irrationality became the national financial culture?

Not all business reporters were at fault. In 1997, the *Wall Street Journal* began an exposure of security firms allocating new stocks at artificially low prices to favored corporate executives, all behind the scenes. The *Wall Street Journal* said it had the earmarks of bribing the best clients of security firms as a way of keeping their business. In 1998, before the scandals burst, *Business Week* printed a cover story with the blazing line: "Corporate Earnings: Who Can You Trust?" If one ignores grammar on the cover of a national magazine, what the story said was predictive. It said that there was a "gnawing sense that companies . . . are regularly pushing the limits, accountants are AWOL, and analysts are too enmeshed with their investment-banking brethren to provide objective advice."[20]

But all was forgotten in the tide of easy millions. Most business reporting trumpeted the "new economy" and the coming of the era of uninterrupted wealth. The majority of business reporters in print and in the "investing" programs on television issued stories that in retrospect seem childlike in their innocence and joy at the new economy.

Three years earlier *Business Week* warned that many company auditors finding undocumented profits among large corporations did not report them in hopes that they would be rehired to do audits in the future.[21] If widely read business journals, read routinely by reporters on business and finance, made these assertions three years before the collapse, apparently the staffs of hundreds of papers and broadcast networks were too excited by the booming stock market to notice.

The Dead Canary No One Noticed

Coal miners used to carry a caged canary into the depths of the mine because canaries are more sensitive than humans to the fatal methane gas that miners dread. When the canary died, the miners knew they were in danger.

Among the continuing cases of failure of the major news media to use readily available information to explain a shocking development within U.S. cities has been its treatment of homelessness. Local news media were generally sympathetic, though retail stores complained that homelessness was bad for business. But all seemed to think this sudden phenomenon of the otherwise prosperous 1980s was an act of God. It wasn't. It was an act of Congress.

The new phenomenon of homelessness was a human tragedy, but it also had a deeper significance that would extend beyond homeless people in the street and have a significance that in the long run involved both domestic and foreign problems. There were causes for homelessness itself that were ignored or treated only superficially by the major media and by political leaders of the country.

In 1985, according to a study of governmental expenditures by the Department of Housing and Urban Development (HUD) and a study on Housing Related Expenditures by the National Low-Income Housing Coalition,[22] the federal government, in one way or another, subsidized $42 billion (measured in 2002 dollars) for low-cost housing, usually paying landlords the difference between costs and normal profits. In 1986, during the Reagan administration, that amount was cut in half. By 2002 the annual expenditures were averaging about $30 billion a year, a drop of almost 30 percent from 1985. During that same period, 1985 to 2002, the number of households in the United States had risen from 88 million to 106 million.[23] Thus, as the number of households needing housing rose more than 20 percent, subsidies for low-cost housing dropped 30 percent.

By 2003, partly obscured by war and plans for future wars, explosive crises were beginning to shake cities and states all over the country. A growing number of cities and counties faced bankruptcy. School funding, which had begun to improve student performance by reducing class size and repairing decrepit buildings, began to shrink again. Local civic services were being cut, some with endangerment to health and family cohesion.

But, with all the fluctuations over the years in the national economy and changes in the American population, the one indicator of fundamental, dangerous instability that was visible, dramatic, and an alarming symptom of social and economic breakdown was a growing number of homeless individuals and families sleeping in streets, abandoned caves, and old cars. Their numbers steadily increased in a process that Americans began to take for granted, but the situation shocked foreigners whose own cities had not seen the same phenomenon.

No developed democratic country can depend on the private home-building and real estate industries to provide low-cost, affordable housing for lower-income families. Private builders and banks that finance them prefer middle-class and upper-class housing. Homes for poor or low-income families are less profitable and less stable. In other developed countries, subsidized housing for low-income families is considered a necessity, as is universal health care and other standard social programs in which private entrepreneurs prefer not to deal.

The news media, whether sympathetic with or angry at the unsightly groups, seemed to behave as though their appearance was a mystery, explainable mainly by addiction, mental illness, or "preference for the streets." There are addicts and the mentally ill among the homeless, but the stereotypes represent national escapism from the realities.[24] There are at least 6 million low-income households that are either homeless or pay half their income for housing. A household with one person working at minimum wage for 40 hours a

week, 52 weeks a year, can afford only $268 monthly for rent
and utilities. Housing costs are higher than this in every
county in the country.

Suffer The Little Children ...

Another shameful and unnecessary consequence of homelessness, for which the news media have provided only
minor or misleading causes, is its effect on children. The
bipartisan Millennial Housing Commission, appointed by
Congress in 2002, issued a report on May 30, 2002, that
stated that the severe housing shortage affects "family stability, the environment for children, and the familiar dis-
rupting of children's lives by having to move constantly in
search [for jobs and] for housing." The problem, the commission found, cascades down to the revenue for cities and
states because housing and jobs have been "the mainstay of
the national economy." The major media gave little serious
attention to the commission's report and almost no attention to the origins of the homeless phenomenon since the
mid-1980s.

For the mentally ill who are among the homeless, the
root cause of their homelessness is a cruel act of oppor-
tunism by states and counties. In the years after World War
II, psychiatric studies showed that the majority of people in
mental institutions would recover or reach stability sooner
if they were treated in community mental clinics. As a result,
most mental hospitals were emptied, with the promise that
the saved money would go into less expensive local clinics.
But few local clinics were created. Federal and state governments used the saved money for unrelated purposes. As
a result, thousands of mentally ill men and women were
abandoned to U.S. city streets, without treatment.

The Love of Money is the Root . . .

The most-read newspapers and the largest audience for broadcast news have been easily lured to the "widows and orphans" approach of tax-cutters that resulted in unfair shifting of financial burdens from corporations and the wealthy to ordinary taxpayers. Beginning with the Reagan administration of the 1980s, tax-cutting members of Congress and many state legislatures campaigned to cut income taxes, claiming that they caused outrageous harassment of people like poor widows and small-business people, who were intimidated by ruthless auditors of the Internal Revenue Service (IRS). Year after year, the cases were highly publicized, all overblown. As a result, drastic cuts were made in the staffing and appropriations of the IRS. The campaign was successful. It crippled the operation of the most efficient and fairest tax, the income tax. (All other methods, like sales taxes, ask the least affluent of the public to pay the highest percentage of their disposable income.) In 2002, the IRS said it lacked auditors to review complex accounts of large corporations, so they had to limit their audits to the returns of middle-class and low-income people. The largest corporations had won the battle to get away with their riches and let working people pay their bills. The media share responsibility in the resulting gross unfairness by reporting uncritically the tax-cutters' horror stories. The "widows and orphans" technique had worked again with the major media, who seem uneducable on the issue of taxes.

By 2002, workers, shareholders, and the national economy were shaken by the dozens of firms like Enron and major banks that collapsed or were weakened when their undetected use of fraudulent practices and theft shook the economy and left workers unemployed. Some study groups suggest that the earlier cutbacks in the IRS contributed to the corporate scandals.[25]

President George W. Bush entered office with the slogan "Leave No Child Behind," but more children live in poverty today than twenty years ago, "and 42 million people, most of them working but still poor, do not have health insurance," according to a report in the *Orange County Register*.[26]

Together with the increasing maldistribution of income in the United States, in which national wealth has been flowing to the richest households, most of the domestic ills of the country in the early years of the twenty-first century are not total mysteries. Growing homelessness was simply an early warning that something was going wrong in the economy and the social machinery of American democracy.

The homeless did not cause the new extremes of maldistributed national income or the epidemic of greed that produced the historic magnitude of 1990s corporate crimes or a war that distracted attention from problems at home. The homeless were one of the most obvious victims, but they were more than that. Their early appearance in the 1980s and their high visibility was a loud alarm. That strange occurrence seemingly out of nowhere meant that, underneath this new surface disruption, something deeper and more fundamental was going wrong in the American social and economic system.

Among the institutions on which the public depends to probe for explanations of a visible disorder in the community are the country's major news media. Sadly, in this case these media were satisfied with what were clearly superficial and basically irrelevant explanations. The major news media are a democracy's early warning system. Once again in the twenty-first century, as too often happened in the twentieth, they failed to report that the canary was dead.

The reports of my death are greatly exaggerated.
MARK TWAIN

CHAPTER SIX

PAPER IN THE DIGITAL AGE

The birth and spectacular growth of the Internet have been accompanied by the last rites pronounced over the impending death of words printed on paper. One inventor, Ray Kurzweil, who works with devices for the blind, has written that by 2030 molecule-size brain implants receiving images and words will eliminate the need for texts. More typical was the 2001 prediction of Ted Padover, CEO of Image Source Company: "Personally . . . I believe that most of us will see near extinction of printed works in our lifetime."[1]

The predictions continue to grow. Computers are reaching ever greater capacities for storing information, accelerating speed, and improving the clarity of text and images on monitor screens. Computer sizes shrink even as their functions multiply and their prices drop. Prototypes of magazine-size digital screen newspapers have articles that are scanned and pages that are turned by push buttons. There are magazines re-created on cell phone screens as well as on full-size computers. And in the 1990s it became possible to buy handheld computers capable of holding ten novels, each e-book selected with a click and its "pages" turned with a button.

Next to the Scaffold:
The Daily Newspaper?

Daily newspapers, now mostly a minor subsidiary among the multitude of other media owned by large conglomerates, have been regarded as cumbersome properties with an unpromising future. On the surface, there was cause for concern. For more than thirty years, daily circulation of printed papers has been falling, as have the number of daily papers in the country. In many ways, the newspaper is the most troublesome medium the conglomerates own. And of all the printed media, it was the first for which most of the end-of-print predictors assumed an early death.

Death announcements of a city daily seem to come with regularity. This deepened Wall Street's poor opinion of newspapers, whose annual profits, compared to those of broadcasting, were merely in the 20–25 percent range (a healthy profit for any company), while broadcasting profits were 30–60 percent.

Big conglomerates are prejudiced for another reason. Multimedia firms prefer properties that are easily converted for reuse among their other media, like novels into movies into videos. Daily news cannot be recycled. An original news item is dead the day it is printed, while a popular sitcom or detective series can have an impressive life span. The TV show *I Love Lucy* began in 1951, and although its star, Lucille Ball, died in 1989, the original show is still being rerun in the twenty-first century and making money worldwide.[2]

It is true that the bare statistics appear ominous, and Wall Street and other financial students, being dedicated to numbers, are understandably pessimistic. In 1970, 62 million papers were sold each weekday, when there were 63 million households, suggesting that almost every home bought a daily paper. In 2002, 56 million papers were sold when there were 106 million households. Apparently, close to half the households in the United States no longer have a daily paper regularly in the home.[3]

Death in the Afternoon

One statistic in particular has fueled predictions of the demise of newspapers. Within the last generation almost half the afternoon dailies in large cities have died or merged with a morning paper. Where once there were an almost equal number of morning and afternoon dailies, by 2002 there were 47 million morning papers sold each day but only 9 million afternoon papers, most of them in smaller cities and towns.[4]

Curiously, a contribution to the shrinkage of newspaper circulation was the 1950s creation of the interstate highway system, which led to a major growth of suburbs.[5] Until the 1960s, most breadwinners still took trolleys, buses, or trains to centralized, downtown factories and offices, often buying two papers, one for home and for reading on the way to work on mass transit, and an afternoon paper to read on the way home and then share with the family for the evening.

Newspaper circulation grew or remained steady from that time to 1970, when commercial offices, factories, and department stores moved to malls in the suburbs, where there was cheap land and ample parking. Increased car ownership and shrinking mass transit led to highways jammed with commuting drivers, most of them listening to the latest radio news (including traffic reports). When car commuters reached home, they usually turned on their TV sets and spent the hours after dinner watching offerings from the multiplying TV channels. These social changes were fatal for big-city afternoon papers. By 2003, barely half of U.S. households had a daily paper in the house.[6]

An Unfulfilled Dream

The endurance of daily papers seems puzzling when people, faced with the pace of modern urban life, constantly complain that "no one has enough time." And in today's miniaturized, portable society, the newspaper seems to have a strange and even ridiculous form. Opened wide, it is a menace on a crowded commuter train. Read outdoors, a sudden breeze can create a comic scene of frantic indignity.

For decades, newspaper publishers themselves have complained about their need to support a large brick-and-mortar building filled with heavy, expensive machinery and to employ a group of unorthodox professional workers, the reportorial staff, with whom publishers maintain a love-hate relationship. The factory part of the newspaper has been simplified because computers eliminated much of the complex machinery. Since the 1970s, reporters have composed their stories on computers, whose keyboards simultaneously transmit them to editors' screens and thence to production units, where a printing machine converts each edited story and headline into a column-wide strip of paper. Relatively unskilled workers paste up the stories to form full pages that then are transformed into steel plates for the high-speed automated presses. At the end, the full papers emerge in rapid succession neatly folded and bundled for delivery.

Publishers are further galled that distribution to the home of each subscriber must still be done one by one. Men and women driving vans or cars up the street hurl a paper out the window onto the lawn or rose bushes of each subscriber or, in big cities, deliver them to newsstands or apartment doors. For a century, publishers have dreamed of electronic transmission of the paper into each home, thereby ending presses and hand deliveries. The dream was so obsessive that it produced more than one comical experiment. Shortly after World War II, many owners bought FM stations, not yet a profitable medium, whose frequencies included the portion usable for remote printing, which could end the labor-intensive delivery system. But even if the idea worked, it was soon clear that it required subscribers to own the primitive fax machines of that day, and the result would be 164 pages of paper—in that era, slimy paper at that—dumped onto their living room floors every dawn.

At another time, desperate publishers tried an experimental device in a delivery van that contained a computerized cannon programmed to shoot the rolled newspaper onto the correct street and house number of each subscriber. But cannon being cannon, after too many projectiles went through living room windows or knocked little boys off their tricycles, the experiment was abandoned.

Stop the Presses? Not Yet.

Newspapers have not yet disappeared, nor are they likely to in the near future. The newspaper survives for reasons that have little to do with clever technology. Its endurance depends, in part, precisely on the reader's need to open with arms outstretched a double page that covers more than 1,000 square inches of columns and stories, 48 inches wide and 22 inches deep. What sounds like a ridiculous expanse of print is, in fact, an advantage. Each reader's eye can scan and select from the expanse the one or two stories of interest to that particular reader and do it more rapidly than scrolling even the sharpest presentation on a computer screen.

The huge expanse of the newspaper page is the result of a seventeenth-century tax dodge. When the British Crown lost patience with uppity London newspapers and placed a ruinous tax on each page, the publishers displayed their historic ability to escape taxes by simply expanding the size of each page so much that the tax-per-page didn't put them out of business. Because the British were the world's source of technology and machinery during the period, ever since, newspaper presses have been built to issue the largest printed page in world publishing.[7]

But a more social factor keeps the newspaper a common artifact in the digital age. Newspapers have a unique social function that their media competitors do not. They are crucial to American local civic life, which, in turn, is a unique part of the U.S. political system. No other industrial democracy leaves to each community the control of its local schools, police, land use, and most taxes. In other countries these are national functions. Thus, every American city and town has voters involved in the performance of the school system in which their children are educated, in the taxes they pay on their property, and in the behavior of their police force. They vote on these, city by city on election day, and the only medium that informs them of these matters in any detail is the printed newspaper.

Because social characteristics are difficult to quantify on the charts of Wall Street analysts (on Wall Street, numbers are Holy Scripture), predictions of an early demise for newspapers will continue.

Though there are an increasing number of U.S. cities without their own daily paper, weekly papers take their place. In villages the gap is filled with copy-machine sheets that post civic and political items in stores and post offices. These social functions are likely to extend the life and solvency of the printed newspaper and keep it a substantial presence in the media scene for many years. Readers can quickly scan forty or one hundred social and political stories and accounts of dozens of cultural events, all capable of detail and background.

Broadcasting can transmit only one item at a time. A current television news item that is 120 seconds is considered "long," a similar news item on the radio even more so. The items over the air must be brief because broadcasters are terrified by something even more fearsome than a poor Nielsen rating: the viewer's hand-held remote control with channel buttons. If confronted with one moment of boredom, uncounted thousands of homes press the dreaded channel button and the broadcaster's program disappears.

The Nonaffluent Need Not Apply

Daily newspapers have refused to die as a national medium, but it would be romantic to ascribe the survival of newspapers to their unblemished virtue. Too many publishers have wanted short-range success with truncated staffs, shrunken news space, and uninterrupted growth of profits. There is still far from universal recognition by owners of newspaper chains that their advantage over competing media is precisely the wide selection of subject matter capable of depth and detail that cannot be copied by other media. Furthermore, most newspapers still reflect in their sources and content the world as seen by leaders of corporate and public high offices. Seldom, if ever, do daily sections deal with continuing needs of ordinary American families, needs that differ from those of the people with whom publishers have lunch.

People who are not affluent seldom see stories about their day-to-day pains and pleasures and consequently see little reason to buy a daily paper. As a result, the daily newspaper has become the medium for the middle and upper classes. Ironically, the daily paper's long, detailed stories are the basis for most reporting in radio and television, which specialize in brief items. In Washington, D.C., almost every high government executive, member of Congress, and head of a government agency begins the day by reading the *New York Times,* the *Wall Street Journal,* and the *Washington Post.* A similar practice exists in state houses and city halls around the country. The newspaper might provide within its details the tidbits used by broadcasters. Using the newspapers as source material permits local station owners to have much smaller news staffs than do newspapers.

Despite their longer and more numerous stories, newspapers share responsibility for the narrow political spectrum in American electoral politics. Newspapers' relatively detailed stories are still clustered around the center-right of politics because their news is mainly drawn from corporate life and major political leaders. It was not always this way, and the country's politics showed it. As described in more detail later in this book, in the late nineteenth century, every American city of any size had half a dozen papers or more, and their politics both in editorials and news emphasis ranged from far left to far right and everything in between.

By the early twenty-first century, literally 99.9 percent of contemporary daily papers are a monopoly in their own cities. That is in sharp contrast to the newspaper scene in other industrialized countries. In London, for example, there are twelve daily papers; in Paris, thirty-three; in Tokyo, thirty-one.[8] The multiple newspapers of all kinds in foreign capitals (whose governments are not decentralized, as in the United States) expose their citizens to a wide range of political and ideological ideas and programs. The U.S. major media display a constricted political spectrum, which is a powerful factor in the relatively narrow range of choices that American voters face each election day.

That 99.9 percent of morning papers are monopolies in their own cities understates the problem. Owners exchange papers with each other or buy and sell papers so each can have as many newspapers as possible in a geographic cluster. This permits individual owners to have something close to a monopoly for daily printed advertising in that region and in many cases to use one regional newsroom to serve all their papers in that cluster.

The consequence has been that, even while all newspaper circulation slowly drops, with big-city afternoon papers rare, the remaining morning papers are more secure than in the past and average profits per paper are almost double their levels thirty years earlier.

The leading newspaper groups (owners prefer "groups" to "chains") are Gannett, with 97 dailies with 7 million total circulation, followed in order by Knight Ridder, with 34 papers and 4 million circulation; the Tribune Company (Chicago), with 11 papers and 3.5 million circulation; Advance Publications (Newhouse), with 27 papers and 3 million circulation; and the New York Times Company, with 17 newspapers and 17 million circulation.[9]

A Medium for Dentists' Offices?

Another printed medium, magazines, did not escape the acquisitions that swept many different media into each of the leading conglomerates. In 2001, there were 17,694 consumer and business magazines published in the United States, but the 10 largest ones had 26 percent of the industry's $27 billion in revenues that year. Time Warner alone owned magazines with 12 percent of national revenues, followed by Hearst, Advance, International Data, Reed Elsevier, and McGraw-Hill.[10]

The printed magazine is alive and well, perhaps the printed form least constricted by the growth of digital media. The proliferation of magazines follows the proliferation of consumer goods. When one kind of product has sufficient sales, it can lead to a new magazine specializing in whatever the subject may be—from motorcycles to sex.

The circulation of a magazine depends on how it is distributed. Some are among the many inserts in Sunday newspapers and have a large distribution, thanks to the newspaper industry having its fattest papers and highest circulations on Sunday, when national circulation hovers around 60 million. It is difficult to know how many of the inserted magazines in those Sunday papers survive the common Sunday morning ritual that throws out unwanted sections and inserts unread. Thus, *Parade* magazine has a circulation of 35 million, but it is in a Sunday newspaper insert, which a family may or may not immediately throw into the recycling bin.

Other magazines are issued by organizations that distribute them as an inducement and promotion for the organization and its goals. The *AARP* magazine of the American Association of Retired Persons, for example, had 21.5 million circulation in 2003 but comes automatically with the very low membership fee, twelve dollars a year.

The once-mighty national magazines of general circulation—*Life, Look,* and *Saturday Evening Post*—all died at the height of their circulation, about 7 million each, in the late 1960s, when high-quality color television finally became a common household appliance. Until then, the only reliable media for advertisers who wanted high-quality color for national distribution were the slick-paper national magazines of general interest. When widespread color television provided a larger audience at less cost per consumer, the former magazine triumvirate died.

By 2003, leading magazines by subscription revenues were *TV Guide, People Weekly, Reader's Digest, Time Magazine, Sports Illustrated, National Geographic, National Enquirer, Better Homes and Garden, Newsweek,* and *Star.*[11] Other magazines are simply adjuncts to popular television programs that are oriented around celebrities like *O, The Oprah Magazine, ESPN The Magazine,* and *Discover.*

The 1960s sexual revolution made illustrated sex scenes in periodicals like *Playboy, Penthouse,* and *Playgirl* almost, though not quite, coffee-table household periodicals. Even the women's magazines, once designed for the former homebody looking for decorating schemes and new diets for husband and children, now stare out from supermarket checkout counters with cover eye-catchers like "12 Different Ways to Drive Your Man Wild in Bed." It has become acceptable that women can also be interested in sex and pornography.

Another supermarket rack is for the ever-present magazines of celebrity gossip, well-known actors breaking up with their fashion model girlfriends, divorcees telling secrets about former husbands, "The Real Story Behind . . ." and stories of "miraculous" events in distant places. The traditional regulars are still displayed, like the *National Enquirer,* but now with fewer stories about a New Zealand wolf giving birth to human twins. Magazine racks in chain and large independent bookstores are often a hundred or more feet in total length, evidence that the new specialized magazines as well as titles of past decades have not forsaken print in favor of their computerized digital forms.[12]

Twenty-three Hundred Years Old but Still Around: The Book Printed on Paper

The book, printed on paper and bound by cloth or glossy heavy paper, was once predicted to be among the first victims condemned to death by computerized forms. But printed books have been obstinate survivors.

Some early Internet executives and experts, and not a few book people, were among the prophets of doom. They predicted that in a short time books as we know them would disappear and argued, with some evidence, that the substitute was at hand and had genuine advantages over the conventional book. The substitute was the e-book, a single handheld device with the capacity of a modest home bookshelf and modern, high-speed reproduction techniques.

The basic rationale was that readers would no longer pay twenty to thirty dollars for a book that weighed around two pounds and was seven inches by ten and contained only one novel or nonfiction work. In contrast, a handheld e-book weighed perhaps eight ounces, could fit comfortably in a shirt pocket or small purse and contain the equivalent of ten full-length novels. There was every reason to believe that the type resolution would be as clear and readable in an e-book as in a well-printed book, and its "pages" turned conveniently when the reader pressed a button.

Why, it was reasoned, would one have to keep running to a bookstore, maintain or build ever larger bookshelves, increase the burden of heavy carry-on bags dragged onto airplanes, or add to the cruelty of ever heavier textbooks stuffed into the bulging backpacks already distorting the spines of students?

But digital books, for all their convenient size and versatility, faced reader preference for the old-fashioned book printed on paper and bound in hardcover or heavy paper. In 2002, the estimated highest average per capita spending on media by U.S. consumers was $212 for basic cable and TV, second was $110 for home videos, followed closely by $100 for books. Trailing books by far were records, newspapers, magazines, movies, and other media.[13]

In 1995, for example, consumers spent $25 million for books of all kinds and in 2000, $32 million.[14] There are at least 350 dictionaries of computer terms—all printed on paper and issued as conventional books.

The Capricious Commodity

In the twenty-first century, books regularly continue to frustrate major media conglomerates. Books are a capricious commodity. Some of the most lavishly financed and promoted books by celebrated mass market authors simply fail to cover their costs, while periodically other books written by unknowns or printed by small publishers, and even some books self-produced and paid for by their authors, occasionally make profits. A few become bestsellers.

Bertelsmann, one of the Big Five media conglomerates, fired a popular editor in the firm's book division, Random House, not because her book sales had failed to make a profit but because they had failed to achieve predetermined "expected profits." Large publicly traded conglomerates that announce "higher expected earnings" are favored by Wall Street because the prospect of merely the announcement itself will attract investors and thus automatically raise share prices, permitting popular analysts to recommend the stock. If an "expected earnings" statement is insufficiently cheerful, investment banks will be less eager to lend the company money or recommend that their clients buy its stock; as a result, its shares will drop on the stock market.

As the corporate disasters of the 1990s demonstrated, under this pressure many firms announced "expected earnings" based on dubious data that in the end failed not only their ordinary shareholders but the national economy.[15] Despite the unpredictability, every major publisher hopes a new book will be a bestseller, even though every book person knows that only a microscopic percentage of books ever make that list, and even some that do so fail to make a profit. But for both authors and publishers, hope springs eternal in the human breast.

When the largest media conglomerate of them all, Time Warner, had to reduce the $29 billion debt it incurred for the marriage of AOL and Time Warner, it decided to raise the money by offering its book division for sale at $400 million but had to lower the price when the high price brought no bids.[16] When the French conglomerate Vivendi began to succumb to its debt, among the first of its media collection sold was Boston's Houghton Mifflin publishing company.[17]

As Verlyn Klinkenborg wrote in the New York Times, "The old assumption of book publishing—that it earned modest, steady profits built on a respected stable of authors and a deep back list—now seems practically prehistoric."[18] The book as we know it, while not prehistoric, is, in fact, twenty-three hundred years old.

The Upstart's Invention

Though today's leading conglomerates worry about their books making sufficient profits, historically the book is the product of a monopoly. In the second century B.C., Egypt's Ptolemy V was the proud inheritor of the greatest library in the world, the 700,000 scrolls in the famous Alexandrian library. The scrolls, containing the learning and histories of the recorded world, were made from flattened Nile River reeds. When Eumenes II, monarch of Pergamum (now Turkey), wanted his own great library equal to the Alexandrian and tried to import reeds from the Nile, Ptolemy V was affronted by the upstart and declared a monopoly on Nile River reeds.

Eumenes was forced to have his scribes write on both sides of animal skins. But squares of cut hides did not make compact scrolls, not even the finest hides, the skins of unborn lambs. They were also unwieldy as a collection of individual sheets, so Eumenes had each particular work prepared for library storage by sewing together one edge to make a hinge. The book was born. The spirit of Eumenes survives in the word *parchment,* derived from his kingdom, Pergamum.[19]

The book was what would be called today a "random access medium." Unlike the scroll, which had to be unrolled all the way if the desired text was near the end, the book could be opened at once to any desired section.

(A mixed fate unfolded for the Alexandrian scrolls. The library became a lover's gift when Cleopatra gave it to one of her favorite lovers, Marc Antony. Finally, when Christian conquerors reached Alexandria, they perceived the scrolls as symbols of a pagan religion and burned down the library.)

The story of books versus scrolls demonstrates a common characteristic of new technologies intruding upon older ones. Books and scrolls co-existed in common use until the thirteenth century. Scrolls are still used today for special ceremonies, like graduation exercises and special proclamations by politicians. A new mass technology seldom removes its predecessor at once. Generally, the two survive side by side for many years, as did farm horses and tractors.

A twenty-first-century version of the Alexandrian library

is a project of the Alexandria Scholars Collective. The plan calls for a new, modernistic structure in the ancient Egyptian city, with its ultimate goal to make a digital record of every book in existence. Using modern technology and the enthusiasm of book and charitable groups, it hopes to become, among other things, an inexpensive and rapid source for sending appropriate books to impoverished countries. It hopes also to become a scholarly depository of the world's published works.[20]

The modern digital world is filled with attempts at private monopolies, not so much for the glory of a leader as for market power in billion-dollar industries. Modern leaders of great industries no longer display their high status in their libraries but by their high compensation, stock options, and lavish pension plans compared with other conglomerate presidents. Entrepreneurs, like IBM in computers and Bill Gates's Microsoft, which is coming close to monopoly in computer operating programs, have led to Eumenes-like counter moves, like Apple in computers and Unix to compete with Windows operating programs.

At one time, big-chain booksellers like Barnes & Noble, looking to their future, announced that they would soon sell books-on-demand. Customers asking for a book not on the shelves of the store could obtain a downloaded digital version when they plugged in their handheld computers. If the customer insisted, a special machine in each Barnes & Noble store would receive the electronic version and, using existing techniques of copying, binding, and paperback covering, hand over a complete book to the customer the next day. A few years later, the plan had failed to become a reality for both technical and economic reasons. But Barnes & Noble continues to be the country's largest bookseller, with more than 1,500 stores, followed closely by Borders Group, with 1,190.[21]

When computers first came into common use in the mid-1980s, it was said that they had ushered in the paperless society. Fifteen years later, the annual consumption of paper in the United States had increased by 67 percent.[22]

The double helix of literate civilization seems to include a gene that programs an appetite for words on paper.

On a discounted cash-flow basis
the earth simply is not worth saving.
S. DAVID FREEMAN, former chairman, TVA;
author of *Time to Choose*

CHAPTER SEVEN

REBELLION AND REMEDIES

There has been much at the turn of the century that is dis-
heartening. The catastrophes visited on the country by the
hijackers of commercial airliners on September 11, 2001 dev-
astated the United States' image of itself and of the rest of the
world. That was followed by the devastation of the country's
belief in the integrity of its economy. The unprecedented
magnitude of corporate fraud, theft, and collusion was not
by fly-by-night sleazy operators but by some of the country's
largest corporations. Gone also in a seeming split second
was the record of trusted auditing firms whose names at the
end of annual reports had always permitted stockholders to
breathe easily. Perhaps more shocking, the country's most
prestigious banks, for more than a century trusted as tem-
ples of fiscal rectitude, had been knowing conspirators in the
squalid tricks.

Government agencies of the past, like the Federal Communications Commission majority in 2000, abandoned their
legal obligation to protect and promote the diverse interests

of the country's media audience. In effect, the commission turned over the public's property—the airwaves—to huge media corporations that then became a law unto themselves. This was aided and abetted by oversight agencies like the Securities and Exchange Commission and the Anti-Trust Division of the Department of Justice, both deliberately weakened over the years by a White House and Congress dependent on corporate contributions to obtain the obscene amounts of money used to run for public office. If all of that were insufficient as an inauspicious opening of a new century, the country declared an open-ended war in one of the most unstable arenas of the globe.

It is precisely in these circumstances that the performance of the country's mass media is tested. The majority of Americans depend on the standard news media for full and realistic reporting with relevant background. With few exceptions the main media failed the challenge.

As noted previously, the early years of the twenty-first century found the country's media world controlled not by the fifty corporations of twenty years earlier, but by all those past media, plus new ones, compacted into five giant conglomerates. These five conglomerates had interlocks with each other. Together they offered only a limited spectrum of the political information and commentary appropriate for a nation of widely differing regions and needs. Yet these five conglomerates are the designated stewards of the absolute necessity in a democracy: citizens in a democracy need full information about their government and the state of their society in order to be sufficiently informed of their true self-interest when they cast ballots on election day. When some of the most pressing domestic problems and a fair spectrum of ideas and commentary have disappeared from the main media, the American public has lost its real choices.

Rays of Light

Within this gloom there is some light. When the first edition of this book was published, it warned, "Each generation has to establish its own priorities and re-invigorate the best principles of the society."[1] That new generation, now joined with veteran allies in the struggle for freedom of significant information, has appeared on the scene. Confronted with the arrogance and avarice of the mass media conglomerates, older reform groups, hardened by their experience with past failures, combined with a new generation seemingly born with inherent skills in the uses of digital technology, has risen to the challenge.

By 2003, there were more than one hundred media reform organizations, a few from the Far Right but most of them moderate or progressive alternatives to the rigid and limited spectrum of the major media. Unlike some past reformers, the new ones possess expertise in not only how the media operate but also the complexities of how these media are linked to the general political system. Skills in new technology have been used for creative, progressive works that are open and surprisingly successful. A generation of mostly youthful Internet journalists and anthologists has bypassed the traditional standard media by providing national and global news not always found in big-media broadcast and printed news.

These emerging workers in the digital media have also mobilized substantial national and worldwide nonviolent protests, almost entirely through the Internet, against some of the traditional centers of world economic power like the World Trade Organization and other financial conferences of global economic institutions. The bankers, powerful controllers of billions and with their counterparts in major governments, once flew to the most prominent and pleasant world capitals, often in their own private jet planes. They now have retreated to obscure and difficult terrain, like alpine villages and Doha, Qatar, to escape the newly sophisticated opposition of the young. Though hardly the final victory of the Davids over the Goliaths, the multiplication of sophisticated Davids, young and old, has made progress in creating possibilities for a more democratic media.

Not Yet Eden

In the new century, progressive reform movements still must deal with a formidable armory of broadcast programs from the Far Right. In 2003, Rush Limbaugh, for example, had an audience of 20 million for his daily diatribes, which were largely against anything left of his own ultra-right policies and stunningly bizarre fantasies.[2] Daytime radio, dominated by the largest owners, has become a right-wing propaganda machine with crudities and right-wing consistency that shock and puzzle observers from other industrial democracies. As noted earlier, the largest radio chain in the country, Clear Channel, has twelve hundred stations that dwarf all lesser radio broadcasters, with its star talk show, Limbaugh's, followed by a similar menu of right-wing commentators specializing in crude diatribes and juvenile vocabularies. The remainder is canned syndicated music censored of any lyrics that hint of social-conscience ideas.

An analysis by the University of Pennsylvania Annenberg Public Policy Center found that 18 percent of U.S. adults listen to at least two political call-in shows a week. About 7 percent listened only to Limbaugh, and 4 percent listened to Limbaugh and others like him. About 2–3 percent of all

Americans listen to a conservative host, but 4–5 percent listen to a moderate or liberal show.[3]

It is some comfort for those looking for social uplift in afternoon TV shows that the lead, by far, is *Oprah*. In addition to her human interest guest interviews, she has become a major influence on serious book reading by regularly recommending a particular book. Most of her choices not only cause euphoria among the publishers but notably contribute to national literacy. Nevertheless, among the top ten afternoon TV shows are several who join Limbaugh as princes of darkness.

Among the country's newspapers, most dailies continue to remain close to the center-right but increasingly include occasional details of social problems and some attempt at balance in their op-ed political columnists. The *New York Times,* long the voice of the political and financial establishment, has shown more initiative in recent years. Many of its investigative initiatives have been uniquely useful, if one excludes the series on the alleged involvement of President and Hillary Clinton in the Arkansas Whitewater scandal, which turned out to be a journalistic indictment without substance.

Readers will notice that I cite the *New York Times* frequently, both as a reliable source and as a failed source. I have used it because it is the only national newspaper for the general audience and has more than 250 print and broadcast news organizations that subscribe to its services, most of which use news or syndicated columnists from the *New York Times* daily. For these same reasons, when the *Times* succeeds or fails it has a disproportionate effect on most of the other printed and broadcast news and, of course, on the American public.

The *Wall Street Journal* and *USA Today* are nationally

distributed but are specialized. The *Journal* news sections carry the most authoritative and detailed reports of corporate life, and *USA Today,* designed mainly for travelers and distributed heavily in airports and hotel rooms, has evolved from its early period of irrelevant novelties to an adulthood of respectable specialized reporting and balanced op-ed debates.

Necessary Remedies

The dominant concern is that the five huge media conglomerates, for all realistic purposes, now control what the American public learns—or does not learn—about its own world. It was once possible to consider excessive concentrated control of the mass media as a distinct entity on its own, a formidable force in the national economy and politics. But it is no longer possible to separate the media giants from other major industries. Ownership of media is now so integrated in political orientation and business connections with all of the largest industries in the American economy that they have become a coalition of power on an international scale. Consequently, remedies that might return media to their proper role as a source of the information needed to sustain the American democracy require laws and regulations that apply not only to the unique qualities of the mass media but also to the entire political economy, with which the mass media have dynamic interlocks.

Antitrust Action

The most obvious remedy for industrial giantism of all kinds is antitrust action by the U.S. Department of Justice. There is a need to break up the Big Five media conglomerates. In past decades, government antitrust actions have responded sharply to domestic monopolies but considered it even more egregious when large conglomerates cooperated with each other by becoming partners in the pattern of cartels. As mentioned earlier, joint ventures are now common among all the Big Five, even to the extent of swapping properties by way of lending money to produce mutual profits for the ostensible "competitors."

The globalization of world economy and communications has been an excuse for suspending antitrust action needed to protect the American public from the excesses of their multinational corporations. But monopolies and cartels in foreign countries that make life harder for large American corporations are quick to hear protests from Washington. In 2003, a status report from the Department of Justice declared, "Since the mid-1990s, the Antitrust Division of the U.S. Department of Justice has employed a strategy of concentrating its enforcement resources on international cartels that victimize American businesses and consumers."[4] Even though the report includes the word *consumers,* the context of the statement is clear that, when consumers are U.S. corporations, the government is outraged that foreign cartels allegedly victimize them, and the Department of Justice is quick to act. U.S. monopolies and cartels that merely "victimize" individual American consumers seem not to be important.

FCC: Obey the Law

It is urgent to repeal or totally revise the 1996 Telecommunications Act, which provided the law and the encouragement for the creation of overpowering media giants. The 1996 Act was created, according to the *Wall Street Journal,* when the "Gingrich class" of 1994 Republicans privately asked the industry what it wanted and almost literally gave them the law they asked for. The indiscriminate passion for deregulation of everything by corporate-minded ideologues has produced unmitigated disaster for cities and states throughout the United States, in the economy and particularly in the relationship or lack of it between the mass media and the American public.

Of special concern to the media audience is the recent record of the Federal Communications Commission (FCC), which controls broadcasting. It flagrantly abandoned its primary legal obligations: to protect the consumer of news and other media, to guarantee cities' access to their own local radio and television stations, and to give each community a voice in approving licenses based on the past performance of their local station.

For decades past, FCC regulations and former broadcast law awarded licenses on the basis of what kinds of programs each applicant for a broadcast license committed itself to provide for the needs of the cities covered by its stations. In contrast, licenses are now granted to whichever corporation has the most money, with no obligations except to operate "in the public interest," a phrase still in communications law, which in recent years has meant less than nothing.

In the past, when a station's license came up for renewal, the station was asked to demonstrate, with its broadcast schedules, whether it had made at least a nominal effort to keep its earlier commitments to the communities in its local market. In addition, any citizens with a serious complaint were able to protest a renewal in a formal hearing.

From 1934 to 1980 that system, with all its imperfections and devious evasions by station owners, did in fact produce access by citizens to their own stations and provide a wide range of programs for a variety of ages and audiences, a range of quantity and quality that began to disappear in the 1980s.

The Fairness Doctrine

The first dramatic change in the country's broadcasting came in the mid-1980s, when a concerted campaign was launched by the National Association of Broadcasters and its member stations to repeal the Fairness Doctrine. The Fairness Doctrine required stations to devote a reasonable time to discussions of serious public issues and allowed equal time for opposing views to be heard. By the mid-1980s, there had been years of broadcasters' complaints that keeping records was too onerous, though their annual profits were among the highest among American industries. The broadcasters insisted that the Fairness Doctrine requirement in fact hampered local and national discussion programs from discussing civic issues and that repeal would increase these community debates on serious matters. The broadcasters succeeded in repealing Fairness; in the next six months, civic discussions on the air dropped 31 percent. Since then, they have almost completely disappeared in major markets.[5]

The impact of conglomeration and loss of diversity is clearly demonstrated in newspaper editorials on the Fairness Doctrine. Before newspapers and their conglomerates began buying broadcast stations, in 1969 when the Supreme Court ruled that the Fairness Doctrine was constitutional, the majority of newspapers editorialized in favor of the Fairness Doctrine. But by 1984, when newspapers had become part of the growing conglomerates that owned both newspapers and broadcast stations, those newspapers had reversed their positions and editorialized against the Fairness Doctrine. At least 84 percent of newspaper editorials then argued that the Fairness Doctrine should no longer be required. Diversity of opinions had begun to shrink and rights of reply disappeared from the U.S. airwaves.[6]

In the past, the Fairness requirement was an incentive

for stations to offer air time to local groups to avoid a battle when their licenses came up for renewal. During the fifty years of Fairness Doctrine, the FCC never revoked a license. (Communications law, from the start, has always forbidden the FCC from mandating specific content for any station.) If the Fairness Doctrine were reinstated now, there would be no inhibition of the Rush Limbaughs and other wild talk shows, but individuals now unfairly accused of being insane or "Nazis"—in this case, the kind of rhetoric used to characterize equal rights for women—would have a chance to reply.

The Public Voice in License Renewal

Another remedial action that has produced at least modest results in the past has been challenges by community groups to stations' license renewals. The renewal period was expanded from three years to eight by the disastrous 1996 Telecommunications Act, which started the removal of restrictions on ownership. Even so, protests against renewal are still a citizen right that in the past permitted excluded major groups to gain air time. It is still possible to launch such a challenge as the date for a local station's license renewal approaches. The FCC combines renewal dates for regional groups of states. Protesters in each region would need to know when to do their recordkeeping as evidence of improper or absent concern with serious news programming on their local stations. They would also have to be reminded, regularly, that they own the air waves and, consequently, control the licenses for its use.

Each group of states has its own eight-year renewal cycle for both radio and television stations in that region. Some examples are the following:

Connecticut, Maine, Massachusetts, New Hampshire,
Rhode Island, and Vermont: radio 2006, TV stations 2009;
New Jersey and New York: radio 2006, TV 2007;
Texas: radio 2005 and 2013, TV 2006 and 2014;
California, radio 2005 and 2013, TV 2006 and 2014;
Ohio and Michigan, radio 2004 and 2012.

In the Absence of Law, Lawlessness

The FCC retreat from real regulation of broadcasting for the
benefit of the general public has resulted in illegal protests,
like pirate, or unlicensed, broadcasts that are transmitted
by individually assembled, portable, low-powered stations
that reach a particular community, now without news about
their cities. The most publicized was "Radio Free Berkeley,"
based in a van that moved to different locations in the hills
about that city and broadcast news of interest and notice
of educational events to the community and its minority
groups. Because unlicensed broadcasting is a federal crime
punishable by fines and imprisonment, one of the earliest pi-
rates, Stephen Dunifer, was eventually located by the FCC,
convicted in court, fined, and placed on probation.[7]

In the meantime, at least one thousand illegal low-powered stations appeared around the country. They seem to
continue in the United States, are common in other countries, and are not likely to disappear. Among a generation
of young people are youths sophisticated in circuitry and a
desire to reach their own neighborhoods and towns. A low-
powered transmitter, small antenna, and amplifier can be
built for about five hundred dollars with parts available at
Radio Shack. Operators broadcast from their garages, attics,
or their own rooms and generally tend to avoid offensive lan-

guage or capricious comments, presumably finding a neighborhood grateful for the only source of news about itself.[8] There are thirty-five hundred applications pending before the FCC for permits for low-power neighborhood broadcasting,[9] feeding the hunger in most communities for local news they do not get from their own stations. A great deal of chaos, illegal transmissions, and theft of legal cable and dish transmissions are likely to continue as long as the FCC permits such a limited variety of programs and such limited public access to its own local stations.

Another major gap is the U.S. limitation to only one noncommercial public broadcasting system, unlike the multiple varied ones in Britain, Japan, and other democracies. Until there is the kind of adequate, multichannel television that is truly noncommercial and devoted to children, education, adult entertainment, and the popular and performing arts, the most technologically advanced and richest country in the world will continue to have the least capacious noncommercial broadcast system among its peer nations.

Ever larger conglomerates will encourage devious escapes unless the U.S. Department of Justice follows the European Community's antitrust prohibitions, typified by its blocking of the merger of Elsevier and Wolters Kluwer in academic publishing (a European act that, ironically, despite U.S. reluctance to use antitrust against its own media conglomerates, benefits U.S. research and development).

Rebellion in the Groves of Academe

In far more quiet and less dramatic actions, the most respectable of institutions, libraries, and universities of the country have been forced to create their own (legal) way of avoiding the prohibitive pricing of the academic monopolies.

Media monopolies have damaged basic institutions of the country, which have been forced to find their own escapes from both intrusive laws and the absence of laws.

Libraries, for example, are faced with rising book costs from conglomerate publishers and increasingly use interlibrary loans to share less commonly used books. At the same time they have had to deal with emergency laws passed after 9/11 that permit the Federal Bureau of Investigation (FBI) to monitor individual users of books and periodicals. Libraries have imposed their own internal policies to minimize official snooping into those who take out books. Judith F. Krug, director of the American Library Association Office for Intellectual Freedom, said, "We believe that what you read is nobody's business but your own."[10]

A teleconference of librarians agreed that they should obey FBI inquiries only when accompanied by a proper court order. Most libraries adopted a policy of keeping as few records as possible and, rather than the former practice of getting rid of unneeded records each week, do so immediately, every day. Enron is not the only organization that knows when and how to keep its shredders busy.

Scholars, Ph.D. versus Dollars, Inc.

There is a quiet corner of U.S. media in which the government's reluctance to use antitrust laws has, in an ironic way, undercut a crucial element in the nation's continued dominance as the world's most powerful superpower. Central to U.S. long-term development is its ability to remain a leading user of basic research and development. It was crucial a century ago in mobilizing its vast continental resources in the Industrial Revolution, and it is crucial today as research and development underlie the country's industry, economic health, and even its dominance in weaponry. The atomic bomb in World War II did not leap unbidden from a corporate boardroom.

What appears to the brokers of legislation and fiscal matters in Washington as literally an academic matter resides in a growing crisis in the libraries of U.S. universities.

Access to the most important literature in intellectual and scientific journals is increasingly threatened by great leaps in prices demanded by a global triumvirate of media monopolists in academic journals. The three dominant companies—Reed Elsevier and Wolters Kluwer in the Netherlands and John Wiley in the United States—can do this because each has the ultimate paradise of a monopoly: a captive market.

Modern scholars must comply with stringent academic requirements before their work is accepted and published. They must first have their long and highly researched dissertations reviewed by two presumably neutral scholars in their field and then be accepted by a reputable academic journal. Completion of this process is required before acceptance into the university faculty with lifetime tenure, the Holy Grail of young scholars.

Professors and would-be professors face the never-ending crisis: "publish or perish." Granted, in the seventeenth century, Galileo Galilei had it harder because he faced "publish *and* perish" when sent to the Inquisition for violating the biblical dogma that the earth is the center of the universe.[11] But today the burning of heretics at the stake has been succeeded by the more profitable practice of exorbitant prices charged by the three global publishing monopolies.

Reed Elsevier, started in 1860, continues to acquire other publishers: in 1993 *The Official Airline Guides;* in 1997 four companies and an alliance with Microsoft; in 1998 Matthew Bender, leading publisher of legal cases; in 2000 four more firms; in 2001 four more, including Harcourt Brace General and the fixture in every bookstore and library of any size, the multivolume *Books in Print*, along with other standard items, librarian and bookseller standard references, *Publishers Weekly*, and *Library Journal*.[12]

The second dominant academic publisher, Wolters Kluwer, also in the Netherlands, has been making acquisitions since its establishment in 1889. Elsevier was about to acquire Wolters Kluwer for $8.8 billion in 1998, but when the European Community Monopoly Commission objected, the merger did not occur.[13]

The third dominant academic and professional book publisher in digital and printed form is the John Wiley Company in the United States, started in 1807. Wiley foresaw the growth of the Industrial Revolution, shifted emphasis to books about science and technology, and has remained a specialist in that genre ever since. In the 1900s, social science and college- and graduate-level textbooks became major products and more recently books on medicine and medical education. In 1997, Wiley acquired Van Nostrand Reinhold and became publisher for the American Cancer Society's journal *Cancer*. They have since acquired Jossey-Bass, Lasser tax guides, and the Dummies computer series. By 2002 their revenues exceeded $700 million.[14]

This great leap in prices for academic and professional work, along with budget cuts of universities as a whole, has caused a crisis for research libraries. "The ... crisis is now in its fourth decade," according to Prof. Peter Suber, of Earlham College.

We're long past the point of damage control and into the era of damage. Prices limit access, and intolerable prices limit access intolerably. Every research institution in the world suffers from intolerable access limitations, no matter how wealthy. Not only must librarians cope by canceling subscriptions and cutting their book budgets, but researchers must do without access to some of the journals critical to their research.[15]

Subscription prices increase steadily. John Wiley and Sons, for example, publishes three specialized journals on polymer science, all of which raised their annual subscription prices by more than 80 percent between 1997 and 2002. Wiley's *Journal of Comparative Neurology* cost $10,056 a year in 1997 and $16,995 in 2002, an almost 70 percent increase. The price of Elsevier's *Atmospheric Environment* increased 67 percent in five years. Elsevier's journal, *Brain*, costs $19,971 a year for a series of 131 special sections.[16]

By 1986, Dr. Michael Rosenzweig, a sociologist at the University of Arizona at Tucson, had had enough. The academic journal he had helped create years before, *Evolutionary Ecology*, had raised its subscription rate to $8,000 a year. Rosenzweig and his wife Carol rebelled. His whole board of editors defected with him, and they issued their own journal, *Evolutionary Ecology Research*. The cost, counting all the detailed preparation and evaluations, was $353 a year. More than one hundred university libraries around the country joined the revolt.[17]

By 2003, the Rosenzweigs' revolt had evolved into a worldwide Scholarly Publishing and Academic Resources Coalition (SPARC) under the auspices of the Association of Research Libraries. SPARC now has members in two hundred universities in North America, Europe, Asia, and Australia. Harvard, Yale, the University of California, and other university groups in the United States and Canada have joined in the worldwide coalition.[18]

Forced to reduce sharply their purchase of new texts and other books, universities have formed regional clusters in which the member campus libraries divide annual journal subscriptions among themselves. When one campus requests a specific article in a journal from the member campus that actually subscribes to it, the requested article usually is sent by Internet. But even here, the monopoly publishers have retaliated. The commercial firms have imposed contractual limitations on digital distribution of their printed works as a condition for subscribing to even one of their journals.[19]

A Digital Commons

Another academic-oriented reaction against monopolists is the Electronic Commons movement, conducted entirely on the Internet. The word *commons* is used metaphorically, not as the grassy public plots that are typical of the community-owned expanses in New England towns (for example, the famous Boston Common). The Electronic Commons has become a worldwide effort to keep as much intellectual property as possible—articles, books, art, film, textbooks, music, and other published material—in the public domain, free of commercial copyright restrictions. Librarians and others reacted to the easy success in recent decades of commercial media corporations using their power in Congress to extend copyrights well beyond earlier limits. Copyright extension stimulated the fear that corporate control was moving toward what would effectively be "perpetual copyright," keeping ever more material the business property of the media conglomerates.

Contributors to the new Commons collection are free to decide whether their material will be licensed for selected use under conditions of their own choosing. Otherwise, the material is open to the public for "noncommercial use." If anyone wishes to use Commons material for profit-making, the author can charge fees. Foundations and a coalition of legal specialists launched the Electronic Commons in 2001.[20]

A similar effort is Wikipedia, an Internet free encyclopedia that consists entirely of volunteer operators and contributors. It, like the Creative Commons, was started in 2001.

Two years after its founding there were almost 150,000 entries in more than ten languages. Its name is derived from the Hawaiian word *wikiwiki,* meaning "fast." Though it contains all the subject categories of a large general encyclopedia, the articles vary in quality and length, from the scholarly to the sketchy.[21]

Though the Wikipedia was created to counter the corporate control of information, a number of commercial firms have started their own fee-based "wiki" Internet sites, which business professionals and corporations can use as a fast-moving bulletin board for large corporate conferences and conventions.[22]

Even a conventional book publisher, Prentice Hall, faced with Internet usage of copyrighted material, is issuing books over the Linux Internet under an "Open Publication License," which permits anyone to download one of their books in this category and make full photocopies. The publisher predicts that this will develop enough goodwill and interest in books reproduced this way that eventually users will want the sturdy, stable conventionally printed hardback books for as much as fifty dollars each.[23]

New Activism of the Young

As mentioned earlier, the active political direction for the country has seen the growth, thanks mostly to the Internet, of movements of mostly younger men and women who have had a serious influence on public thinking on policy matters and in voting. That and the Internet have activated what used to be the lowest age-group participation in voting, the 18- to 24-year-old citizens. The Twenty-sixth Amendment to the Constitution passed in 1971, granting the right to vote to any citizen eighteen years old or above (on the basis that if they were sent to fight in Vietnam, they deserved the right to vote). It enfranchised 11.5 million young voters, but in the first presidential election afterward only half of the eligible voters actually cast ballots. Whether the new activism among the young will change politics significantly and for how long remains to be seen. It could be a fundamental factor in elections. By 2000, the 14.4 percent, or 27 million, men and women of the voting age population 18 to 25 years old who were actually U.S. citizens and therefore eligible to vote had increased their registration to vote to 60 percent. According to the Youth Vote Coalition, other young adults and younger politicians are the most attractive to them, at 70 percent. In 2000, only 24 percent found the president elected that year to be legitimate, and what most concerned them was terrorism, 17 percent; jobs and the economy, 15 percent; and crime, 13 percent.[24]

Media Reform Groups

The large majority of media reform groups concentrate on a variety of what they see as needed changes. The Democratic Media Reform, originally funded by the Social Sciences and Humanities Research Council of Canada, explores the condition of all English-language media in the country. In the United States it works in conjunction with Free Press in Northampton, Mass. (mediareform.net), and major centers like the Association for Progressive Communications in San Francisco; the Association of Independent Video and Filmakers, Big Noise Tactical Media, and Brennan Center for Justice in New York City; the Benton Foundation and Campaign Legal Center in Washington; and the Center for Communication and Community in Los Angeles.

Other significant national media reform and monitoring groups include Jeff Chester, an indefatigable monitor of media matters in Congress and the FCC, who has created the Center for Digital Democracy, Center for Media Education, and Teledemocracy Project, all based in Washington; *Extra!* the publication of FAIR (Fairness and Accuracy in Reporting), regularly reports errors and omissions in the major news media; the National Writers Union's *Action Alerts;* Free Speech TV, which broadcasts twenty-four hours a day via satellite DISH Network Channel 9415, advocates diversity oriented around social progress and the environment, covers protest marches, and produces films;[25] and Zine, which publishes anthologies of independent publishers with circulation of less than five thousand.[26] A reflection of the speed with which a new generation has become accustomed to rapidly changing images and commercials requiring near-subconscious impressions is a Ten Seconds Competition film festival. The event is held each year to select the best of one thousand entries that demonstrate ways to squeeze their messages into the world of standard commercials.

The new protests against entrenched media power are local, national, and international. Some local groups monitor citywide or regional press and broadcasting, and some national and others, like the World-Information Organization and UNESCO, are international and hold periodic conferences of new-generation activists in various regions of the world. As corporate media giants have become international in scope, so have media reform organizations.

The Corrupting Disease

While reform concentrating on the mass media must continue, it must fight the formidable barrier inhibiting all social progress in the United States. A fundamental change on which media and other reforms depend is the removal of the magnitude of corporate money given to the major political parties. It tests the patience of any citizen to take seriously the claim by politicians that the millions of dollars from corporations does not influence their votes. If that were true, one must assume that for the last generation, as corporate contributions to politicians have grown to historic highs, the corporations making those massive contributions are incurably stupid and continue to throw away ineffective millions year after year out of pure caprice or philanthropic virtue.

Before mass media reforms can become real and substantial, the political system requires changes that seemed almost impossible before the Internet generation used the technique to organize protests. But as long as hundreds of millions of dollars continue to be given to candidates and officeholders, there will be powerful influence on the laws and agencies of the U.S. government, given that corporations, including media corporations, constitute 75 percent of all political contributions. The influence of media corporations on broadcast laws, for example, is an example of the results—almost complete disappearance of serious national and worldwide news from local radio and television stations, low-budget television programs that coarsen the culture—though broadcast profits are among the highest in American industry.

Public Objection on the Rise

Public objection to the misuses of corporate power, especially by media corporations, is increasingly evident, and that is encouraging. A new generation of young people, once notoriously uninterested in national and world politics, has become an effective corrective on the American media scene. They have, probably well beyond that of their elders, skill in marshaling information and using it to produce public policies.

An aroused adult generation and activist younger one is in the tradition of the country's first trust-buster, President Theodore Roosevelt, who took on the great conglomerates and monopolies of his time and broke their conspiratorial hold on the American consumers. He died forty years before the first crude Internet was born, but in 1903 the first message he sent to Congress as president of the United States rings true today: "The first essential in determining how to deal with the great industrial corporations is knowledge of the facts."[27]

James Madison, fourth president of the United States, died sixty years before the first crude radio was born, but what he wrote more than two hundred years ago proclaims the same principle: "A people who mean to be their own governors must arm themselves with the power which knowledge gives. A popular government without popular information, or the means of acquiring it, is but a prologue to a farce or a tragedy or perhaps both."[28]

*There are still quite a few executive officers
who are accustomed to giving orders and
who resent the media for not taking them.*
KENNETH A. RANDALL, 1980[1]

CHAPTER EIGHT

"WON'T THEY EVER LEARN?"

As Joseph Pulitzer approached the end of his career, he worried about the future of his newspaper. Would his heirs be competent and committed? Or would they sell to greedy new owners? He decided to follow the example of the *London Times* and to name trustees instructed by will to operate the paper in the public interest.

The trustee device generally has failed. Voices from the grave seldom win debates; where there is a will there is a lawyer to break it. But 1904 was a more innocent age, and Pulitzer set out to find distinguished citizens as trustees to preserve the integrity of his *New York World*. He was impressed with the character of the presiding justice of New York State's highest court, Morgan K. Stanley. He took the judge horseback riding and explained his plan. The judge seemed amenable. The two men tentatively agreed that Stanley would be a trustee. They rode on for a while before Pulitzer asked, "What do you think of the *World*?"

"It is a great paper. But it has one defect."
"What is that?"
"It never stands by its friends."
"A newspaper should have no friends," Pulitzer replied sharply.
"I think it should," the judge answered just as sharply.
"If that is your opinion," Pulitzer said, "I wouldn't make you one of my trustees if you gave me a million dollars."[2]

Pulitzer was serious. In his newsroom a sign announced ominously, "The *World* has no friends."

But almost all news media have friends who are given preferential treatment in the news, who are immune to criticism, who can keep out embarrassing information, or who are guaranteed a positive image. In the newsrooms of America, these friends are called "sacred cows." They frequently include the owner, the owner's family and friends, major advertisers, and the owner's political causes. Sacred cows in the news run the gamut from petunias to presidents. In one northeastern city the sacred cow is civic flowerbeds donated by the publisher's spouse; in another city it is an order that any picture of Richard Nixon must show him smiling.

The sacred cows in American newsrooms leave residues common to all cows. But no sacred cow has been so protected and has left more generous residues in the news than the American corporation. So it is ironic that in the last decade the most bitter attacks on the news media have come from the American corporate system. The irony becomes exquisite when, in the 1980s, the segment of American life that most hates the news increasingly comes to own it.

Large classes of people are ignored in the news, are reported as exotic fads, or appear only at their worst—minorities, blue-collar workers, the lower middle class, the poor. They become publicized mainly when they are in spectacular accidents, go on strike, or are arrested. Other groups and institutions—government, schools, universities, and nonestablished political movements—are subjected to periodic criticism. Minor tribes like athletes, fashion designers, and actors receive routine praise. But since World War I hardly a mainstream American news medium has failed to grant its most favored treatment to corporate life.

There has been much to celebrate in the history of corporate industry and technology. Great cities rose and flourished, material goods flowed to the populace, cash spread to new classes of people, standards of living rose, and life was prolonged in developed countries.

There have also been ugliness and injustice in corporate wielding of power—bloody repressions of workers who tried to organize unions, corruption of government, theft of public franchises. But through it all, most of the mass media depicted corporate life as benevolent and patriotic.

The Ghost at the Banquet

In the late 1950s, ghosts appeared at industry's banquet. Raw materials had been extracted in astounding volumes, and some were near exhaustion. Economic benefits of industrialization were spread unevenly, causing political turbulence. As ever, entrepreneurs contended for dominion over the earth's crust, this time wielding its bitter fruit—uranium. In some forms the ghosts were literally invisible. Since the start of the Industrial Revolution, new vapors, 200 billion tons of carbon dioxide alone, were added to the atmosphere, changing climates and human organs.[3] Thousands of new chemicals, like DDT, soon resided in every living tissue and, like radiation, created ominous biological alterations. By the 1980s some wastes of industry, 77 billion pounds a year, were so hazardous that it was not clear whether the planet could safely contain them. Corporate products and wastes began to poison drinking water, food, and in some cases whole communities. In the past itinerant merchants sold harmful products that could sicken or kill hundreds, but now great international organizations poured out avalanches of products which, if unsafe, threatened millions. One in four Americans came to die of cancer.

In earlier periods, death and disease were accepted as acts of God. If a tunnel collapsed on miners or textile workers died coughing blood, it was all in the hand of God or random bad luck. But when industry's ghost of pollution and disease materialized in the last half of the twentieth century, the problems drew attention not, as before, to the hand of God but to the organizations that owned and operated most of industrial civilization—the great corporations.

Corporate unease became sharper when a president whom corporations considered their own, Dwight D. Eisenhower, left office in 1961 warning against the bloated power of what he called "the military-industrial complex." Later that same year twenty-nine major corporations, some with household names like Westinghouse and General Electric, were convicted of conspiracies in selling $7 billion worth of electrical equipment, and some executives actually served short jail sentences.[4] More shocks to the corporate status quo came in quick succession. Racial tensions, suppressed for centuries, burst into a mass movement in the 1960s. The Vietnam War protests raised an additional specter of rebellion in the streets. Another president the corporations regarded as their champion, Richard Nixon, left office in disgrace in 1974, partly because of accusations of corruption involving prominent corporations.

When the twenty-nine corporations were convicted of conspiracy in 1961, a lawyer for one of the defendants told the judge that the executives should not be punished because their acts were "a way of life—everybody's doing it." Thus, even before massive corporate fraud, dishonest bookkeeping, executive theft, and collusion of the country's largest banks and accounting firms at the turn of the twenty-first century, a permissive corporate culture of "everybody's doing it" had paved the way for decades in the past.

In 1979 the Department of Justice found that, of the 582 largest American corporations, more than 60 percent were guilty of at least one illegal action, including evasion of taxes, unfair labor practices, dangerous working conditions, price fixing, pollution, and illegal kickbacks. At the "West Point of capitalism," the Harvard Graduate School of Business Administration, the *Harvard Business Review* found that corporate ethical practices, poor in 1961, were even worse in 1976. Its survey of industrial leaders showed common practices like cheating customers, bribing political officials, and using call girls for business purposes.[5] Two separate 1976 surveys of corporate executives by corporations themselves—Pitney Bowes and Uniroyal—found that a majority of business managers "feel pressured to compromise personal ethics to achieve corporate goals," including selling "off-standard and possibly dangerous items."[6]

Nevertheless, nothing in government or law prevented the two hundred largest corporations from increasing their control of all manufacturing from 45 percent in 1947 to 60 percent in 1979,[7] and nothing lessened corporate crime, which produces $44 billion in losses a year compared with $4 billion in property losses resulting from crimes committed by individuals.[8]

Courts have always been lenient with corporations, though in recent years even that has not satisfied the corporate world. Conservative foundations give judges and their families all-expenses-paid trips to Miami so they can take courses in the laissez-faire doctrines of Milton Friedman, focusing on the necessity of leaving corporations untouched by regulation and minimally touched by law. By 1980 one-fifth of the entire federal judiciary had taken the courses.[9]

Added judicial sympathy would not have seemed necessary. In the 1961 conviction of the twenty-nine corporations involved in the electrical equipment conspiracy, all the cases had been delayed for ten years or more, some for twenty-five years, while the offenses continued.[10] When the Aluminum Company of America was found guilty of illegal damage to competitors, massive legal defenses by the company delayed court action for sixteen years.[11] Though the Internal Revenue Service regularly jails between 600 and 700 tax evaders each year, some for relatively small amounts,[12] when the Firestone Tire & Rubber Company pleaded guilty to concealing $12.6 million income in two deliberately false tax returns and to conspiring to obstruct legal audits of their books, the corporation received a fine of only $10,000.[13]

In addition to their ability to evade or soften the legal consequences of their actions, corporations are protected by their special positions in government. After laws are passed or before regulations are designed, outside advisory committees sit with government leaders to help shape official actions. In 1974, for example, AT&T had 130 positions on these advisory bodies, RCA 104, General Electric 74, and ITT 53.[14] Defense industry executives sit on the Pentagon's Industry Advisory Council, oil executives sit on the National Petroleum Council, and some of the heaviest-polluting industries have executives on the National Industrial Pollution Control Council.[15] The most powerful business lobby, the Business Roundtable, has been able to use its membership on such committees to kill crucial legislation on the verge of passage, like the unexpected collapse in 1974 of a bill in the House of Representatives that would have established a consumer protection agency.[16]

In universities, as in government, corporate values have

steadily and quietly become dominant in the scientific research community. Corporate executives are the largest single group represented on governing boards of colleges and universities. In the public schools corporate materials have always been prominent, and their presence is increasing.[17] Only 1 percent of already tight school budgets are used for instructional materials, and industry has been quick to fill the gap with largely self-serving publications. Free classroom materials are produced by 64 percent of the five hundred largest American industrial corporations, 90 percent of industrial trade associations, and 90 percent of utility companies. The materials concentrate on nutrition, energy, environment, and economics, almost all supplied by industries with a stake in their own answer to the problems posed in the materials. "Free marketplace" and nonregulation of business is the predominant classroom economics lesson, presented largely through materials from a business group, the Advertising Council. The only nonscholastic source of classroom material larger than corporations is the Department of Defense.

A New Irreverence

While corporate influence remained almost untouched in the last few decades, changes occurred at the grass roots. Fueled by the irreverence of the 1960s protesters, critical attitudes toward corporations for the first time in recent American history went beyond the small enclaves of the Left and reached the middle class. In the early 1970s, corporate abuse became an issue when an ecology movement cut across political and class lines. Government, responding to its demands, looked more closely at corporate crime. A new consumer movement, built around the nucleus of Ralph

Nader and skilled university students, produced systematic data on dangerous consumer goods and unfair business practices. Slow-acting malignancies caused by asbestos and other carcinogens began raising morbidity and death rates among industrial employees, drawing attention to the hazards in the workplace.

At about the same time Western capitalism entered a period of crisis. The spiral of prosperity faltered. In country after country, including the United States, standard remedies failed or made things worse. What seemed at first to be an isolated phenomenon of escalated oil prices became a more fundamental malaise. Undeveloped nations that were once docile sources of raw materials vital to the new industrial civilization became less docile. Leaders of business and finance had always insisted, at least in public, on the infallibility of the self-righting mechanisms of their marketplace. And yet the marketplace defied their pronouncements. That malfunction, too, turned the public's attention to the great corporations.

In most walks of public life, corporations are accustomed to a smooth path edged with indulgence. Criticism in the United States had tended to be short-lived if it came from government or established sources. Longer-lasting criticism came from public health authorities, social scientists, union, liberal and left activists, and other specialized voices. In both cases, either criticism failed to be reported in the mass media or the reports were brief or even neutralized by the media's criticism of the critics.

The standard media—mainstream newspapers, magazines, and broadcasters—had always been reliable promoters of the corporate ethic. Whole sections of newspapers were always devoted to unrelieved glorification of business people, not just in advertisements where corporations pay for self-praise but in "news" that is assumed to be dispassionate. Most business sections of daily papers seldom apply to corporations the same criteria of validation and critical judgment applied to other subjects. Most business pages consist of corporate propaganda in the form of press releases run without significant changes or printed verbatim. Each day millions of expensive pages of stock market quotations are printed, even though only a small minority of American households actively trade in the stock market. Editorially, corporate causes almost invariably become news media causes. Among the most commonly suppressed news items each year are stories involving corporations that are reported in the major media.[18] The integration of corporate values into the national pieties could not have been established without prolonged indoctrination by the main body of American news organizations.

In the years after 1970, mounting public anger at some corporate behavior does occasionally find expression in print and on the air, as when the public was asked to sacrifice warm homes and car travel during a gas shortage while the major oil companies reported their highest profits in history. Or local demonstrations against polluting industries became melodrama that met the criteria for conflict news. Or a spectacular trial, like the Ford Motor Company defense against criminal charges of neglect for its defective Pinto gas tanks, caught the media's attention. The barriers against damaging news about corporations were high but not impassable. Journalism had slowly changed so that in a few standard media, including, ironically, the daily bible of business, the *Wall Street Journal*, there were more than brief flurries of items about bad public performances of big business. There was still no significant criticism of the corporate system, simply reporting of isolated cases, but for the first time there was a breach in the almost uniform litany of unremitting praise and promotion of corporate behavior.

Corporate leaders were outraged. They criticized government agencies that reported corporate culpability. In their political action committees they raised the largest campaign war chests in electoral history to defeat candidates they considered hostile to business, and in 1980 they elected a national administration dedicated to wiping out half a century of social legislation and regulation of business.[19] They created intellectual think tanks to counter academic studies damaging to corporations. But the corporations reserved their greatest wrath for the news media. Hell hath no fury like the sacred cow desanctified.

Business had special advantages in its attack on the media. It had privileged access to media executives through common corporate associations and lobbies, and it could produce large-scale advertisements to counter antibusiness news and, increasingly, to use as threats of withdrawal against hostile media. And corporate leaders could invoke against the media that peculiar American belief (ironically created more by the media than by any other source) that to criticize big business is to attack American democracy.

Criticizing the media is neither unnatural nor harmful. The difference in the corporate attack was that the campaign attempted to discredit the whole system of American news as subversive to American values and to characterize journalists as a class of careless "economic illiterates" biased against business.

Some specific corporate complaints were justified. Throughout journalism there is more carelessness and sloth than should be tolerated. Most reporters are "economic illiterates" in the sense that they lack skills to analyze business records and they seldom have the sophistication to comprehend world economic forces. But the accusation that standard American reporting was biased against business was absurd. It was absurd, but beginning in the 1970s it was relentless.

In 1976 the vice chairman of Bethlehem Steel, Frederic West Jr., told the American Newspaper Publishers Association: "People in business have a lot of gripes about the press. Anytime a bunch of executives get together these days you can be sure somebody will start talking about what's wrong with the news media."[20] In 1977 the president of Union Pacific said, "There is a basic bias that big business is bad."[21] In 1981 the president of a major advertising agency, Needham, Harper & Steers/Issues and Images, said: "All too frequently some rather rabid anticorporate messages are aired as part of the regular daily news schedule ... I assure you that I echo the sentiments of most people on the corporate side who've been stung repeatedly by the slanted coverage of their activities. Especially those stories about corporate profits."[22]

A vice president of Shell Oil complained to a Senate committee about bias in the news. He displayed headlines as evidence. "I have brought along a few articles clipped from our daily newspaper as examples of what I mean." The headlines were:

Nader Charges Energy Scare Designed to Double Oil Prices
Aspin Claims Oil Companies Gouging Public
Senator Claims Oil Shortage Put-Up Job
Jackson Says Oil Firms Irk Public with Evasions[23]

These news items usually originated with documented studies or with reports of established agencies. Lawrence K. Fouraker, dean of the Harvard Graduate School of Business

Administration, echoing the complaints of those (including media companies and journalists themselves) who want only pleasant news about their work, said that business reporters "tend to be gullible about business, if it is not good news."[24]

No other news sources, including high government officials, have been as effective as corporate executives in causing reporters to be fired, demoted, or removed from their beats. If the routine reporting of negative news about business from official sources was enraging, the idea of journalists taking the initiative in their own investigation of business, as they do with government, welfare recipients, and organized crime, tended to produce hysteria.

"Overzealous Reporters?"

Leonard Matthews, president of the American Association of Advertising Agencies, said that "business and the entire free enterprise system need to be supported by the media" but that this "mutually healthy relationship" had been "impaired in recent years by the overzealous actions of a small but very visible group of investigative reporters who have made a practice of slugging advertisers while their associates in the sales department were accepting an order from the same company."[25]

In the 1980s there were more investigative reporters than ever before. They had their own organization, Investigative Reporters and Editors. And the stereotype of the journalist as radical and antibusiness does not match the facts. An authoritative study by Stephen Hess showed that 58 percent of Washington correspondents consider themselves "middle of the road" or "conservative" politically. "In the past," Hess wrote, "the Washington press corps was liberal . . . a stereo-type of the news corps that is no longer accurate."[26]

It does not excuse journalists, who should become competent in the subjects they cover, but genuine economic literacy throughout the American population is remarkably low for a society in which economics has become the center of national politics. It is even more remarkable that business people themselves are among the most economically illiterate. A survey of three thousand persons by the business-oriented Advertising Council showed that "only 8% of all U.S. businessmen can correctly define the functions of these five groups—business, labor, the consumer, the investor, and advertising."[27]

One of the most caustic critics of business reporting had been Walter B. Wriston, chairman of Citibank. He insisted that journalists are interested only in bad news about the economy. "The media, supported by some academic 'liberals,' would have us believe that things are not just going badly, they are growing progressively and rapidly worse," Wriston said in 1975.[28] Wriston's own 1975 prediction was "I am convinced inflation is going to moderate very, very substantially" and "I don't think there is any question that the price of oil will come down." Five years later, the consumer price index had risen more than 50 percent, and the price index for refined petroleum products was up 150 percent.[29] Eventually, inflation and oil prices did fall, but "eventually" is not convincing evidence that a leading banker had any more foresight than the "economic illiterates" who happened to be less euphoric than the bankers.

The vigorous corporate campaign against alleged bias in the news contained a large element of cynicism along with whatever genuine anger was involved. Most corporate leaders did not experience criticism by the media. David Finn, leader of a major industrial public relations firm, Ruder and Finn, conducted a survey of the one thousand largest industries for the American Management Association in 1981. When chief executive officers were asked to describe how the media had treated their companies, their responses were

Poor, 6%
Fair, 28%
Good, 47%
Excellent, 19%[30]

Two-thirds of the leading industrial chiefs of the country believe the media treatment of their companies is good or excellent, and only 6 percent feel it is poor. Corporations must constitute the best-treated complainers in society.

A few corporate leaders have said that the corporate antimedia campaign is misdirected. J. Peter Grace, president of W. R. Grace Company, says the public's bad image of business originated "because business has countenanced dishonesty in dealing with government employees and purchasing agents on a world-wide basis." William F. May, chairman of American Can Company, said, "There is a tendency for business to stand on tippy toes and communicate only the favorable. We need to present more unvarnished information."[31]

Senator Abraham Ribicoff of Connecticut told a meeting of top business executives in 1979:

Businessmen are always getting mad and blaming someone else when the blame lies squarely on your shoulders. You let the Japanese beat you in the small-car market. You treat every regulation as an attack when you know very well that some regulation is beneficial to you. You also seem to forget that the American people are concerned for their health, life and safety.[32]

Corporations as Heroes

Perhaps nowhere is the cynicism more blatant than in the newly energized activity known as corporate advertising. This constitutes printed and broadcast ads designed not to sell goods and services but to promote the politics and benevolent image of the corporation—and to attack anything that spoils the image. Ideology-image ads as a category of all ads doubled in the 1970s and had become a half-billion dollar-a-year enterprise.

The head of a large advertising agency described the purpose:

It presents the corporation as hero, a responsible citizen, a force for good, presenting information on the work the company is doing in community relations, assisting the less fortunate, minimizing pollution, controlling drugs, ameliorating poverty.[33]

The publication *Media Decisions* estimated that as much as $3 billion in corporate money goes into all methods of promoting the corporation as hero and into "explanations of the capitalistic system," including massive use of corporate books and teaching materials in the schools, almost all tax deductible.[34]

The energy crises of the 1970s and 1980s intensified the corporate campaign against the media, led this time by the petroleum industry. Extraordinary escalation of consumer prices for energy was accompanied by multiplied profits to the oil companies. The corporate profit announcements were intended, as usual, to impress international investors, and the general public apparently was not supposed to notice. But it did. The public demanded that legislators, civic groups, and the media explain why private citizens were asked to sacrifice but oil companies were not. A survey showed that 25 percent of the American population favored nationalization of the oil industry.

The structure and inner finances of the oil industry are among the most byzantine in the world. Journalists had remained ignorant and for the most part are still ignorant of the realities of energy economics. Journalistic negligence has damaged the public, but it has been to the advantage of oil companies.

In the 1980s the most vigorous promoter of the corporation as hero and the most relentless critic of the news media was Mobil Oil. In 1981 Mobil and its petroleum allies gave the journalistic world an object lesson in the penalties for journalists who stray from the paths of corporate piety.

Mobil Oil was the third largest industrial corporation in the country (Exxon was second), and it had taken the lead among American corporations in attacking the news media for alleged antibusiness bias.[35] In 1972 it began using some of its $21 million annual public relations budget for advertisements directed against the news media and succeeded in guaranteeing its ads a place on the editorial pages of a dozen major papers (a spot next to editorials that came to be known in the newspaper trade as "the Mobil position"). During the 1973 Arab oil crisis Mobil's editorial ads appeared in hundreds of papers. The company also ran a column called "Observations" in Sunday supplements distributed to thousands of community newspapers. Mobil has an informal network of television stations that carry its political and antimedia commercials. It sponsors books and publishes some books under its own imprint and others by regular trade and university presses. Its book *The Genius of Arab Civilization*, published by New York University Press, is one of a series promoting countries where it has oil interests. Other books and reports it has sponsored have been published by MIT Press and Hudson Institute.

Mobil's own accuracy in advertising has not always been the best model for the journalists it lectures so sternly. In 1980 the company agreed under threat of official penalty to undo the inaccuracy of a Mobil ad that claimed a product would save up to 25 percent in oil consumption when in fact it often increased oil consumption.[36]

Mobil's most noticeable and influential ads against the media have appeared in the editorial space of the *New York Times*, the *Wall Street Journal*, the *Washington Post*, and other major metropolitan newspapers. The ads express anger at error in the media, weariness at media ignorance, and sarcasm at lack of devotion to the true principles of the First Amendment. Unfortunately, Mobil seemed to define one First Amendment for the news media and a different one for the oil company.

One Mobil ad declared, "Any restraint on free discussion is dangerous. Any policy that restricts flow of information or ideas is potentially harmful."[37] It is a noble idea. But shortly afterward, Mobil Oil, a major sponsor of public broadcasting, urged the Public Broadcasting System to suppress the showing of a film that would upset its oil partner, Saudi Arabia.[38]

In 1981 Mobil ran one of its editorial ads in ten major newspapers with a total of 7 million circulation. The ad exploited the Benedictine Sisters against their will. The Sisters complained. Only one of the papers, the *Los Angeles Times*, ran the letter of complaint. Mobil's multimillion-dollar editorial ad campaign obviously was more convincing to the other nine papers than grievances of the nonpaying Benedictine Sisters.[39]

Other Mobil editorial ads praised the company itself for sensitive attention to pollution.[40] When a national business group of which it is a member, the Council of Economic Priorities, issued a pollution report that mentioned Mobil's poor record on pollution, Mobil withdrew its support from the council. When Columbia University created a program to give training in economics to business reporters, a project aiming to diminish journalistic "economic illiteracy," Mobil's action may provide a hint at the nature of the "economic literacy" it desired. Mobil was a contributor to the Columbia program but, when the university named the director of the program, Mobil withdrew its support because the director had once criticized the oil industry.

When a smaller company used a front organization to criticize Mobil, a vice president of Mobil announced indignantly, "The public has a right to know who is behind any advocacy effect." This prompted the Jack O'Dwyer public relations newsletter to disclose that Mobil is the sponsor of pro-oil, antigovernment cartoons that appear in hundreds of newspapers around the country masquerading as the newspapers' own, with Mobil the unidentified propagandist.

The cynicism of ads focusing on corporate policy is not always subtle.[41] One Mobil ad said the company needed all its profits for drilling because only 1.7 percent of its wells struck oil. The ad did not explain that this was true for only a small category of drilling and that the average success rate for all drilling is about 60 percent. Even less subtle was the Mobil ad that declared in 1979: "Can oil companies be trusted to put additional revenues into the search for new energy supplies? History says yes."

Sadly, history says no. The top twenty oil companies have used profits to purchase so many firms outside of oil production and distribution that the value of their nonoil properties in 1979, the year the Mobil ad appeared, totaled $35 billion.[42] Mobil itself was investing much of its profits "in search for new energy supplies" by purchasing such assorted nonoil companies as Montgomery Ward, Container Corporation of America, restaurants in Kansas City, condominiums in Hong Kong, and W. F. Hall, of Chicago, one of the largest commercial printing plants in the world. Mobil indulged its profits "in search for new energy supplies" by printing *Playboy* magazine, *National Geographic,* and Bantam and Random House paperback books.[43]

Oil Versus a Journalist

The quiet power of a large corporation to suppress damaging information and to silence the journalist who brings it to light can be seen in the attack by Mobil and its oil industry allies on an economics reporter for United Press International (UPI), then a leading American news agency.

Major oil companies based in the United States pay an extremely low U.S. income tax. The meager percentages are obscured by oil industry finances that are so arcane that even the Securities and Exchange Commission has said that they cannot be dealt with by ordinary accounting methods. But when the complexities of industry finances were expressed in plain language, Mobil and its friends decided to discredit the correspondent who accomplished the task.

The reporter selected for treatment was a poor example of the corporate stereotype of a liberal-radical journalist hostile to business. Edward F. Roby of UPI is a graduate of West Point, was awarded a Silver Star for Vietnam combat, is a devotee of conservative economist Milton Friedman, and personally believes that corporations should pay no income taxes. But he also believes in reporting the news and making it clear.

On June 5, 1981, Roby received a routine government report in the Washington bureau of UPI. It was a study of oil company revenues and taxes prepared by the Financial Reporting System of the U.S. Department of Energy.[44] He noticed that the effective tax rate for the twenty-six largest energy firms, including Mobil, Exxon, and Gulf, was surprisingly low for the adjusted gross income. The adjusted gross income for the oil companies was the income of the parent firm within the United States after the firm had been forgiven U.S. taxes for any taxes paid in other countries.

The nominal corporate income tax was 46 percent, but in fact the average tax paid by all U.S. corporations in 1979 was 23.7 percent. The twenty-six largest energy companies, according to the report, paid even less—12.4 percent—at a time of record-high oil industry profits. The 12.4 percent income tax rate for the biggest oil company was, Roby learned from the Internal Revenue Service, the same rate that would be paid by a private citizen who made less than twenty thousand dollars a year. He wrote that information in a story that appeared on UPI news wires in June 1981.

Shortly after Roby's story went out on the wires,[45] a Mobil ad appeared in "the Mobil position" in eleven influential American newspapers under the headline: Won't They Ever Learn? "Once again," the ad began, "newspaper readers across the country were recently presented with a massive dose of misinformation on oil industry taxes."

After its usual denunciation of a news article about oil profits being "misleading" and "blatantly incorrect," the Mobil ad concluded, "This is not the first time the oil industry has been falsely accused of underpaying its taxes ... we hope that UPI will set the record straight so the American public can make judgments based on accurate and reliable data."

The ad told readers that oil company income is

taxed by the country in which it is earned according to the country's corporate tax rate. These foreign income taxes—and only income taxes—are credited by U.S. law against taxes on that foreign income to avoid double taxation on the same income . . . Despite the fact that we have pointed it out hundreds of times, reporters still can't seem to get it right. [Emphasis Mobil's] [46]

But Roby and UPI were correct.

A Lesson on Taxes

What Mobil had not pointed out hundreds of times—or ever—was the strange arrangement it had made to define "income tax" in its foreign tax credits. Mobil was a member of Aramco, the consortium of four oil companies—Mobil, Exxon, Socal, and Texaco—that dealt with Saudi Arabia for oil. In 1950 the Saudis announced an increase in the price of oil to its partners. Ordinarily, this would mean that Aramco would pay higher royalties for the oil and deduct from its revenues as a cost of doing business this added cost of its raw material, in the same way that an individual taxpayer can deduct from his or her total income (not from taxes) some of the amount he or she pays for doctor bills. But that is not what happened.

In 1977 Representative Benjamin Rosenthal of New York produced secret Internal Revenue Service documents going back to 1950.[47] They showed that the tax laws of Saudi Arabia were drafted with the help of Aramco to call the added price of oil not a "royalty" or "cost of doing business," as was proper, but an "income tax." The Saudis did this knowing that income tax paid to a foreign country is deductible from the income taxes an oil company pays the United States on all income received in the United States by the parent firm.

At the same time, the U.S. Department of the Treasury called this "royalty exacted in the guise of income tax" a "sham." But the power of the oil industry within government is almost unmatched, and the unorthodox provision was accepted by the Treasury. A 1977 calculation by the House Ways and Means Committee showed that about 75 percent of what the oil companies paid Saudi Arabia for oil was counted as "income tax," reducing their U.S. taxes so much that it cost other U.S. taxpayers more than $2 billion a year. It is such a highly profitable avoidance of domestic taxes that it has motivated the major oil companies to emphasize Middle East oil despite its high price and unstable future.

The Mobil ad did not explain the "sham." Instead it denounced accurate news.

Recently officials in China, which has no income tax, were startled when American oil companies, negotiating for drilling contracts, asked the Chinese to exact an income tax. Presumably this request did not arise so much from a desire to pay taxes to a Marxist regime as from a desire to pay artificially low taxes to the United States.[48]

A few days after Mobil's attack on the Roby-UPI story, Exxon, possibly in an attempt to help an ally in its offensive, attacked another Roby story and mentioned Roby by name. Roby had reported what had earlier been reported by the *Wall Street Journal* and industry trade papers.[49] Secretary of the Interior James Watt, in his philosophy of maximum exploitation of natural resources, had announced that a vast area of the oceanic outer continental shelf was open for drilling bids by oil companies. Roby wrote that some oil companies thought Watt had opened too large an area at that time. It was news that oil companies wanted less, not more, acreage to explore. Roby, in the seventeenth paragraph of his story, had written that Exxon recommended "offering much less acreage in each sale." The Exxon communication to Secretary Watt said precisely that, recommending "offering much less acreage in each sale."

Exxon in teletypes, telegrams, and mailings to editors all over the country simply denounced Roby and UPI as "misrepresenting Exxon's position."[50] Exxon did not tell the editors what Exxon had said to Watt and what Roby had reported. It simply said the company was misrepresented. UPI depends for its existence on the faith newspaper and broadcast clients have in its reports. A major advertiser calling its stories inaccurate could hurt. And Roby, as an individual journalist, was about to be badly damaged by the oil company campaign against his accurate reporting.

Other oil companies had joined Exxon in recommending that less acreage be offered for drilling. These companies included Atlantic Richfield, Union Oil, Sohio, and Marathon. Their requests for reduced acreage are on record in their own files, in government files, and in their own releases sent to news media. Yet in dutiful support of Exxon in its attack on the media, Charles DiBona, president of the American Petroleum Institute, the oil industry's main lobby, issued his own press release to the news media, saying: "I know of no company which has said that over time it wants less offshore land opened to inventory."[51]

Tony Dinigro, media manager for Mobil Oil, told a meeting sponsored by the right-wing group Accuracy in the Media that the "Won't They Ever Learn?" ad was designed to embarrass the wire services. Dinigro said, "We hope this ad will serve to put the reporter, the wire service and other reporters who are writing about this subject—about Mobil—on notice to make sure they take the time to . . . do an accurate piece."[52]

The concerted attack on Roby worked. UPI told him to do no further stories about Mobil and no in-depth stories on oil and taxes, even though his specialty in the UPI Washington bureau was energy and environment and even though his superiors agreed that his stories about the oil companies had been accurate. Shortly afterward, Roby left UPI and became a European correspondent for another major American news organization.

Why did Exxon pick on Roby when the same passage was reported independently by papers like the *Wall Street Journal*, the *Washington Post*, and other news organizations? One possibility is that Roby's story about all oil company income taxes had made him a target.

An object lesson in the Corporate School of Journalism had been given. Corporations have multimillion-dollar budgets to dissect and attack news reports they dislike. But with each passing year they have yet another power: They are not only hostile to independent journalists. They are their employers.

On October 19, 1981, UPI dutifully reported another attack on American news media. A corporate executive said: "What our country needs worse than anything is freedom from the press.... The press is absolutely intolerable today."

The speaker was Arthur Temple. Temple at the time was vice chairman of Temple-Eastex, which was the largest single stockholder in Time, Inc., the largest magazine publisher in the country and employer of hundreds of journalists whom Mr. Temple, then a director at Time, Inc., considered "absolutely intolerable." Among the publications over which Mr. Temple had responsibilities, as a director, was a major reporter on American business, *Fortune* magazine.

NEUHARTH SAYS 1-PAPER
TOWNS DON'T EXIST
Headline in trade magazine

No Gannett newspaper has
any direct competition.[1]
ALLEN NEUHARTH, chairman of
Gannet Co., to Wall Street analysts

CHAPTER NINE

FROM MYTHOLOGY TO THEOLOGY

Anthropologists, looking in history for what journalism is supposed to look for daily—the literal truth—know that there is a curious quality to epic poems. The mythological men and women are more courageous and loyal than in real life. Turning life's natural mixture of the noble and ignoble into unrelieved heroism is done by those who, like editors of the old *Soviet Encyclopedia*, believe it is their religious duty to mislead the public for its own good or who convince themselves that their heroes' sins are merely misunderstood philanthropy.

Every culture has its official folklore. In ancient times medicine men transformed tribal legends to enhance their own status. The twentieth century is no different, but the high priests who communicate mythic dogmas now do so

through great centralized machines of communication—
newspaper chains, broadcast networks, magazine groups,
conglomerate book publishers, and movie studios. Operators of these systems disseminate their own version of the
world. And of all the legends they generate none are so
heroic as the myths they propagate about themselves.

The largest and most aggressive newspaper chain in
the United States was not so different from other corporate
media giants. It was neither the best nor the worst. But Gannett Company, Inc., is an outstanding contemporary performer of the ancient rite of creating self-serving myths, of
committing acts of greed and exploitation but describing
them through its own machinery as heroic epics. In real life
Gannett has violated laws, doctrines of free enterprise, and
journalistic ideals of truthfulness. But its official proclamations are a modern exercise, with appropriate Madison
Avenue gloss, of the ancient privilege of the storyteller
—transforming the shrieks of private sins into hymns of public virtue.

Forbidden Words

In the beginning there was Frank E. Gannett.[2] He was tall,
big-jowled, and genial; he never drank or smoked and only
in extremis would utter, "My goodness!" In the mythic tradition, he worked his way through Cornell University and
became part owner in 1906 of the tiny *Elmira* (New York)
Star-Gazette. From this humble beginning came America's
largest newspaper chain. (The word *chain*, with its implication of captivity, is shunned by the newspaper industry; the
preferred term is *group*, with its appealing connotation of
harmony and mutual aid.)

Through his lifetime, Gannett's papers were inflexibly

conservative. But Frank Gannett praised the sacred dogma of freedom for his local editors and reporters. He or his foundation might own a local paper but the local editor would work without interference from above. Carl Lindstrom, editor of the *Hartford Times*, described what happened when a Gannett official addressed the staff after the chain bought the *Hartford Times* in 1928:

Nobody must ever use the word, "chain," in regard to Gannett newspaper properties. The word must not appear in the paper. It must not be voiced. If outsiders were so indiscreet or ignorant as to utter it they must immediately be apprised that in referring to Gannett newspapers, the word was "group." [3]

Having thus laid down a command from headquarters, the official next declared, "It must be explained ... that the cardinal principle of Mr. Gannett in operating his papers was local autonomy."

While the Greeks had Homeric poems for their epics, modern corporations have other art forms: executive speeches, press conferences, and publicity releases that are reported in fulsome detail through their own media. Above all else are full-page ads that celebrate the corporations' own spirituality and social service. Gannett has always been a devoted practitioner of the art.

In 1936 a Gannett full-page ad announced transfer of Frank Gannett's nineteen papers to the Frank E. Gannett Newspaper Foundation, whose self-perpetuating directors were all appointed by Frank E. Gannett. The ad did not mention anything as mundane as superior tax benefits. The announced purpose of the reorganization was to provide more service to the community:

Not newspapers for profit to ownership, but profit to the communities in which they are published. Not newspapers produced with a minimum of expense ... but rather newspapers that reflect an extravagant hand, yet designed to be commercially successful, but with whatever remaining profits ploughed back into the ground from which they sprung.[4]

One year later, Frank Gannett ploughed back into the ground from which they had sprung two of his paper in Albany, New York. Killing these papers removed direct competition for the Albany papers of William Randolph Hearst.[5] At about the same time, it so happened, Hearst killed his two Rochester, New York, papers, giving Gannett a monopoly there. Perhaps it was fitting that Gannett should have no rivals in Rochester, which was to become the seat of his empire. But there were ungenerous souls who regarded this remarkable coincidence—not a rarity among chains with competing papers—as an unconvincing demonstration of free enterprise. It violated the capitalist dogma of uninhibited competition that they proclaimed with religious fervor in their editorials. In the Homeric tradition Hearst and Gannett announced these acts in their papers as enlarged public service.

Only a year later Gannett suffered an irreverent interpretation of his dedication to journalism without fear or favor. It was a period of rapid growth of electric generating systems owned by states and municipalities and of fierce counterattacks by private power company groups, called in those days "trusts." A. R. Graustein, president of International Paper and Power Company, testified before a Senate committee that his company had secretly financed the expansion of the Gannett chain, giving the private power trust influence over Gannett (and other chains for which the power company did the same thing). Senator George W. Norris, who chaired the committee, said this was part of a "campaign going on all over the country by the power trust to get control of the generation and distribution of electrical energy." [6]

It may have been a coincidence that the Gannett papers were enthusiastic supporters of the power trust and scathing attackers of public ownership of generating plants. Frank Gannett died in 1957 and was succeeded as head of the chain by Paul Miller. Miller, like Gannett, was tall but, unlike Gannett, handsome and imposing. Though patrician in manner, he was born in Diamond, Missouri, and grew up in a small town in Oklahoma. It was this rustic background he stressed when he visited owners of local papers, with whom he established fatherlike relations of friendship and trust. When local owners were confronted with impending estate taxes or heirs fighting over their papers, it seemed natural to turn to Paul Miller for advice and, as it happened, as a buyer for their papers. Under Miller, Gannett's tradition of growth accelerated. So did the tradition of epic mythology, including, in one instance, Homeric invocation of the dead.

Misquoting an Icon

On February 11, 1963, Paul Miller received the William Allen White Award at the University of Kansas. William Allen White had been owner, editor, and publisher of the Kansas *Emporia Gazette*, a small paper he bought in 1895 and turned into a national voice of liberal Republicanism, humanistic ideals, and sensitive prose. His voice, always based in Emporia, carried civilized ideas into the corridors of power. He was a confidant of presidents, including, when it finally came into vogue, a Democratic one. He was one of the few genuine demigods of justified reverence in newspaper publishing. He could even get away with criticizing his fellow publishers for narrowness and greed, or what he called their "unconscious arrogance of conscious wealth." When he died in 1944 he was mourned in solemn resolutions of condolence by publishers who regularly ignored his precepts.

On the occasion of his receiving the William Allen White Award in 1963, Paul Miller asked his audience an interesting question:

Would William Allen White have approved of chains?

Would he feel that "chain" newspapers are having good effects or bad on American journalism? Or none at all?

Could he have reached world eminence as an editor of a so-called "group newspaper"?

My answers to all . . . of these questions are optimistic and affirmative.[7]

How well William Allen White would have maintained his iconoclastic independence in the Gannett chain may be judged in a moment. In the meantime, it may be worth noting that White hated chains. He hated the idea of all large corporate influence on newspapers. He once wrote:

As the newspapers' interest has become a mercantile or industrial proposition, the dangers of commercial corruption of the press become greater and greater. The power trust of course is buying the newspapers in order to control the old vestige of leadership, the remaining fragment of professional status that still remains in the newspaper business.

As a commercial investment the newspaper is yielding good returns for investment. But as a political weapon it is worth to self-seeking corporations hundreds of dollars of undercover influence where it is worth dollars in direct returns.[8]

White's most eloquent view of chains and chain owners was expressed in an obituary he wrote in the *Emporia Gazette* on the death of Frank Munsey, the great newspaper chain operator of his day.

Frank Munsey, the great publisher, is dead.

*Frank Munsey contributed to the journalism of his day the talent of
a meatpacker, the morals of a money changer, and the manners of an un-
dertaker. He and his kind have about succeeded in transforming a once-
noble profession into an eight percent security.*

May he rest in trust.[9]

When Plato, that great promoter of the elite, was elimi-
nating unpleasant realities from Homer, he said, "We must
beg Homer not be angry if we delete them." White, safely
dead nineteen years when Miller invoked his blessings from
the grave, would have had a few choice words about Plato
and Paul Miller.

The year 1963 had added importance in Gannett history:
Allen Harold Neuharth had arrived at Rochester headquarters.[10] Frank Gannett had a limited vision, Miller broadened
it, and Neuharth built it into a modern conglomerate empire.
Clever, good looking in an impudent way, engagingly frank
in love of power and pomp, Neuharth could have starred
in dramas of corporate conquest, possibly produced by one
of the two television companies he eventually bought. He
makes more than $1 million a year, travels in a company jet
whose imperial *G* is woven, etched, embossed, and printed
on all visible appointments, has a taste for Pouilly-Fuissé
and sharkskin suits (of which a friend said, "When Al wears
a sharkskin suit, it's hard to tell where the shark stops and
he begins"). As Neuharth's mentor, Miller gradually relinquished his titles and Neuharth became company president,
chief executive officer, and chairman.

Another crucial year was 1967. That year, Gannett joined
large newspaper chains that, beginning in 1963, entered the
arena of international finance by listing their shares on Wall
Street. In 1967, Gannett had 28 newspapers and $250 million
in annual revenues.[11] Under Neuharth's driving energy the

corporation, financed by Wall Street, grew to 93 daily papers, 40 weeklies, 15 radio and 8 television stations, 40,000 billboards, Lou Harris Public Opinion Poll, TV productions, a half-interest in McNeil-Lehrer Productions for television and cable, satellite operations in thirty-six states, and more than $2 billion in annual revenues. It had a spectacular record of ever-increasing quarterly earnings.

Accent on Money

More than anyone else in American newspaper publishing, Neuharth reversed the public posture of corporate journalism. In the past, newspaper owners, their private finances known largely to themselves and their local banks, publicly pictured themselves as penniless keepers of freedom of the press. They cried poverty and the First Amendment to fend off antitrust indictments, child labor and wages-and-hours laws, unions, workers' appeals for higher wages, advertisers' complaints of high rates, and politicians' accusations of monopoly bias. Each newspaper failure was reported as proof of the imminent collapse of the industry. In fact, the number of daily papers in the country had remained constant for thirty years; some die and others are born. The failure rate for papers had been remarkably low.[12] For decades the newspaper industry had been one of the most profitable in America.

Neuharth recognized that entry of the newspaper business into the New York Stock Exchange changed all this. Big investors are not enamored of small enterprises on the verge of collapse. Like other leading industrialists of the period Neuharth also recognized that it was no longer profitable to conceal the emergence of giantism. Big investors look for giant cash flow. He discarded the mendicant's cup and pitiful whine and began to celebrate power and size as synonymous with efficiency, social responsibility—and profits. He began to use the dreaded five-letter word *chain* in mixed company. He met regularly, as do all corporate leaders, with Wall Street analysts who question executives so they can then give inside investment advice to important clients. During one meeting, Neuharth was asked whether the corporate name should be pronounced *GAN-nett* or *Gan-NETT*. Neuharth smiled and said the correct pronunciation was *MONEY*.

Gannett (accent on the last syllable) used a great deal of Wall Street money and produced a great deal more. The company went eighteen years, from 1967 to 1985, with each quarterly profit greater than the one before. When all manufacturing return on stockholder equity averaged 15 percent, Gannett's was 21 percent.[13] Even to hard-boiled investors, the profit margin on some Gannett papers was astonishing—30 to 50 percent a year.[14]

But in one respect Neuharth conformed to tradition. Publishers publicly like to insist that there is no such thing as a newspaper monopoly.[15] The word *monopoly* evokes specters of trust busting by the government. It boils the blood of advertisers and of communities in which papers are the only dailies. So publishers created the charming concept of "media voices" that included, when rhetorically necessary, anything and everything printed, uttered, broadcast, seen, or heard in and by a community. Thus, no daily paper is a monopoly. Unfortunately, almost all of them are. By 2000, of all cities with a daily paper, 99 percent had only one newspaper management (in 1910 more than half of all newspaper cities had local daily competition, typically five or six papers).

But if customers and excluded community groups hate

monopolies, Wall Street loves them. Otis Chandler, at the time head of another giant newspaper conglomerate, Times Mirror Company, publisher, among other things, of the *Los Angeles Times*, said: "If a newspaper is noncompetitive, it gives you a franchise to do what you want with profitability. You can engineer your profits. You can control expenses and generate revenues arbitrarily."[16]

So Neuharth, like other publishers, insisted in public that there are no monopolies, but in private—with investors— he insists that there are. In 1979, *Editor & Publisher*, the newspaper-publishing trade magazine, headlined a story about a Neuharth speech: Neuharth Says 1-Paper Towns Don't Exist.[17] In his speech Neuharth gave as an example his paper in Boise, Idaho. He told his audience (which was in another state) that he had nine local competitors in Boise— "ten choices for the reader." He referred to dispensing boxes around the leading hotel in Boise, but he did not add that these boxes included specialized papers like the *Wall Street Journal*, the *Christian Science Monitor*, and free advertising circulars, none with local news. Nor did he mention that none of the other papers is published in the county where his daily circulates. Not surprisingly, the Gannett paper in Boise had 99.5 percent of all daily sales in the county.[18]

But in private, Neuharth spoke differently. In 1976 he told Wall Street analysts, "No Gannett newspaper has any direct competition ... in any community in which we published." His appointed publisher in Wilmington, Del., told *Advertising Age* that the chain bought the Delaware papers because "they are the only game in town."

In 1986, Gannett finally bought a big-city paper with competition, the *Detroit News*, close in circulation with Knight-Ridder's *Free Press*. But soon afterward, both papers asked for exemption from antitrust law in order to become business partners. Later the same year, Gannett bought another competing daily, the *Arkansas Gazette*, which had a comfortable 60/40 lead over its rival, the *Democrat*. It was a sign that there are few profitable monopolies left.

As the chain mushroomed in the 1970s, complaints of monopolistic arrogance threatened Gannett's image, so the company turned to the great corporation art form. A series of full-page celebration ads began to appear in major newspapers and magazines seen by journalists, financiers, and prospective sellers of newspapers. The ads used the Gannett slogan: Gannett—A World of Different Voices Where Freedom Speaks.[19] A standard ad proclaimed: "Gannett believes in the freedom of the people to know."[20]

From time to time the ads referred to reality. Some of Gannett's thousands of journalists do produce individual pieces of admirable journalism. These become the stuff of the full-page ads. But most of the empire consists of vast silent domains where ruthless demands for ever-increasing profits crush journalistic enterprise and block adequate coverage of the news in their communities.

It does not detract from the positive social benefits of some Gannett policies to note that they were forced on the corporation.

In 1978 Gannett announced its intention to merge with Combined Communications Corporation, at the time the biggest media merger in the country. The merger was crucial to Gannett's leap into the national conglomerate arena. Neuharth said it was a "marriage made in heaven." But some objectors at the wedding were not prepared to forever hold their peace.

A black media group protested that Gannett's history of hiring women and minorities was "worse than the industry average."[21] It said the company had conflicts of interest: In Rochester, for example, its papers had refused to print Urban League reports of supermarket price discrimination in black neighborhoods for fear of offending advertisers. And it said the Gannett papers reported poorly on issues like nuclear power, race, and human relations, perhaps, it said, because Paul Miller was close to Richard Nixon.

Manufacturing Modern Myths

The Federal Communications Commission, which had to agree to the merger, said the combined companies would exceed the legal limit of broadcast stations allowed to any business entity. And the FCC had doubts about permitting Gannett to continue to own its Rochester television station in a city where it owned the only daily newspapers.

Gannett resorted to the twentieth-century form of Greek mythology.[22] It hired the advertising agency Young & Rubicam to produce a $1.5 million public relations campaign to create a heroic image of Gannett. It sold its Rochester television station to black business people (at a record high price). It appointed a black editor for its Oakland, Calif., paper which it had reluctantly acquired as part of the merger (reluctant because Oakland had too many civic problems and too much adjacent competition for a typical Gannett operation; a few years later, Gannett sold the Oakland newspaper to its black editor, adding to the chain's new program of assisting blacks. It began to promote women aggressively. The FCC approved the merger.

Neuharth stepped up his public speeches. Though the Department of Justice has been comatose on the subject of newspaper mergers, the image of corporation as hero helps maintain government indifference. More immediate was the need to polish the picture of Gannett benevolence for practical corporate reasons. Gannett was in the business of acquiring other firms. Unlike most corporate acquisitions, newspapers are intensely local and highly personal. Advertisers and community groups care about the nature of their local newspaper and who owns it. Staffs work in peculiar operations that require hourly synchronization. If they become demoralized at the prospect of a ruthless owner they can defect and lower the price of the paper asked by the original owner. The local owner often has to remain in the community and face angry peers for selling to an outside exploiter. A bad image is not good for business. Local owners, most of all, like high bidders. But they also like buyers who look nice.

Gannett ads were designed to make any prospective seller feel that selling to Gannett was a patriotic act. The ads and the Neuharth speeches stressed the theme that big corporations can protect freedom of the press better than small corporations can. In 1980, for example, Neuharth said the real danger to freedom of the press came not from networks and big papers but "in Pumpkin Center, S. Dak.; or Paducah, Ky.; or Pocatello, Idaho—the smaller communities across the country—where the resources of the media are more limited and the balance of power shifts to police and sheriffs and lawyers bent on stilling the local voices."[23]

Gannett presumably would never be "bent on stilling local voices." But in Salem, Ore., as in ancient Troy, there was heavy translation between reality and myth.

In 1974, Gannett bought, from the owning family in Salem, a company that published the morning and evening papers. It did so with the standard speech with which chain owners bless each new acquisition, telling the new community they admire and respect the existing papers and would never think of telling editors how to operate in this special and wonderful city.

And so it was in Salem. But after the speeches there is, typically, a quiet set of events. If the old owners had two papers, one morning and one afternoon, as they had in Salem, one of the papers—gradually and with a diplomatic passage of time—is quietly folded into the other. The emerging single paper is more profitable. On the other hand, if they lacked a Sunday edition, produced mostly for its masses of ads, one may be started with no proportional increase in news reporting. If reporters leave or retire they are not replaced, quietly reducing the staff and local news. Outside news services paid for by previous owners are discouraged and the systemwide Gannett service encouraged.

Most important and least visible are the financial expectations most chains impose on their new acquisitions, Gannett with more precision and punishment than most. The local team was given its profit orders.[24] These used to be called "Profit Plan," but as Gannett gained skill in bureaucratic euphemisms the term was changed to "Progress Plan." The local publisher was told precisely how much he or she must produce in profits for each three-month period. Each local quota was carefully orchestrated in Rochester. It was not keyed to the needs of the local community, except as a guess at maximum possible extraction, but is derived for the total system's impact on Wall Street. Every quarter, the profits must increase. This maintains the price of stock, big banks are happy to lend the chain money for more expansion, and it entices future sellers of independent papers to sell not for cash but for easy pieces of paper, share of the ever-rising value of Gannett stock.

Local editors and publishers who met their profit quotas had considerable freedom. Those who did not were punished. They either lost their jobs or relinquished control to Gannett's regional or national headquarters. When they failed they forfeited the goal of most local chain editors and publishers—the chance to be promoted to a larger paper or, ultimately, to the hierarchy of the national organization. In either case, the reward was far from their current local community, their "commitment" to whose future is so often the subject of the full-page ads.

The manager in Salem was shown the list of annual profit increases in other Gannett papers. It was supposed to impress him. It did. For calendar year 1975, one year after the Salem acquisition, some of the figures of increased profit on Gannett papers were hard to believe: 113.6, 90.9, 58.8, 45.3, 32.8 percent. Each "unit"—newspaper, radio station, or television station—had to meet its quota. Salem was told to double its previous profits. Or else. So in Salem, after the echo of the Acquisition Ceremony had faded, changes were made. Former discounts to advertisers were eliminated.[25] In one year ad rates increased 42 percent. The year before Gannett bought the paper, profits were $700,000. In its first year of ownership Gannett raised profits to $1,500,000 and the year after that to $2.1 million—tripled in two years.

Advertisers rebelled at the new high rates of the only paper in town. They called in an outside organization to start a free-circulation paper to carry their ads for less money. The new paper, started by Community Publications, Inc., soon had 20 percent of all ads in Salem.

The Gannett empire struck back. Neuharth appointed a new publisher with orders to "fatally cripple the Community Press." Gannett salespeople were given a bonus for every ad taken away from the other paper. Advertisers were offered cash to abandon the competitor (one was offered $13,000). Hesitant advertisers were taken on expenses-paid trips to Reno and Lake Tahoe. Long-term contracts with attractive terms were offered on condition that all ads would be withdrawn from the competing paper.

When a major advertiser, K-Mart, still balked, national executives of Gannett visited national executives of K-Mart, told them that the other paper was doomed and if K-Mart did not switch soon the Gannett paper, when it returned to being the only paper in town, might not take K-Mart ads on pleasant terms. When the store's executives still wavered, Gannett made intimations about the local K-Mart manager, who said in a sworn deposition that Gannett officials talking to his superiors tried to make him "look absurd from all standpoints, from our decision-making to taking graft and being involved in graft and corruption."

Ultimately, Gannett drove the other paper out of business. The other paper sued. Gannett settled out of court but for a time some of the court documents in the lawsuit were available to the public. When reporters began to look at them Gannett quickly petitioned the court to seal the records. Cassandra Tate, a free-lance writer, asked Allen Neuharth how all his corporate advertising could stress the public's right to know, proclaim the sanctity of open court records, and then make the Gannett court records secret. She cited one Gannett ad that asked: "Can you imagine up to 90 percent of all court cases settled in secret? Gannett could not." [26] Why didn't that apply to Gannett's own court records?

Freedom of the Press?

Neuharth answered, "That's business. I don't think it has anything at all to do with the First Amendment."

It was not the first time Gannett had exempted itself from its slogans. In 1974 Gannett supervisors were at the Rochester Institute of Technology (in the Frank E. Gannett Building) being trained to break a possible strike by Gannett's union printers. [27] An alternative paper in Rochester, the *Patriot*, sent a photographer to take a picture of the scene. The photographer was firmly escorted out of the room while some Gannett supervisors yelled, "Confiscate his film!"

When Gannett, notoriously poor at competing, decided

to sell the *Hartford Times* in the 1970s because it had local competition, the new owner sued Gannett and won, having charged the chain with fraud.[28] The chain's managers had created a letterhead "survey" company that issued a false report exaggerating the *Time*'s circulation.

In 1979 Neuharth said, "Diversity of news and views and quality of journalism has been greatly enhanced in this decade by growth in newspaper chains."[29] Publicly owned chains, he said, "are providing better news and service to their readers." A large ad in the *New York Times*, obviously aimed at investors and potential sellers, asked, "What happens to a family newspaper when it joins Gannett?"[30] The answer: "It gets better."

How can one know it gets better? Neuharth believed he knew. In a *Los Angeles Times* interview in 1978 he said a locally owned newspaper that gives too much sophisticated news is "out of touch with its community." Chain papers, he said, are realistic, give the readers what they want, and consequently gain circulation. [31]

The Gannett papers failed their tests. From 1973 to 1978 Gannett papers lost 6 percent in circulation while other dailies of the same circulation size gained circulation.[32]

Neuharth singled out as excessively concerned with quality and quantity of news two papers whose owners had been firm in announcing their rejection of chain ownership, the *Riverside* (California) *Press-Enterprise* and the *St. Petersburg* (Florida) *Independent-Times*. While Gannett was losing circulation during the five years preceding Neuharth's statement, the independent papers "out of touch" with their communities were gaining more than 8 percent circulation.[33]

Occasional embarrassments like these increased the need for more mythology. The full-page ads increased. Neuharth made even more speeches, which were reported more fully in his papers. In 1977 he said that in the first eight years of the 1970s, "A total of seventy-four Pulitzer Prizes have been awarded to U.S. newspapers and their staffs. Sixty-one of those seventy-four went to newspapers of group owners." [34]

His wording was careful. Strictly speaking he was correct, if one counted as "newspapers of group owners" papers like the *New York Times* and the *Washington Post*. These and other large, prestigious papers had in recent years bought other, smaller newspapers. But if one counted papers that were developed independently and only lately had acquired other papers, the independently developed papers won most of the Pulitzer Prizes (the *New York Times* won eight during the period Gannett cited, the *Washington Post* eight, the *Boston Globe* five, the *Chicago Sun-Times* five, the *Chicago Tribune* four, and so on).[35] Papers that achieved their distinction as the sole papers of their owners won 77 percent of the Pulitzers. Once-independent papers run by chains won only 23 percent of the prizes, even though they were a majority of all American dailies.

Don't Be Too Serious

Neuharth himself may have disclosed one cause of the Gannett chain's failure to gain circulation for its monopolies. In a 1978 speech to the American Society of Newspaper Editors, in Washington, D.C., he ridiculed smaller papers that try to be too serious. When it comes to national and international news, he said, "Coffeyville Kansas, Muskogee, Oklahoma, they don't give a damn; the less they hear about Washington and New York the better they feel about it."[36]

The editor of the *Emporia Gazette*, still owned by heirs of William Allen White, was in the audience. Coffeyville, a site of a recent Gannett acquisition, is near Emporia. The Emporia editor wrote: "It was my first meeting so I was too shy to go to the microphone and tell Mr. Neuharth that Coffeyville is not a backwoods hillbilly town ... and that his remarks were an insult to the then newest Gannett property, the *Coffeyville Journal.*"[37]

The *Coffeyville Journal*, it turned out, had been greatly respected and its circulation had grown steadily before Gannett bought it.[38] Its former owner, Richard Seaton, and editor, Daniel Hamrick, had won prizes for the fight against attempts by the John Birch Society to take over the city council. After Gannett bought the paper, the amount of news was reduced. When an accurate news story offended an advertiser, the Gannett headquarters told the local editor to make peace. When reactionaries complained about stories the paper had always run, a Gannett regional director supported the complaints and a Gannett senior vice president said he was grateful for being informed that the local editor was "failing to do a proper news reporting job for its community."

The editor of many years, Daniel Hamrick, quit. A nearby paper, the *Parsons* (Kansas) *Sun*, editorialized: "Its neighbors have watched with dismay the decline of the *Journal* in recent months. Its news content, under chain ownership, had become increasingly small."[39]

The *Emporia Gazette* wrote: "One of the state's best editors quit his job last week because he could not get along with some executives of the Gannett chain that bought the paper ..."[40]

What happened to news in Salem, in Coffeyville, and in other Gannett cities was not unusual for Gannett local papers or for almost all chain-owned local papers. Profit squeezes and indifference to comprehensive local news is the norm. Systematic studies by researchers over the years made clear that despite grandiloquent rhetoric, chain papers had given their communities less serious news than did independent papers.

A study reported in the standard scholarly journalistic publication *Journalism Quarterly* found that papers that were once competitive but were made monopolies by chains produced "higher prices and lower quality."[41] Another study at Brookings Institution showed that chain-owned papers charged 7 percent more for ads than independent papers, but where the chains had competition their rates were 15 percent lower than for counterpart monopoly papers.[42] A 1978 study at George Washington University showed that chain papers gave their readers 8 percent less news than independently owned papers.[43] This was confirmed in a separate study by Kristine Keller, who found that of serious current news (as opposed to "soft" features) independent papers printed 23 percent more than did chain dailies.[44]

The most pervasive changes made in independent papers acquired by chains are typically to increase advertising and subscription rates, to introduce cosmetic alterations of page design and makeup to give the impression of modernity, and to quietly reduce the amount of serious news. It was conventional wisdom among publishers that readers are uninterested in "serious" news. As we will see later, this is not true. The real reason publishers shun serious news is that it is more expensive than features. The "serious" papers Neuharth ridiculed gained circulation while his own lost circulation. Detailed and comprehensive news requires experienced reporters who devote substantial time to each story, particularly local stories. The reporters are paid by the local paper, they have fringe benefits, and they often form unions. "Soft" features, in addition to attracting advertising, are inexpensive: they can be bought from a syndicate and delivered by mail or computer from a machine that is cheap, requires no fringe benefits, and never forms unions. It is possible to issue a mediocre paper with a large staff but it is not possible to produce a good paper with too small a staff. Unfortunately, in a monopoly city it is possible even with deficient news to extract excessive advertising revenues.

In 1966, before Gannett began its drive to create its international empire, its 26 daily and 6 Sunday papers averaged approximately 45 news employees per paper.[45] By 1980, when it had 81 daily, 53 Sunday, and 23 less-than-daily papers (and had added Saturday editions to acquired papers that previously had none), it averaged 26 news employees per paper. During this period, the average circulation size of its papers remained the same, about 44,000.

Editorial vigor diminishes under chain ownership. A *Journalism Quarterly* study published in 1975 said that more than 85 percent of chain papers have uniform political endorsements. "These data run counter to the insistence of chain spokesmen that their endorsement policies are independent of chain direction," the report said.

The Cox chain, once the ninth largest in circulation, in one election ordered all its papers to endorse the same national candidates.[46] Scripps-Howard, once the seventh-largest chain, has done the same and annually adopted a uniform stand on major issues. The Panax chain fired editors who refused to put the publisher's propagandistic views on page 1 as news.[47] Copley Newspapers, with dailies in Illinois and California, once ran national ads proclaiming its editorial position, "the birth of Jesus Christ, God's only begotten Son," in order to argue against "the defiant polemics of some theologians."[48] Presumably, it was a position that readers of its papers, even if they happened to disbelieve fundamentalist polemics or happened to be Jews, Moslems, and other nonfundamentalists, had to accept from the only paper in their town. Freedom Newspapers, a substantial chain, spent years promoting its founder's libertarian philosophy of dissolving almost all government in favor of private enterprise.[49] When one branch of the family moderated the doctrinaire approach, the papers became far more profitable and popular. But the chain's management was sued by other heirs who feared that the papers were drifting from libertarianism to conventional conservatism.

Chain papers are divided in their political drive. Either they pursue the doctrines of their owners, like Freedom or the chains that impose centralized endorsements, or they become bland to avoid controversy. Editorials that take a stand may offend advertisers or community groups. In general, as all organizations become large and directed from afar, they value predictability and bureaucratic smoothness. Another *Journalism Quarterly* study of editorials over a fifteen-year period found that after an independent paper is bought by a chain the general result "is not helpful to readers who seek guidance on local matters when they turn to the editorial pages of their daily papers."[50]

Chains tend to hire less-qualified journalists. Stephen Hess in a study of Washington correspondents found that when chains had 75 percent of all American daily circulation, they had only 29 percent of the correspondents working for individual papers, and their correspondents had significantly less education than those working for independent papers.[51]

No Control—Just Fire the Editor

There is seldom daily or detailed interference in the chain papers' news. Given the large number of rapid decisions reached hourly, such interference would be impossible. Instead, there are chain policies. The chain hires and fires its local editors and publishers, the most definitive mechanism of control possible. It controls the budget, another persuasive influence. Gannett had another way of controlling community newspaper money: In 1979 it announced that bank deposits of its local papers, beyond daily operations needs, would be transferred nightly to Rochester—about $4 million a day, not a small loss to the economy of its communities.[52]

There are additional persuasive measures that permitted Gannett to publicly declare local independence and private commitment while ruthlessly extracting every possible dollar from the local community. Stock options permitted managers to buy Gannett stock at an artificially low price. If, through maximum profit making, they could drive up the price of the stock, they might make a fortune in the future.

In 1981, a Gannett executive told Wall Street analysts that local Gannett managers are offered stock options in the parent company to make certain they will push for profits and, as she expressed it, "to tighten the golden handcuffs."[53] The intriguing title of this executive is senior vice-president for human resources. The title would have been applauded by the Homeric rewrite artists.

Of all the Homeric incantations of chains, the most resounding is the folklore of Local Autonomy. It is the centerpiece of every speech, press release, and ceremony on the occasion of a chain's purchase of a local paper.

Three themes are mandatory in the ritual speech: The new acquisition is a splendid paper that the outside company has no intention of changing; the chain acquired the paper in order to offer its larger resources for even greater service to the community; and the new owner believes, absolutely, completely, and without mental reservation in Local Autonomy. This is the unholy trinity of newspaper acquisition speeches. And the greatest of these is Local Autonomy.

Gannett's ceremonies were strictly orthodox.

Tucson, Ariz., December 1976: "From long association with the top executives of Gannett I know them to be men of high principle ... They believe in local autonomy."[54]

Three weeks later, in Reno, Nev., on the occasion of another Gannett takeover: "Both companies have long had policies of local autonomy. This approach guarantees that all news and editorial decisions will continue to be made by local editors and publishers."[55]

Nashville, Tenn., July 1979: "In keeping with Gannett's policy of local autonomy [the present editor] will have full responsibility for all news and editorial matters."[56]

Allen Neuharth, in 1978, about all his papers: "We believe completely in the concept of local autonomy."[57]

But alas, periodically the golden handcuffs come apart and the hymns of local service turn sour.

On the morning of February 27, 1976, journalistic hierarchs conducted the Local Autonomy rite in Santa Fe, New Mex. Gannett had bought the local monopoly daily, the *New Mexican*, founded in 1849 and owned since 1949 by Robert McKinney. McKinney was a tough, irascible man who sold to Gannett with an ironclad contract for Local Autonomy. The contract gave McKinney continued total control of his paper for several years, during which he would be chairman, chief executive officer, publisher, and editor-in-chief. The contract specified that McKinney, suffering from heart trouble, would necessarily be out of Santa Fe, with its 7,000-foot altitude, much of the time. But he would still be boss and his deputy, Stephen E. Watkins, would, as in the past, run the paper as president and chief operating officer.

On that February morning in Santa Fe, Paul Miller, then chairman of Gannett, conducted the ceremonies: "The *New Mexican* will add to our group one of the nation's distinguished papers and the West's oldest.... It is generally regarded as one of the best studied, best printed and best managed in the country."

Allen Neuharth uttered the benediction: "Mr. McKinney has developed a splendid newspaper that exercises a positive, useful influence throughout its area. He has laid the groundwork for continuing growth and we look forward to his further leadership."[58] Once the ceremonies were concluded and the sacred words had their obligatory reproduction on page 1 of the purchased paper, the curtain was drawn on the stage. Behind the curtain all was not peace. Watkins was given his marching orders from Rochester, including his profit quota.[59] He was stunned when he saw the profits other Gannett papers were making but he tried his best to meet the quota. One year after Gannett took over, Watkins had produced the sixteenth-highest increase in profit in the chain. Local news was cut, as it usually is, and replaced by inexpensive syndicated matter from afar. Hispanic news, important for New Mexico, was sharply curtailed. Cartoonist Bill Mauldin, who had lived in Santa Fe for years, said of the Gannett-style *New Mexican*, "It could be printed in Hutchinson, Kansas, or Amarillo, or Pecos, Texas. Essentially it lacks character. It particularly lacks the character of the place it's being printed in."[60]

Inside the chain, memorandums circulated and meetings were called as executives planned how to circumvent the tough McKinney contract to produce a standard Gannett paper. Gannett's western regional vice president proposed one option to a Gannett operative on the scene: "Look, this is the way the contract reads, so be nice to the old coot and tell him what you've done after you've done it and be sure that his empty office is kept dusted in case he ever drops in."[61]

When McKinney ordered an editorial endorsing Democratic candidate Bruce King for governor in June of 1978, the Gannett appointee did it reluctantly and, against McKinney's orders, criticized King in the endorsing editorial.

A little later, Gannett fired Watkins, McKinney's chief in Santa Fe. Watkins's replacement was referred to as "Quinn's spy on the scene." John C. Quinn is Gannett senior vice president for news.

Finally, McKinney sued for fraud and breach of contract. The trial lasted fourteen weeks, at the time the longest in New Mexico history. A jury in U.S. District Court found Gannett guilty of breach of contract. Judge Santiago E. Campos ordered the paper returned to McKinney. The judge's official order was not kind. He noted that Watkins had pushed for the big profits Gannett demanded to match its other papers. He cited one paper, in Bellingham, Wash., with 50 percent annual profit and another in Olympia, Wash., with 36 percent profit. The judge wrote:

This worried Watkins. A precipitous rise in profits, he felt, would damage the quality of the newspaper and lead to its eventual demise. Watkins became defensive toward the profit push. This convinced Gannett officials that he was standing in the way of progress....

Gannett has already wrought, and daily continues, an unconscionable and malicious deprivation of precious rights belonging to McKinney ... the right to control editorial policy of the only newspaper published in the capital city of the state of New Mexico....

One of the greatest sources of wonder to me at trial was the attitude of some of the Gannett men when they addressed McKinney's right of "complete charge" and "complete authority"... They attempted to project sincere impressions that these contractual provisions did not really mean what they clearly state.... The effort failed. Neuharth, for example, cavalierly characterized McKinney's solid and substantial contract rights of "complete charge" and "complete authority" as "window dressing."... McKinney would not have entered into the bargain if he had contemplated that Gannett would not keep its word.... He was attracted to Gannett because of its policy of "local autonomy." [62]

On June 27, 1980, the jury in New Mexico found that Gannett had violated its contract that granted McKinney autonomy. Four months later, Gannett, in the tradition of Soviet revisionists, ran full-page ads. They depicted two stern and determined men, marching to their own drumbeats, on the keys of massive typewriters, giants of integrity. The headline read: Different Voices of Freedom. The text was inspiring:

Each Gannett newspaper forms its own editorial opinions. Nobody tells local editors what to think.

Each Gannett editor marches to his or her own beat, and these are as different as the pulses of each editor's community. That is why Gannett newspapers, broadcast stations and other media are "A World of Different Voices Where Freedom Speaks."[63]

The Soviet rewrite artists would have been envious.

More people are bribed by their
own money than anybody else's.
JONATHAN DANIELS[1]

CHAPTER TEN

"DEAR MR. PRESIDENT..."

"Dear Mr. President," the letter began, nothing extraordinary in a country where every day hundreds of citizens write to the president of the United States. But this was not an ordinary letter. The recipient on this July day in 1969 was President Richard M. Nixon. The writer was Richard E. Berlin. The name of Berlin and six other men whose cause he invoked meant nothing to the general public, but they meant a great deal to Richard Nixon. And in the symbiotic equation of power, Richard Nixon meant a great deal to them.

Berlin was asking the president to use his influence to exempt him and his friends from a federal law that in previous years had sent other corporate executives to jail.[2] That is why they needed the president. The reason President Nixon needed them was nearly as obvious.

Richard Berlin, as noted on his stationery, was president and chief executive officer of the Hearst Corporation in New York. At the time, the Hearst Corporation owned nine newspapers, ten broadcasting stations, twenty-six magazines, and a book publishing house.[3] Berlin spoke for his corporation and for six others, so his letter represented a massive complex of popular communications—dozens of newspapers, national magazines, cable systems, radio and television stations, book publishers, and the country's second-largest news service. These media produced news and information that helped create the country's perception of the world in general and of Richard Nixon in particular.

No politician likes to lose the sympathy of even a single newspaper or radio station. For a national leader to lose the support of a major portion of all American media can be a political disaster. Richard Nixon needed no education on the subject, but Berlin was not famous for subtlety. In the unlikely event that the president missed the point, Berlin took pains to hint that if Nixon did not come across with the favor Berlin requested, the media chiefs would remember this when Nixon ran for reelection in 1972.

The Hearst executive and his fellow publishers were not conducting a novel experiment. By the nature of their positions they were all familiar with power: Many corporations lobby for favorable government treatment, but only media corporations control access to the American mind. The more media power possessed by a media corporation, the more a government leader has reason to feel its displeasure.

Few media corporations deny that they have power. They usually assert that they would never use their power for selfish purposes. But no corporation, media or otherwise, will fail to use its power if it feels a threat to its future or to its profits. The threat could be a national political movement it dislikes, as the New Deal seemed to most newspaper publishers during the Great Depression. Or it could be a threat to profits that makes them urge creation of loopholes in the law, like the Newspaper Preservation Act.

Whatever the provocation, when a media corporation executive approaches a politician for a favor or to deliver a threat, there is no doubt in the mind of either party what is at stake.

Lionel Van Deerlin, an ex-journalist, was former chairman of the House Subcommittee on Communications. He said that every member of Congress is familiar with the special power of broadcasters and publishers. Van Deerlin described it simply: "They can make or break you."[4]

Frank Leeming, when publisher of the *Kingsport* (Tennessee) *Times-News,* said that on the occasions when he asked his delegations in Congress for favorable action, "When they look at Kingsport they would see me both as a businessman and as the person who controls the editorial policy of the paper."

The late Katharine Graham, when head of the Washington Post media empire, as president of the American Newspaper Publishers Association lobbied personally for legal restrictions to prevent AT&T from competing with newspapers. That is a normal activity for the head of any trade organization. She also spoke to the editorial writers and reporters covering the issue for the *Washington Post.* That, too, is normal for trade associations seeking public support. It is not normal that the lobbyist looking for media support is also the employer of the journalists being lobbied.

Joseph Costello once owned five radio stations in Louisville. When he went to Washington to lobby for deregulation of radio, he said of each of the members of Congress in the various districts covered by his stations: "He knows he's got to buy time on my radio station, so he's going to lend me an ear. We're keeping them alive back home and that's why the newspaper and radio and TV people are more effective lobbyists."

The National Association of Broadcasters, even in 1969 with a $7 million budget and 6,000 members, lobbies in Washington for broadcasters and presents large speaking fees to members of Congress who, through their committees, have influence over broadcast legislation. It uses a special network to mobilize individual stations to bring pressure on their local members of the Senate and House. It says that it uses this lobbying power to "preserve the American way of broadcasting," which Jonathan Miller of *TV Guide* said really means "preserving their hegemony over the eyeballs of America." [5]

The results over the years have been impressive. Newspapers have obtained special favors to exempt them from child labor laws and to obtain favorable postal rates, tariffs on imported newsprint, and media taxes. Broadcasters were able to hold back cable broadcasting for more than ten years, obtained the deregulation of radio, and moved toward deregulation in television.

TV Blackout on TV

Important issues can be promoted by the media, but at strategic times they can also be ignored. On March 29, 1979, Van Deerlin made a historic announcement: a bill for the first basic alteration of communications law in forty-five years. It would give commercial broadcasters what they had lobbied for—semipermanent possession of their station licenses, cancellation of the requirement to provide equal access for political candidates, and no further need to present community issues or to do it fairly. It proposed a fundamental change in the law controlling the most pervasive common experience in American life, the seven and a half hours a day that the average household uses its TV set. When Van Deerlin made the announcement of the proposed change, there were two hundred persons present at the press conference, including representatives of the television networks. That night no television network in the country mentioned the event. [6]

A fair report on the Van Deerlin proposal might have said

that the station the viewers were watching and all other stations would, under the proposal, no longer be required to operate in the public interest, to be fair in their presentation of issues and candidates, or to give equal time for rebuttals. It was important news, but it was not broadcast.

Huge umbrella corporations with control over a variety of media can use one medium they control to enhance another, and at times the leverage is used to change the news in order to woo governments. United Press (now United Press International), like the Associated Press, not only reports the news but sells its services to news systems which, in many countries, means selling it to governments. Colin Miller is the syndicate consultant who helped create what was once the most popular political column on the continent, "Washington Merry-Go-Round," by Drew Pearson and Robert Allen. Miller, Pearson, and Allen planned a special column that would do for Latin American papers what they did for American ones — expose political malpractices in the country. The column was distributed by United Features, which was corporately controlled by United Press International. Miller testified before a Senate committee:

When word of this reached the front office of United Press, we were ordered to drop the idea. They were afraid that what Pearson and Allen might expose in Lima, Peru, or Asunción, Paraguay, or Rio de Janeiro, might evolve to become a negative factor insofar as the governments were concerned and, through the governments, upon the papers to which the United Press sold its service.[7]

In 1981 two editors of the national news agency of Canada, Canadian Press, told a Canadian government commission that the news service edited its news about the media in ways to please major media owners.[8] The press service was bought by 110 newspapers, forty of which are owned by the Thomson chain. The two editors said that a news account of a Thomson paper strike was deliberately reduced to three paragraphs and that a speech by the president of the Ontario Federation of Labor criticizing the Thomson organization was killed. When a branch of Canadian government investigated to see if a series of birth defects in women employees of Thomson was caused by electronic terminals used in the newspaper's plants, the wire service delayed the story for twelve hours until they saw what the Thomson paper would report about itself.

Time, Inc. owned book publishing houses, national news magazines, and book clubs, among other media properties. *Time* magazine had been a steady supporter of the policies of Henry Kissinger. The Time, Inc. book house, Little, Brown, published both volumes of Kissinger's memoirs and his ideas on foreign policy. *Time* magazine excerpted large sections of the books and ran Kissinger's picture on the magazine's cover. Kissinger's books were also selections in the biggest book club in the country, Book-of-the-Month Club, owned by Time, Inc. These coordinated promotions of Kissinger's books could have been coincidental but it is a coincidence experienced by few authors and publishers who lack control of so many media.

Large media corporations have their own political action committees to give money to favored candidates or, in the growing fashion, to defeat unfavored ones. Some media corporations also own other industries that will benefit from the right candidates.

Time, Inc., which owned and operated *Time, Life, Fortune, Sports Illustrated, People*, and *Money* magazines, had a political action committee in its own name. Candidates receiving contributions from a Time, Inc. political committee were quite aware that they had become special beneficiaries of the media empire, whose reporting could affect their political careers. In 1986, after General Electric acquired the

National Broadcasting Company, it installed a GE president who informed employees of its new radio and television unit that they were expected to support General Electric's political goals, including a political action committee to influence legislation. The head of the news staffs said that those employees would be exempted. The rest of NBC presumably would be expected to support the corporate politics.

It is not every American business person who easily makes appointments with the president of the United States or, like Richard Berlin, is certain to have his or her letters read and acted upon by the president. Berlin's letter created serious change within the Nixon administration even though the favor Berlin asked affected only one Hearst newspaper, the *San Francisco Examiner*. The other publishers whose names he invoked were not much more involved. Cox had only one paper affected, Knight had only one, Worrell one, Block one, Newhouse two, and Scripps-Howard seven (while Berlin mentioned all of the chains, there is nothing to indicate that the others participated in his letter to the president, though they, too, were actively pressing for the change Berlin pursued). But, as noted, Berlin and his colleagues were speaking not with the power of fourteen papers, but with the power of seventy-four. In addition to their total newspaper holdings, they spoke with the media power and influence over public attitudes that flowed from their magazines, books, and broadcasting stations. Most of the publishers' properties would be unaffected by the requested law, but all of their media properties could be used to influence the president.

Berlin wanted President Nixon's influence to exempt a group of newspapers from antimonopoly law, which forbids competing firms to perform the act usually described in headlines as "rigging prices"—quietly agreeing on prices among themselves while appearing to compete.[9] Fixing prices is also contrary to the rhetoric of free enterprise with which the same media flood the public. Only occasionally does unpleasant reality puncture the surface appearance, as in 1961 when executives of some of the country's best-known corporations were jailed for conspiring to fix the prices of electrical equipment. Now a few newspapers had somewhat the same problem.

In twenty-two cities of the country, ostensibly competing local papers had, over the years, agreed to become business partners, fixing prices and sharing profits while maintaining separate newsrooms. In 1965 a U.S. district court found this a violation of the antitrust law. The newspapers appealed that decision and began lobbying for special exemption from the law for any competitive newspaper that felt it might be failing financially. The effort was rejected by Lyndon Johnson's Democratic and Richard Nixon's Republican administrations in 1967, 1968, and the summer of 1969, on grounds that it was harmful social policy. If newspaper companies were permitted to ignore antitrust laws, other kinds of firms would demand the same exemption.

In 1969 the U.S. Supreme Court upheld the finding that the forty-four papers were in violation of the law. The publishers felt an impending crisis. Faced with the terrifying prospect of competing in the open market, they became desperate. Richard Berlin, speaking for the most powerful operators, became a crucial operative.

"Faithfully, Dick ..."

Berlin shrewdly sent two letters. The one to the president was partly Uriah Heep proclaiming loyalty before the majesty of the president. The letter ends with a conventionally typed "Sincerely." But Berlin, who presumably had no hesitation in asking secretaries to retype letters to the president of the United States, used his pen to scratch out the "Sincerely" and in a heavy hand wrote in large letters, "Faithfully, Dick."

Even in the Nixon letter, Berlin permitted the scent of power to escape.

I am taking the liberty of addressing myself to a matter of common interest to both you and me.... Many other important publishers and friends of your administration (including Scripps-Howard who are involved in seven of these arrangements) are similarly situated. All of us look to you for assistance.

But at the same time Berlin wrote a different kind of letter to Nixon's assistant attorney general in charge of antitrust, Richard W. McLaren. There was no Uriah Heep in the McLaren letter. It was a tough demand with a clear threat:

Those of us who strongly supported the present administration in the last election are the ones most seriously concerned and endangered by failure to adopt the Newspaper Preservation Act ... the fact remains that there was almost unanimous support of the Administration by the newspapers who are proponents of the Newspaper Preservation Act. It therefore seems to me that those newspapers should, at the very least, receive a most friendly consideration.

Berlin again made certain that his threat to Nixon and the Republican party could not be misunderstood.

Those of us ... now find that, by supporting that person and that party which we thought best exemplified those very ideals, we have become the victims and the targets of a narrow and tortured economic concept advanced and implemented by those in whom we placed the highest confidence.

Berlin sent a copy of this letter to President Nixon.

The "narrow and tortured economic concept" was the Sherman Act, a law in effect since 1890, which simply codified the supposedly sacred catechism of capitalism that is endlessly enunciated by most newspapers, magazines, broadcasters, and movie studios—that competition is the life of trade and that free enterprise requires the marketplace to decide who shall survive.

There followed a strange minuet by the Nixon administration.

In June, before the Berlin letters, Assistant Attorney General McLaren, speaking for the administration, testified against the publishers' bill. The chairman of the committee handling the bill, the late Senator Philip A. Hart of Michigan, responded:

I want to congratulate you and the Nixon Administration for the position you have taken ... I know it would be easier for all of us in public office to grant newspapers special favors because they deal with us intimately every day.[10]

Decision Reversed

But Senator Hart's congratulations were premature. Several weeks later, after the Berlin letters, the Nixon administration reversed itself and announced that it was now in favor of the bill. The publishers obtained their Newspaper Preservation Act and President Nixon was given his political reward, the support of the large media organizations.

In his letter to the president, Berlin had referred to "many important publishers" who wanted the bill. He meant seven chains, a few of whose dailies were in quiet business partnership with their local competitors. The chains owned only fourteen of the forty-four newspapers involved in the Newspaper Preservation Act. But it did not take an angel from heaven to inform Richard Nixon that when the Hearst executive issued a threat he was not speaking merely with the power of the one Hearst paper needing the favor. Nixon knew he was dealing with seven chains that owned seventy-four daily newspapers with 40 million circulation—at least 80 million readers—in twenty-six states, including the major states without whose electoral votes no presidential candidate can win an election. When Berlin raised the issue of political support for Richard Nixon he was talking about papers read by more people than would vote in the next election.

These same corporations had additional ways to influence the public. Hearst was a major owner of magazines, broadcasting stations, and book publishing. Scripps-Howard owned sixteen newspapers, and its parent corporation operated broadcasting stations, United Press International, and United Features, a leading syndicator of feature and political commentary. Cox, in addition to owning a major chain of newspapers, was in book publishing and film distribution.

Some newspapers were opposed to the special exemption, frightened—justifiably, as events proved—that it would permit controlled prices that would make life difficult for independent competitors. But 40 million combined circulation and other media power is more politically persuasive than the thirty-five thousand circulation of the average single daily paper.

The performance of American daily papers in the 1972 presidential election was bizarre. For four years the Nixon administration had attacked not only the news media but their constitutional rights. Nixon had sent his vice president on a crusade attacking newspapers that criticized the White House or ran news of negative events that were normal fare in ordinary reportage. In the Pentagon Papers case the Nixon administration obtained the first court-ordered cessation of publication in the country's history. In the summer of 1972, months before the election, the first Watergate stories began to disclose the profound corruption permeating the White House. But in early October, directors of the American Newspaper Publishers Association were reported "chary of taking any action that implied criticism of the President's policies."[11] At a time when the first Watergate stories should have been of greatest value to voters, the response outside a minority of papers was strange. A study of major papers around the country—dailies with a quarter of all national circulation, including papers in the Hearst, Scripps-Howard, and Cox chains—showed that in the months before the election "pro-Nixon papers had a much higher tendency to suppress damaging Watergate stories than papers making no endorsements." These included the papers who had obtained their antitrust favor from Nixon.[12]

In 1972, Richard Nixon received the highest percentage of newspaper endorsements of any candidate in modern times.

Prominent in this massive support of the man who most threatened their journalistic freedom were chains whose names Berlin invoked in his letters. In the previous three presidential elections—contrary to Berlin's assertion that there was "almost unanimous support of the Administration"—a third of all Hearst papers had endorsed the Democratic candidate, as had a third of the Cox papers and half of the Scripps-Howard papers. In 1972, after passage of the Newspaper Preservation Act, every Hearst paper, every Cox paper, and every Scripps-Howard paper endorsed Nixon. Scripps-Howard ordered a standard pro-Nixon editorial into all its dailies. Cox ordered all its editors to endorse Nixon (causing one editor to resign in protest).[13]

It is likely that Nixon might have won the 1972 election without this wholesale shift to his support and the sympathetic reluctance to print Watergate disclosures before the election. But it was not long after the election, when Watergate stories finally broke through the barriers of publishers' protection, that the president's power began to crumble. Studies throughout the years have shown that any bias in the news tends to follow a paper's editorial opinions.

Without the chains whose local papers benefited from the White House reversal on the Newspaper Preservation Act, Richard Nixon would have had, with the exception of Barry Goldwater in 1964, the lowest newspaper support of any Republican candidate since World War II. Instead, he had the highest newspaper support of any candidate in U.S. history. Without this massive support from the press, much of it implicitly sealed in 1969 by the mutual exchange of favors, Richard Nixon and his aides might have been less confident in their illegal activities.

The rhetoric of media corporations is consistent: They do not interfere with the professional selection of content for their newspapers, magazines, broadcast stations, book houses, and movie studios. This book shows that this is technically true for most operators in day-to-day, hour-by-hour operations, but it is not true for larger issues in which the media corporations have a strong self-interest. In the case of the Newspaper Preservation Act, three media operators, with a stroke of a pen, ordered their professionals to endorse for president a man who had previously attacked their constitutional freedoms but who had recently granted them a corporate favor. And because of the high degree of concentrated control over the mass media, the seven chains that benefited from Richard Nixon's change of mind owned papers read by most of the voters.

Protection of independence in the gathering and disseminating of news and other public information depends on something more than rhetorical declarations of freedom of expression.

Richard Nixon's depredations of freedom of the press

were the gravest since the Alien and Sedition Acts of 1798. Ten years after his departure from office in disgrace, the momentum he initiated had become a continuing crisis. But the dominant newspaper publishers were willing to support the suppressor of freedoms of the press in return for a corporate favor. Nixon's favor was not crucial in the life of the three corporations that ordered their papers to endorse Nixon. Their nine local newspapers were saved not from extinction but merely from competition. The Hearst, Cox, and Scripps-Howard chains had sixty-five other, unaffected newspapers plus a large body of profitable properties in other media. Yet in exchange for so small a prize they were willing to order all their papers—not just the nine—to support a corrupt administration hostile to an independent press. It is not reassuring to consider what might happen to the integrity of national news if dominant media corporations felt their basic power threatened.

We make no effort to sell to the mob.
DANIEL NIZEN, senior vice president,
New York Times[1]

CHAPTER ELEVEN

ONLY THE AFFLUENT NEED APPLY

Nothing in American publishing approached the profitable heresies of *The New Yorker* magazine in the 1960s. In an era when magazine editors regard covers with eye-catching headlines and striking graphics as imperative for survival, *New Yorker* covers typically were subdued watercolors of idyllic scenes. While other magazines assume that modern Americans don't read, *New Yorker* articles were incredibly long and weighted with detail. The magazine's cartoons ridicule many of its readers, the fashionably affluent who are portrayed in their Upper East Side penthouses speaking Ivy League patois. Editorial doctrine on other leading magazines calls for short, punchy sentences, but *The New Yorker* was almost the last repository of the style and tone of Henry David Thoreau and Matthew Arnold, its chaste, old-fashioned columns breathing the quietude of nineteenth-century essays.

New Yorker advertisements still are in a different world. They celebrate the ostentatious jet set. Christmas ads offer gold, diamond-encrusted wristwatches without prices, the implied message being that if you have to ask you have no business looking. A display of Jaeger-Le Coulture advised that the wristwatch "can be pivoted to reveal ... your coat of arms." One ad for Audeman Piquet watches suggested giving three to impress a woman, while another ad did suggest a price, murmuring in fine print, "From $10,500."

There are some homely products, like a Jeep station wagon. But it was displayed with a polo field in the background and was redeemed by other ads like the one that shows a couple in evening clothes embracing in the cockpit of an executive jet. Even in advertisements for products that cost less than $5,000, the characters seem to come from adjacent ads where cuff links were offered at $675, earrings at $3,500, a bracelet at $6,000, a brooch at $14,000. A Jean Patou perfume ad has no vulgar listing of price, but said in bold letters what the spirit of all *New Yorker* ads seem to proclaim: "So rare ... and available to so few."

Despite its violation of the most commanding conventions of what makes a magazine sell, *The New Yorker* for decades had been a leader in making money.

Over the years the magazine was the envy of the periodical industry in the standard measure of financial success — the number of advertising pages sold annually. Year after year, *The New Yorker* was first or second, so fixed in its reputation that other magazines promoting their effectiveness would tell prospective advertisers that they were first or second "after *The New Yorker*," the implication being that, like 1950s baseball and the New York Yankees, first place was unassailable.

That was true until 1967. The year before was a record one for *The New Yorker*. Most people in the industry believe that in 1966 the magazine attained the largest number of ad pages sold in a year by any magazine of general circulation in the history of publishing. In 1966 *The New Yorker* sold

6,100 pages of ads. Its circulation was at its usual level, around 448,000.[2]

In 1967 a strange disease struck. *The New Yorker*'s circulation remained the same but the number of ad pages dropped disastrously. In a few years 2,500 pages of ads disappeared, a loss of 40 percent. The magazine's net profits shrank from the 1966 level of $3 million to less than $1 million. Dividends per share, $10.93 in 1966, were down to $3.69 by 1970.

The disastrous loss of advertising occurred despite a continued high level of circulation which, to lay observers, would seem the only statistic needed for a magazine's success. The popular assumption is that if enough people care enough about a publication or a television program to buy it or to turn to it, advertisers will beat a path to their doorway. That clearly was not happening at *The New Yorker*.

The High Cost of Truth

The onset of *The New Yorker*'s malady can be traced to July 15, 1967. That issue of the magazine carried a typically long report under the typically ambiguous title "Reporter at Large." That was the standing head for *New Yorker* articles dealing in depth with subjects as diverse as the history of oranges, the socialization of rats, and the culture of an Irish saloon. This time the subject was a report from the village of Ben Suc in Vietnam.[3]

The author was Jonathan Schell, a recent Harvard graduate who, after commencement, visited his brother, Orville, in Taiwan, where Orville was doing Chinese studies. Once in Taiwan, Jonathan decided to take a trip to Vietnam, where, according to the standard press, the American war against the Vietcong was going well. In Saigon, Schell was liked and "adopted" by the colonels, perhaps because he had proper establishment connections: He carried an expired *Harvard Crimson* press pass and his father was a successful Manhattan lawyer. The military gave him treatment ordinarily reserved for famous correspondents sympathetic to the war. In addition to attending the daily military briefing sessions in Saigon, the basis for most reports back to the United States, Schell was also taken on helicopter assaults and bombing and strafing missions and given ground transportation to battle scenes.

The assumption of his hosts was that the nice kid from Harvard would be impressed with the power and purpose of the American mission. But Schell was appalled. The war, it seemed to him, was not the neat containment of Soviet-Chinese aggression that had been advertised at home or the attempt of humane Americans to save democracy-loving natives from the barbaric Vietcong. Like all wars, this one was mutually brutal. Americans shot, bombed, and uprooted civilians in massive campaigns that resulted in the disintegration of Vietnamese social structures. And the Americans were not winning the war.

Schell returned to the United States disturbed by his findings. He visited a family friend, William Shawn, the quiet, eccentric editor of *The New Yorker*, who had known the Schell children since childhood. Shawn listened to Schell's story and asked him to try writing about his experiences. Schell produced what Shawn called "a perfect piece of *New Yorker* reporting." The story, which ran in the July 15, 1967, issue, told in clear, quiet detail what the assault on one village meant to the villagers and to the American soldiers.

Shawn said he had serious doubts about the war before Schell appeared, "but certainly I saw it differently talking to him and reading what he wrote. That was when I became convinced that we shouldn't be there and the war was a mistake."

Thereafter *The New Yorker* in issue after issue spoke simply and clearly against the war. It was not the first publication to do so, but at the time most important media followed the general line that the war was needed to stop international communism and to save the Vietnamese and that the United States was on the verge of victory. Most newspapers, including the two most influential dailies in the country, the *New York Times* and the *Washington Post*, editorially supported the war. There were growing popular protests but the mass marches were yet to come. Neither the My Lai massacre nor the Tet offensive had occurred, and the exposure of the Pentagon Papers detailing a long history of government lying about Indochina was still four years away.

The New Yorker was the voice of the elite, the repository of advertisements for the hedonistic rich, of genteel essays on the first day of spring, of temperate profiles of aesthetes, of humor so sophisticated that it seemed designed solely for intelligent graduates of the best schools. The *Wall Street Journal* once labeled it "Urbanity, Inc." When the magazine spoke clearly against the war, it was a significant event in the course of public attitude toward the American enterprise in Vietnam. If this apolitical organ of the elite said the war was morally wrong, it was saying it to the country's establishment.

The Kids Are Reading ...

At the same time, the magazine was giving the message to a quite different constituency. A *New Yorker* staff member recalled that in 1967, "Our writers would come back from speaking on campuses and say that the kids are reading *The New Yorker* out loud in the dormitories."

Ordinarily this is a happy event in the life of a magazine. There is always a need for some younger readers so that when older subscribers die the magazine will not die with them. But advertisers live in the present. Throughout its crisis years after 1966, *The New Yorker* audience actually grew in numbers. But while the median age of readers in 1966 was 48.7—the age when executives would be at the peak of their spending power—by 1974 *New Yorker* subscribers' median age was 34, a number brought down by the infusion of college students in their late teens and early twenties.[4] Many college students will form the affluent elite of the future, but at the moment they are not buying $10,500 wristwatches and $14,000 brooches. They were buying the magazine because of its clear and moral stand against the war and its quiet, detailed reporting from the scene.

It was then that ad pages began their drastic disappearance. An easy explanation would be that conservative corporations withdrew their ads in political protest. Some did. But the majority of the losses came from a more impersonal process, one of profound significance to the character of contemporary American mass media. *The New Yorker* had begun to attract "the wrong kind" of reader. Circulation remained the same, but the magazine had become the victim, as it had formerly been the beneficiary, of an iron rule of advertising-supported media: It is less important that people buy your publication (or listen to your program) than that they be "the right kind" of people.

The "right kind" usually means affluent consumers eighteen to forty-nine years of age, the heavy buying years, with above-median family income. Newspapers, magazines, and radio and television operators publicly boast of their audience size, which is a significant factor. But when they sit down at conferences with big advertisers, they do not present simple numbers but reams of computer printouts that show the characteristics of their audience in income, age, sex, marital status, ethnic background, social habits, residence, family structure, occupation, and buying patterns. These are the compelling components of that crucial element in modern media—demographics, the study of characteristics of the human population.

The standard cure for "bad demographics" in newspapers, magazines, radio and television is simple: Change the content. Fill the publication or the programs with material that will attract the kind of people the advertisers want. The general manager of *Rolling Stone* expressed it when that magazine wanted to attract a higher level of advertiser: "We had to deliver a more high-quality reader. The only way to deliver a different kind of reader is to change editorial." If an editor refuses or fails to change, the editor is fired.[5]

The New Yorker faced this problem but it did not fire the editor; nor did the editor "change editorial." It is almost certain that for conventional corporate ownership the "cure" would be quick and decisive. William Shawn would have "changed editorial," which would have meant dropping the insistent line on the war in Vietnam, or he would have been fired. In the place of the Vietnam reporting and commentary there would have been less controversial material that would adjust demographics back to the affluent population of buying age and assuage the anger of those corporations that disliked the magazine's position on the war.

But at the time, *The New Yorker* was not the property of a conglomerate. Later, in 1986, it would be sold to the Newhouse publishing group. The new owner altered advertising and promotion policies but left editorial content the same. After a year, however, the new owner replaced the editor, William Shawn.

Shawn, a Dickensian man, modest in manner and speech, reddens in indignation when asked whether, during the critical 1967–1974 period, the business leaders of the magazine informed him that his editorial content was attracting the wrong kind of reader.

The Unthinkable Becomes Thinkable

It would be unthinkable for the advertising and business people to tell me that ... I didn't hear about it until the early 1970s. ... It gradually sank in on me that The New Yorker *was being read by younger people. I didn't know it in any formal way. Who the readers are I really don't want to know. I don't want to know because we edit the magazine for ourselves and hope there will be people like ourselves and people like our writers who will find it interesting and worthwhile.*

Shawn's words are standard rhetoric of publishers and editors when they are asked about separation of editorial independence and advertising. The rhetoric usually has little relation to reality. Increasingly, editorial content of publications and broadcasting is dictated by the computer printouts on advertising agency desks, not the other way around. When there is a conflict between the printouts and an independent editor, the printouts win. Were it not for the incontrovertible behavior of *The New Yorker* during the Vietnam War, it would be difficult not to regard Shawn's words as the standard mythic rhetoric.

"We never talk about 'the readers,'" Shawn said. "I won't permit that—if I may put it so arrogantly. I don't want to speak about our readers as a 'market.' I don't want them to feel that they are just consumers to us. I find that obnoxious."

The full-page ads of other newspapers, magazines, and broadcast networks in the *New York Times* and the *Wall Street Journal* are often puzzling to the lay reader. They do not urge people to read and listen. They seem to be filled with statistics of little interest to potential subscribers or viewers. They are intended to show the advertising industry that the demographics of the publication or station are "correct," that their audience is made up not of a cross-section of the population but of people in the "right" age and income brackets.

Eventually during the 1967–1974 period Shawn did hear what he called "murmurings":

There were murmurings in the background about three things: The magazine was getting too serious, the magazine was getting too much into politics, and the pieces were getting too long. My reaction was that we should do nothing about it. Whatever change took place did so gradually and spontaneously as we saw the world ... There's only one way to do it: Did we think it was the right thing to do? Did we take the right editorial stand? ... To be silent when something is going on that shouldn't be going on would be cowardly. We published information we believed the public should have and we said what we believed. If the magazine was serious it was no more serious than we were. If there was too much politics, it was because politics became more important and it was on our minds ... I wish we could remain out of politics but we can't ... I could enjoy life more if we could do nothing but be funny, which I love ... but The New Yorker has gradually changed as the world changed.

Shawn noted that the Time-Life and Reader's Digest empires succeeded because they were started by men who expressed their own values regardless of the market and thereby established an identity that made for long-range success.

Now the whole idea is that you edit for a market and if possible design a magazine with that in mind. Now magazines aren't started with the desire for someone to express what he believes. I think the whole trend is so destructive and so unpromising so far as journalism is concerned that it is very worrisome. Younger editors and writers are growing up in that atmosphere. "We want to edit the magazine to give the audience what they want. What do we give them?"

There is a fallacy in that calculation . . . That fallacy is if you edit that way, to give back to the readers only what they think they want, you'll never give them something new they didn't know about. You stagnate. It's just this back-and-forth and you end up with the networks, TV and the movies. The whole thing begins to be circular. Creativity and originality and spontaneity goes out of it. The new tendency is to discourage this creative process and kill originality.

We sometimes publish a piece that I'm afraid not more than one hundred readers will want. Perhaps it's too difficult, too obscure. But it's important to have. That's how people learn and grow. This other way is bad for our entire society and we're suffering from it in almost all forms of communications.

I don't know if you tried to start up a New Yorker *today if you could get anybody to back you.*

"It happens regularly"

A magazine industry executive was asked if a magazine owned by a conventional corporation would have supported Shawn during the lean years. He answered: "Are you kidding? One bad year like the one *New Yorker* had in 1967 and either the editorial formula would change or the editor would be out on his ear. It happens regularly."

By the 1980s *The New Yorker* was economically healthy again. Its circulation in 1980 was more than 500,000, it was running 4,220 pages of ads a year, fourth among all American magazines, and its profits were back above $3 million.[6] That seems to be a heartwarming morality lesson in the rewards of integrity. But a few years later, even *The New Yorker* would become another conglomerate property. Newspapers and magazines in the main do not want merely readers; they want affluent readers. Broadcasters do not want just any listeners; they want rich ones. Those who are not going to buy are not invited to read, hear, or watch.

Media executives don't tell the general public that only the affluent are wanted. But just as there is sometimes unguarded truth in wine, there is sometimes unguarded truth in the heat of competition. When individual media companies fight for business, or one medium tries to lure advertisers from another medium, the unvarnished truth escapes from behind high-sounding rhetoric. In 1978 the American Broadcasting Company emerged as the leading television network in size of audience; other networks fought to maintain their advertising revenues by deprecating the "quality" of ABC's audience. Paul Klein, then program director of NBC-TV, said ABC's audience might be the largest but it is "kids and dummies."

Reminded that ABC had large ratings "in homes making $20,000 and over," Klein said:

Well, that is the kids watching in those homes, and sometimes the adults. ... We would like to pull away those adults, and leave ABC with the children ... [ABC] may still have a very big audience but their audience will be worthless.

Broadcasting Magazine reported:

More specifically, Mr. Klein defined as his target audience 18- to 49-year-old women who are in reasonably secure financial situations — "the women with some money to buy a product and the necessity to buy it." Since the cardinal rule of program demographics is that people like to watch people like themselves, Mr. Klein is pouring females into his prime-time programs ... Sexually oriented plots are also becoming increasingly prominent.[7]

In counterattack, ABC issued a booklet to impress potential advertisers. One section of the booklet was entitled

"Some people are more valuable than others." When word of this title reached the nonadvertising world, ABC, not wishing to appear nonegalitarian in public, withdrew the booklet — but retained the demographic boast.[8]

Broadcasters can safely be blunt in trade publications seen by advertising agencies. *Broadcasting Magazine*, for example, carries a great deal of corporate promotion aimed at advertisers. One ad announced in heavy type over a photograph of Mike Douglas, the talk show host:

Women 18–49: Mike's Got Your Number!
  The Mike Douglas Show today delivers more women in its audience 18–49 ... a higher percentage of women 18–49 in its audience than the John Davidson Show.[9]

Such advertising is also crucial for magazines in closed business circles. An issue of *Public Relations Journal* carried the following full-page ad:

Wanted: 77,000,000 Movers and Shakers
  Did they go to college? Are they professionals or managers? Are their household incomes $20,000 plus? Are their homes $40,000 plus? Are their corporate securities $20,000 plus? Have they played active roles in local civic issues? Have they written any elected officials or editors lately? Have they written any books or articles? Have they addressed any public meetings or worked for any political parties?
  Only 77,136,000 adults can answer yes to one or more of those questions ... they're big on magazines and not so big on television ... Make this your year to re-evaluate the balance of power between television and magazines in your media planning ...
  Magazines. The Balance of Power.[10]

The original mass medium, newspapers, in its early period carried ads that were marginal in the medium's economics. But in the late 1800s mass production of consumer goods expanded beyond normal consumption. At the time advertisers spent an average of $28.39 a year per household urging people to buy goods and services.[11] By 1980 they were spending $691 per household, an increase far greater than the rate of inflation, with 29 percent of ad money going to newspapers, 21 percent to television, 7 percent to radio, and 6 percent to magazines. By now newspapers get 80 percent of their revenues from ads, general-circulation magazines 50 percent, and broadcasting almost 100 percent.

With more than $247 billion spent in 2001 on those media each year, advertisers do not leave to chance who will see their ads. Surveys and computers make it possible now to describe with some precision the income, education, occupation, and spending habits of newspaper and magazine subscribers and broadcast audiences, though each medium tends to exaggerate the "quality" of its audience. Media operators fear "the wrong kind" of audience—too young or too old, or not affluent enough. The greater the pressure on newspapers, magazines, and broadcasters to increase their profits, the more they push not just for larger audiences but for higher-quality audiences, as each newspaper, each magazine, each broadcast station insists to the major advertisers that it has the highest-quality audience.

With billions in ads and more billions in product sales at stake, advertisers no longer leave the demographics of their ad carriers to rhetoric and speculation. They now insist on carefully audited subscription statistics and scientifically gathered audience data, with sophisticated computer analysis of exactly the kind of individual who is exposed to a particular kind of advertisement in a newspaper, magazine, or broadcast. And they are increasingly interested in the context of their ads in the medium—the surrounding articles in newspapers and magazines and the type of broadcast program in which their commercials are inserted. An ad for a sable fur coat next to an article on world starvation is not the most effective association for making a sale.

Thus, both the "quality" of an audience and the nonadvertising content around the ads have become dominant in the thinking of major advertisers. Not surprisingly, those factors have consequently become dominant in the thinking of owners of newspapers, magazines, and broadcast stations.

The president of Harte-Hanks Century Newspaper Group, owner of twenty-eight daily papers in the United States, said in 1980 that the company's editors are losing what he called their "prejudices" about separating news content from the desire to reach advertisers' model audience. "The traditional view has been for editors to focus only on the total circulation figures. Today we are seeing more editor emphasis on the quality of circulation."[12]

The largest newspaper chain in the country, Gannett, owns ninety-four daily papers. A study of the Gannett chain by William B. Blankenburg of the University of Wisconsin concluded that the chain aims at fewer subscribers who are richer: "The lost subscribers, if less wealthy . . . may not have fitted into their marketing scheme."[13]

Otis Chandler, once the head of the Times Mirror empire, owner of the *Los Angeles Times* and the fourth-largest newspaper chain, said, "The target audience of the *Times* is . . . in the middle class and . . . the upper class. . . . We are not trying to get mass circulation, but quality circulation."[14] On another occasion, he said, "We arbitrarily cut back some of our low-income circulation. . . . The economics of American newspaper publishing is based on an advertising base, not a circulation base."[15]

Wine by the Case

Years after the near-fatal disease struck *The New Yorker*, when recovery had set in, the magazine's Market Research Department commissioned a professional survey to analyze its subscribers.[16] For the edification of prospective advertisers in *The New Yorker*, its salespeople could display 134 pages of statistical tables that showed that the magazine's readers were 58.5 percent male, 63.8 percent married (6.6% widowed, 8.1% separated or divorced); 94.0 percent had attended college or had degrees (21.8% had Ph.D.s); 71.0 percent were in business, industry, or professions; 19.3 percent were in top management; 16.6 percent were members of corporate boards of directors; 40.1 percent collected original paintings and sculptures; 26.1 percent bought wine by the case; 59.3 percent owned corporate stock, which had an average value of $70,500 (though a scrupulous footnote to this datum says, "In order not to distort the average ... one respondent reporting $25,000,000 was omitted from the calculation"); and the median age was 48.4. In other words, the elite audience was "the right kind" for advertising expensive merchandise.

By 1981 *The New Yorker* had recovered enough of its high-quality demographics to make it a desirable carrier for a full-page ad by the Magazine Publishers Association. The ad pursued the theme that magazines are superior for advertising because they don't want readers who aren't going to buy. The headline on the ad read: A Magazine Doesn't Waste Words on Window Shoppers.[17]

Neither does any newspaper or broadcast station that makes most of its money from advertising.

*I would rather be the man who bought the
Brooklyn Bridge than the man who sold it.*
WILL ROGERS

CHAPTER TWELVE

DR. BRANDRETH HAS GONE TO HARVARD

James Gordon Bennett, founder of the *New York Herald,* is one of American journalism's bad boys. In August of 1835 his Ann Street plant suffered a disastrous fire, but the *Herald* was back on the street nineteen days later with this pronouncement:

We are again in the field . . . more independent than ever. The Ann Street conflagration consumed types, presses, manuscripts, paper, some bad poetry, subscription books—all the outward appearance of the Herald, *but its soul was saved.*[1]

The *Herald* was "again in the field" but not "more independent than ever." After the fire Bennett was saved by a large advertising contract from a "Doctor Brandreth," a quack who sold phony cure-all pills. After the *Herald* was back in circulation, the Brandreth ads appeared in profusion. But so did a steady diet of "news" stories, presuming to be straight reporting, "more independent than ever," recounting heroic cures effected by none other than Dr. Brandreth's

233

pills. While other pill makers complained that Brandreth was getting front-page news accounts as well as ads, Bennett replied in his news columns:

Send us more advertisements than Dr. Brandreth does—give us higher prices—we'll cut Dr. Brandreth dead—or at least curtail his space. Business is business—money is money—and Dr. Brandreth is no more to us than "Mr. Money Broker."[2]

Nine months later, when Brandreth canceled his advertising contract, Bennett, in print, called the good doctor a "most impudent charlatan" who "deceived and cheated."

In the new dignity of modern American journalism, this kind of corruption in the news is a thing of the past, having occurred only in the bad old days before the turn of the century. Modern media, it is said, are immunized by professional ethics from letting advertising influence editorial content.

Contemporary news and entertainment are, to use Bennett's phrase, "more independent than ever." Newspapers make 80 percent of their revenues from ads and devote about 65 percent of their daily space to them. Magazines, similarly clothed in virtue, make roughly half their money from ads, though they used to make more, and they usually insist that their advertising departments never shape the articles, stories, and columns produced by professional editors and writers. Radio and television, the most pervasive media in American life, have varied nonadvertising content like game shows, situation comedies, cops-and-robbers serials, news, talk shows, documentaries, and musical recordings.

Broadcasters vary in their separation of commercials and programs. Some, no longer satisfied with a brand name product simply appearing in the background of a scene, now have the commercial product integrated into the dialogue of the program itself. The whole idea is to escape the viewer's mute button. This new insidious technique has been given the name of its predecessor, "infotainment," a repellent word that is alleged to be in the English language."[3]

In short, nineteenth-century money changers of advertisers have not been invited into the temple, they have been given the deed to the temple.

Present-day Brandreths have changed their technique. So have the contemporary Bennetts. The advertiser does not barge through the front door announcing, "I am Dr. Brandreth. I pay money to this network (newspaper, magazine, radio station) and I am pleased to introduce to you the producer (reporter, editor, writer) who, with all the powers vested by society in independent journalism, will proclaim the wonder of my pills." Except for a few clumsy operators, such a tactic is much too crude for the twenty-first century.

Today Dr. Brandreth makes his proper appearance in his ads. He then leaves politely by the front door, goes to the back of the television station (radio studio, newspaper newsroom, magazine editorial offices), and puts on the costume of a professional producer (reporter, editor, writer) whom you have been told to trust: "Through professional research and critical analysis, it is my independent judgment that Dr. Brandreth's pills, politics, ideology, and industry are the salvation of our national soul."

The Subtle Corruption

Modern corruption is more subtle. Today, or in recent times, advertisers have *successfully* demanded that the following ideas appear in programs around their ads.

All businessmen are good or, if not, are always condemned by other businessmen. All wars are humane. The status quo is wonderful. Also wonderful are all grocery stores, bakeries, drug companies, restaurants, and laundries. Religionists, especially clergy, are perfect. All users of cigarettes are gentle, graceful, healthy, youthful people. In fact, anyone who uses a tobacco product is a hero. People who commit suicide never do it with pills. All financial institutions are always in good shape. The American way of life is beyond criticism.

The above messages, to cite only a few, have not been vague inferences. Major advertisers have insisted that these specific ideas be expressed not in the ads but in the ostensibly "independent" news reporting, editorial content, or entertainment programs of newspapers, magazines, radio, and television. The readers, listeners, and viewers did not know that these messages were planted by advertisers. They were not supposed to know. They were supposed to think that these ideas were the independent work of professional journalists and playwrights detached from anything commercial. If the audiences were told that the ideas represented explicit demands of corporations who advertised, the messages would lose their impact.

But for too long, the taboo against criticism of the system of contemporary enterprise, in its subtle way, was almost as complete within mainstream journalism and broadcast programming in the United States as criticism of communism was explicitly in the Soviet Union. The forbidden criticism of the system of free enterprise that experienced spectacular explosions of Enron, Tyco, and other giants of the free market economy in 2001 can be better appreciated by considering what used to be inflexible demands once made and obeyed by broadcasters in, for example, the case of Procter & Gamble and, of course, tobacco products.

The entry of pro-corporate ideas into news and entertainment was specific. Procter & Gamble, once the largest advertiser in television, is now the fourth largest. For years it has been one of the leaders in creating promotions in all media, including commercials inserted into television programs. It has always appreciated the power of advertising. The company was created in 1837 with a soap called, simply, White Soap.[4] But in 1879 Harley Procter, a descendant of the founder, read in the Forty-fifth Psalm, "All thy garments smell of myrrh and aloes and cassia out of the ivory palaces. . . ." Ivory Soap was born and with it the first of the full-page ads for the product. Within a decade Procter & Gamble was selling 30 million cakes of the soap a day. Since then, the company has been spectacularly successful, combining soap, detergent, Christian religion, patriotism, and profit making. After World War II it projected its ideas to television programs in the form of advertising.

They, like most major advertisers, do not merely buy a certain number of commercials, deliver the tapes to the networks and local stations, and let the commercials fall where they may. Some television and radio ads are bought on that basis but not, usually, those of major advertisers. Big advertisers in particular want to know what time of day their commercials will be shown, since that helps define the makeup and size of the audience they are buying. And they want to know the nature of the program into which their commercials will be inserted.

In the early years of television, advertisers sponsored and produced entire news and entertainment programs. This gave them direct control over the nonadvertising part of the program and they inserted or deleted whatever suited their commercial and ideological purposes. NBC's news program in the early 1950s was called *Camel News Caravan* after its sponsor, Camel cigarettes, which banned all film of news that happened to take place where a No Smoking sign could be seen in the background.[5]

After the 1950s, networks produced their own shows and

advertisers bought commercials of varying lengths for insertion during the networks' programming. Advertising was allotted six, then twelve, and now almost unlimited minutes per hour of prime-time evening hours and longer periods at other times of the day. But no network produces a program without considering whether sponsors will like it. Prospective shows usually are discussed with major advertisers, who look at plans or tentative scenes and reject, approve, or suggest changes.

Major advertisers like Procter & Gamble do not leave their desires in doubt.

Wars without Horror

The Federal Communications Commission (FCC) held hearings in 1965 to determine how much influence advertisers had on noncommercial content of television and radio. Albert N. Halverstadt, general advertising manager of Procter & Gamble, testified that the company established directives for programs in which Procter & Gamble would advertise. These policies were to create standards of "decency and common sense. . . . I do not think it constitutes control."[6] He then gave the FCC the formal requirements for television programs, as established by the medium's largest advertiser in their memorandums of instruction to their advertising agency:

Where it seems fitting, the characters in Procter & Gamble dramas should reflect recognition and acceptance of the world situation in their thoughts and actions, although in dealing with war, our writers should minimize the "horror" aspects. The writers should be guided by the fact that any scene that contributes negatively to public morale is not acceptable. Men in uniform shall not be cast as heavy villains or portrayed as engaging in any criminal activity.[7]

Procter & Gamble was particularly interested in the image of business and business people on television programs:

There will be no material on any of our programs which could in any way further the concept of business as cold, ruthless, and lacking all sentiment or spiritual motivation.

If a businessman is cast in the role of villain, it must be made clear that he is not typical but is as much despised by his fellow businessmen as he is by other members of society.

Special attention shall be given to any mention, however innocuous, of the grocery and drug business as well as any other group of customers of the company. This includes industrial users of the company's products, such as bakeries, restaurants, and laundries.

The company view of religion and patriotism is built into programs. If, in a drama or documentary, a character attacks what the memo called "some basic conception of the American way of life," then a rejoinder "must be completely and convincingly made someplace in the same broadcast."

The same is true of what Procter & Gamble called "positive social forces": "Ministers, priests and similar representatives of positive social forces shall not be cast as villains or represented as committing a crime or be placed in any unsympathetic antisocial role."

The memo specifies, "If there is any question whatever about such material, it should be deleted."

Halverstadt testified that these policies were applied both to entertainment programs in which Procter & Gamble commercials appeared and to news and public affairs documentaries.[8]

Thus, corporate ideology was built into entertainment and documentary programming that the audience believes is presented independent of thirty-second and sixty-second commercials that happen to appear in the program. It is sobering that these demands are made of a medium reaching 100 million homes for seven and a half hours every day.

But insertion of corporate ideology and commercial themes in the nonadvertising portion of television programming is not limited to Procter & Gamble. An executive of Brown & Williamson Tobacco Corporation placed into evidence before the FCC the company's policy on programs carrying cigarette commercials, directives that prevailed until the end of televised cigarette commercials in 1970:

Tobacco products should not be used in a derogatory or harmful way. And no reference or gesture of disgust, dissatisfaction or distaste be made in connection with them. Example: cigarettes should not be ground out violently in an ashtray or stamped out underfoot.

Whenever cigarettes are used by antagonists or questionable characters, they should be regular size, plain ends and unidentifiable.

But no cigarette should be used as a prop to depict an undesirable character. Cigarettes used by meritorious characters should be Brown & Williamson brands and they may be identifiable or not.

A vice president of an advertiser of headache tablets, Whitehall Laboratories, told the FCC that the company demanded of networks that "if a scene depicted somebody committing suicide by taking a bottle of tablets, we would not want this to be on the air."

A vice president of Prudential Insurance Company, sponsor of public affairs programs, said that a positive image of business and finance was important to sustain on the air. The company rejected the idea for a program on the bank holiday during the Depression because "it cast a little doubt on all financial institutions."

All major advertisers, it seems, would concur with a statement made by a Procter & Gamble vice president for advertising in 1979: "We're in programming first to assure a good environment for our advertising."[9]

Corporate demands on television programs underlie

what many consider the most grievous weakness of American television—superficiality, materialism, blandness, and escapism. The television industry invariably responds that the networks are only giving people what the people demand. But it is not what the public says it wants: It is what the advertisers demand.

The Best Atmosphere for Selling

At one time the Bell & Howell Company attempted to break the pattern of escapist, superficial prime-time programs by sponsoring news documentaries.[10] The president of the company told the FCC that this was tried to help counter the standards applied by most advertisers, which he described, disapprovingly, as consisting of the following requirements:

One should not associate with controversy; one should always reach for the highest ratings; one should never forget that there is safety in numbers; one should always remember that comedy, adventure and escapism provide the best atmosphere for selling.

Even if a nonescapist program becomes a commercial success, it is likely to be canceled by the networks or major local stations. In the early days of television, there were outstanding serious programs, including live, original drama: *Kraft Television Theatre, Goodyear Playhouse, Studio One, Robert Montgomery Presents, U.S. Steel Hour, Revlon Theater, Omnibus, Motorola TV Hour, The Elgin Hour, Matinee Theater,* and *Playhouse 90.* It was the era of striking television plays by playwrights such as Paddy Chayefsky, who said he had discovered "the marvelous world" of drama in the lives of ordinary people.

Erik Barnouw in his definitive history of American broadcasting writes:

That this "marvelous world" fascinated millions is abundantly clear from statistics. These plays—akin to the genre paintings—held consistently high ratings. But one group hated them: the advertising profession . . . Most advertisers were selling magic. Their commercials posed the same problems that Chayefsky drama dealt with: people who feared failure in love and in business. But in the commercials there was always a solution as clear-cut as the snap of a finger: the problem could be solved by a new pill, deodorant, toothpaste, shampoo, shaving lotion, hair tonic, car, girdle, coffee, muffin recipe, or floor wax.[11]

That was a generation ago. Today's audience is more jaded and sophisticated. So commercials are more insidious and clever. They use humor, self-deprecation, even satire of the product in such a way to leave the viewer with a sympathetic, warm smile that becomes associated with the brand name product.

There is another reason networks and advertising agencies resist serious or nonescapist programs. Networks make most of their money between the hours of 8:00 and 11:00 P.M.—prime time. They wish to keep the audience tuned from one half-hour segment to the next and they prefer the "buying mood" sustained as well. A serious half-hour program in that period that has high ratings may, nevertheless, be questioned because it will interrupt the evening's flow of lightness and fantasy. In that sense, the whole evening is a single block of atmosphere—a selling atmosphere.

Programs like *Roots* on the origins of American black slavery had very large audiences but no comparable commercial support at the level an audience that size ordinarily receives. The forcible seizure of West African men and women and their shackled boat trip on the Atlantic Ocean with dumping sick ones overboard did not create "a buying mood."

The printed media have not escaped the pressure, or the desire, to shape their nonadvertising content to support the mood and sometimes the explicit ideas of advertisers. Magazines were the first medium to carry sophisticated, artistic advertisements.[12] Magazines had graphic capabilities superior to newspapers, with better printing and color illustrations (the first successful national magazine, *Godey's Lady Book*, begun in 1830, hired 150 women to tint the magazine's illustrations by hand). Until late in the 1800s ads were a minor part of magazine publishing, but once national merchandising organizations grew, this national medium responded. By 1900 *Harper's*, for example, was carrying more ads in one year than it had in its previous twenty-two years.

"Bait the editorial pages . . ."

Before television emerged in the 1950s, successful magazines were 65 percent ads. By that time, most magazines were fundamentally designed for advertising rather than editorial matter. The philosophy of Condé Nast had triumphed. Nast, who had created *Vogue, Vanity Fair, Glamour, Mademoiselle,* and *House and Garden*, regarded his mission "to bait the editorial pages in such a way to lift out of all the millions of Americans just the hundred thousand cultivated persons who can buy these quality goods."[13]

The role of most magazines, as seen by their owners, was to act as a broker in bringing together the buyers and sellers of goods. There was, and still is, a significant difference among magazines in how far they go to sell their readers to advertisers. But the influence of advertisers on magazine content continues.

A 1940 *Esquire* article declared that the guitar is a better accompaniment to singing than a piano. A few months later the magazine ran an apology, "We lost all our piano ads . . . We can and do beg the pardon of the piano manufacturers." By then the fiery owners of the magazine had already been tamed. Two years earlier they had started *Ken*, a magazine of liberal idealism that seemed to start with great promise. Advertisers disliked the liberal ideas in its articles and not only refused to advertise in the new publication but threatened to pull out their ads from *Esquire* as well. So the owners of *Esquire* killed *Ken*, even though it met its circulation plans.[14]

In 1962 Paul Willis, president of the Grocery Manufacturers Association, warned television operators that they had better run more programs boosting the food industry. He boasted that a similar warning had worked with national magazines.

We suggested to the publishers that the day was here when their editorial department and business department might better understand their interdependent relationships . . . as their operations may affect the advertiser — their bread and butter.[15]

The periodical *Advertising Age* said Willis "pointed with pride" to favorable food articles printed thereafter by "*Look, Reader's Digest, American Weekly, This Week, Saturday Evening Post, Good Housekeeping, Ladies' Home Journal, Family Circle,* and *Woman's Day,* among others."

If, like Bennett's *Herald*, this was merely the bad old days, there has been little evidence to give comfort in recent years. Condé Nast could create *Vogue* in 1909 with his philosophy of using his articles to get "the cultivated person who can buy these quality goods." In 1972, with *Vogue* under a new owner (S. I. Newhouse, the newspaper chain, which bought the Condé Nast magazines in 1959), it seemed to make no difference. Richard Shortway, publisher of *Vogue*, sixty-three years after Nast's candid statement, made his own candid statement: "The cold, hard facts of magazine publishing mean that those who advertise get editorial coverage."[16]

Magazines have been the Achilles' heel of corporations who also own book houses. The New York Times Company is a conglomerate involved in magazines, books, and broadcasting, as well as newspapers. In 1976 the *New York Times* published a series of articles on medical malpractice.[17] The news series angered the medical industry, including pharmaceutical firms. They could not retaliate effectively against the *New York Times*, which does not carry much medical advertising. But medicine-related advertisers were crucial to magazines published by the New York Times Company, including a periodical called *Modern Medicine*. Pharmaceutical firms threatened to withdraw 260 pages of their ads from *Modern Medicine*, a loss of half a million dollars, and the Times Company sold its medical magazines to Harcourt Brace Jovanovich.

The Permissible Lies

Reader's Digest Association owns the magazine *Reader's Digest* and Funk & Wagnalls book publishing.[18] In 1968 Funk & Wagnalls prepared to publish a book, *The Permissible Lie*, which criticized the advertising industry. A month before publication date, Reader's Digest ordered its book subsidiary to cancel the book. Reader's Digest advertising revenues in its magazine, at that date, were $50 million a year and the association presumably felt threatened by loss of advertising from its magazine if its book subsidiary offended the advertising agency.

Newspapers are considered the most scrupulous of all the media subsidized by advertising. It had been a sacred edict in official newspaper ethics that church and state— news and advertising—are separate and that when there is any doubt each is clearly labeled. This is a relatively recent change. Thirty years ago it was common for newspapers to resist any news that offended a major advertiser. Department store fires, safety violations in stores, public health actions against restaurants that advertised, and lawsuits against car dealers seldom made their way into print. The average paper printed stories about some advertiser or prospective advertiser that were solely promotional propaganda. A standard fixture in almost every newspaper was the memorandum from the business office—B.O.M., or "business office must," meaning that the news department was ordered to run a story for purposes of pleasing an advertiser.

Over the years, in most newspapers—but not all—those blatant corruptions of news had diminished. But censoring of information offensive to advertisers continues. News that might damage an advertiser generally must pass a higher threshold of drama and documentation than other kinds of news. But as more papers become properties of large media conglomerates where profit levels are dictated by Wall Street and distant CEOs, pressure has increased to subdue news that might offend an important advertisers. More common in contemporary papers is the large quantity of "fluff"—material that is not news in any real sense but is nonadvertising material supporting of advertisers.

A 1978 study by the Housing Research Group of the Center for Responsive Law found that

*most newspaper real estate sections serve the real estate industry far bet-
ter than they serve consumers and general readers ... Articles that appear as "news" frequently are promotional pieces for developers, real
estate agents, or industry associations.*[19]

Examples in the study included the following: the *Birmingham* (Alabama) *News* printed four industry press releases
without more than cosmetic rewriting on the front page of its
real estate section; one issue of the *Sacramento Union* had
more than a dozen articles promoting new subdivisions;
press releases were substituted for news articles in the *Baltimore Sun, Birmingham News, Boston Herald American,
New York Post, Philadelphia Evening Bulletin,* and *Washington Star.*

Bigger papers, including some of the country's most
prestigious, often printed more real estate propaganda than
did some smaller papers. The reports said:

*We were surprised to discover half a dozen smaller newspapers ... that
had a small but respectable real estate section. Their success in presenting real estate news in an objective, informative fashion compared quite
favorably with some much larger newspapers.*

These smaller papers were *Indianapolis Star, New Orleans Times-Picayune, Memphis Commercial Appeal,* and *St.
Petersburg* (Florida) *Times.*

The study seemed to have little influence. A year later a
number of newspapers not only kept up the flood of industry promotional material masquerading as news but actually
took real estate reporting out of the hands of reporters and
gave it directly to the advertising department. These papers
include the *Van Nuys* (California) *Valley News, Los Angeles
Herald Examiner, Houston Chronicle,* and *Dallas Morning
News.* Mainly because so many newspaper readers are world
travelers for pleasure and business, a few notes of realism

are found in travel columns. A description of a lovely white-sanded tropical beach may add "Take your DEET to ward off the sand fleas."

The bulk of "news" in the newspaper is contained in similar special sections. The fashion section, for example, is almost always either taken from press releases submitted by designers and fashion houses or written by fashion editors who attend the fashion shows with all expenses paid by the fashion houses. The result is an annual flood of gushy promotion of exotic garments, all in a "news" section. The contamination becomes more blatant with time. In 1980 John Brooks, director of communications for the *Toronto Star*, said that when the paper created a new fashion section,

> all market research was turned over to the editorial department so that planning of editorial content would be consistent with the wants and needs of readers and prospective readers. The Family Editor, under whose jurisdiction Fashion/80 would fall, spent a lot of time with advertising department personnel in meetings with advertisers.[20]

The same is true of travel and usually food sections. A survey in 1977 showed that 94 percent of food editors use food company releases for recipes and 38 percent attend food events at the expense of food companies. This, too, has not changed in the twenty-first century.[21]

Nothing Controversial

The growing trend among newspapers to turn over sections of the "news" to the advertising department usually produces copy that is not marked "advertising" but is full of promotional material under the guise of news. The advertising department of the *Houston Chronicle*, for example, provided all the "news" for the following sections of the paper: home, townhouse, apartments, travel, technology, livestock, and swimming pools. The vice president of sales and marketing of the *Chronicle* said: "We do nothing controversial. We're not in the investigative business. Our only concern is giving editorial support to our ad projects."[22]

One of the most compelling needs for readers in the dramatic inflation of the 1970s was reliable information about comparative shopping, yet it is one of the weakest elements in American newspapers. The consumer information most needed by families concerns industries with control over the advertising income of newspapers—food, transportation, and clothing. A feature that has always been extremely popular with readers during its spasmodic and brief appearances is the market basket survey. A reporter periodically buys the items on a typical family shopping list and writes a story about price changes in major supermarkets. It is not a story that grocery store advertisers like, so it has practically disappeared in American papers precisely when it is most needed. Even when the market basket surveys are conducted by university researchers, as at Purdue University, most papers refuse to carry the reports, one admitting it bent to advertisers' pressure.[23]

In 1980 the *Washington Star* announced a five-part series on the pros and cons of shopping coupons that have become common in newspapers, but the series was killed after the first story for fear of discouraging advertisers who bought space in the *Star* for shopping coupons.[24]

Given the eagerness with which newspapers protect major advertisers, it is understandable that by now advertisers expect that when the interests of readers are in competition with the interests of advertisers, the newspapers will protect the advertisers.

A senior vice president of MGM told newspaper executives in 1981 that he had seen too many negative reviews of movies and warned newspapers that the $500 million worth of movie ads

cannot be taken for granted and you've got to get this word to your editorial counterparts... Today the daily newspaper does not always create a climate that is supportive and favorable to the motion picture industry ... gratuitous and hateful reviews threaten to cause the romance between newspapers and the motion picture industry to wither on the vine.[25]

Death for Sale

The most shameful conspiracy in the history of American news and a major advertiser was the prolonged complicity of the news and advertising media in suppressing or neutralizing the irrefutable evidence that smoking cigarettes kills. According to the British medical journal *Lancet,* as late as the 1990s, in the United States, Europe, Canada, Japan, Australia, and New Zealand, 21 million people died tobacco-related deaths, usually after pain and suffering. The World Health Organization estimated that 3 million people die each year from tobacco.[26]

For decades, newspapers, with rare exceptions, kept smoking deaths out of the news, even after a 1927 definitive study in England made it inexcusable. As late as fourteen years after the Surgeon General of the United States cited serious health risks from smoking, and seven years after the Surgeon General declared that even secondhand smoke may cause lung cancer, 64 million Americans, obviously already addicted, smoked an average of twenty-six cigarettes a day.[27]

But for years newspapers (for whom the top three or four advertisers were always tobacco companies) faithfully reprinted the reports of the tobacco industry public relations operation, the Tobacco Institute, that there was no proven cause-and-effect between smoking and cancer. It seemed that the science of epidemiology that solved the problem of the bubonic plague, typhoid fever, and many other notorious killers of human beings was not applicable to tobacco. Perhaps only after the chromosomes of the cancer cell under the microscope spelled out the name "Brown & Williamson" would the Tobacco Institute at most say that it required "more research and the major news media obediently report it with a straight face.

The prolonged behavior of newspapers was worse, given their ability to be unambiguous about mass deaths based on mounting scientific evidence. In 1971 tobacco advertising was banned from television—or television networks "voluntarily" banned it when it became clear that it was going to be made into communications law anyway. Significantly, thereafter, television was much more willing to highlight antismoking research than was the printed press.[28]

If there is a date beyond which there appears to be the obstinate suppression of the link between tobacco and widespread death, it is 1954. In 1953, the year the AMA banned tobacco ads from its journals, the *New York Times Index*, reflecting probably the best newspaper reporting on the tobacco-cancer link, had 248 entries under "Cancer" and "Smoking" and "Tobacco." Ninety-two percent said nothing about the link; of the 8 percent that did, only 2 percent were articles mainly about the tobacco-disease connection; the other 6 percent were mostly denials of this from the tobacco industry. In 1954, the year of the American Cancer Society's study, the *New York Times Index* had 302 entries under the same titles. Of the stories dealing mainly with tobacco's link to disease, 32 percent were about the tobacco industry's denials and only 20 percent dealt with medical evidence.

In 1980, sixteen years later, there were still more stories in the daily press about the causes of influenza, polio, and tuberculosis than about the cause of one of every seven deaths in the United States.

A Media Disease

There began to be suspicions of a strictly media disease: a strange paralysis whenever solid news pointed at tobacco as a definitive cause of disease and death. For years, up to the present, medical evidence on tobacco and disease has been treated differently than any other information about carriers of disease that do not advertise. The print and broadcast media might make page 1 drama of a junior researcher's paper about a rare disease. But if it involves the 300,000 annual deaths from tobacco-related illness, the media either do not report it or they report it as a controversial item subject to rebuttal by the tobacco industry.

It is a history filled with curious events. In 1963, for example, Hudson Vitamin Products produced Smokurb, a substitute for cigarettes. The company had trouble getting its ads in newspapers and magazines and on the air. Eli Schonberger, president of Hudson's ad agency, said, "We didn't create this campaign to get into a fight with anyone, but some media just stall and put us off in the hope that we'll go away."[29]

This was, of course, strange behavior for media that are anxious for as much advertising as they can get. One major magazine told the company its product was "unacceptable."

The tobacco industry once spent $4 a year for every American man, woman, and child for its cigarette advertising. At the same time, the government's primary agency for educating the public about the dangers of cigarettes, the Department of Health and Human Services, spent one-third of a cent a year for every citizen.

National publications, especially the news magazines, are notorious for publishing dramatic stories about health and disease. *Time* and *Newsweek* have both had cover stories on cancer. *Newsweek*, for example, had a cover story January 26, 1978, entitled "What Causes Cancer?" The article was six pages long. On the third page it whispered about the leading cause—in a phrase it said that tobacco is the least disputed "carcinogen of all." The article said no more about the statistics or the medical findings of the tobacco-cancer link, except in a table, which listed the ten most suspected carcinogens—alphabetically, putting tobacco in a next-to-last place. A week later, *Time*, in a common competitive duplication between the two magazines, ran a two-column article on the causes of cancer. The only reference it made to tobacco was that "smoking and drinking alcohol have been linked to cancer." A few weeks earlier, a *Time* essay urged smokers to organize to defeat antismoking legislation.

When R. C. Smith of *Columbia Journalism Review* studied seven years of magazine content after 1970, when cigarette ads were banned from television, he found:

> In magazines that accept cigarette advertising I was unable to find a single article, in several years of publication, that would have given readers any clear notion of the nature and extent of the medical and social havoc wreaked by the cigarette-smoking habit.[30]

The few magazines that refused cigarette ads did much better at their reporting, he said. (The most prominent magazines that refused cigarette ads were *Reader's Digest* and *The New Yorker*.)

The magazines that carried accurate articles on the

tobacco-disease link suffered for it. In July 1957 *Reader's Digest* ran a strong article on medical evidence against tobacco. Later that month, the advertising agency the magazine used for twenty-eight years said it no longer wanted the *Digest* as a client. The agency, Batten, Barton, Durstine and Osborn, had $1.3 million in business a year from the magazine. But another client, the American Tobacco Company, which spent $22 million a year with the agency, had asked the agency to choose between it and *Reader's Digest*.

In 1980 a liberal-left magazine, *Mother Jones*, ran a series of articles on the link between tobacco and cancer and heart disease, after which tobacco companies canceled their ads with the magazine.[31]

Elizabeth Whelan reported, "I frequently wrote on health topics for women's magazines, and have been told repeatedly by editors to stay away from the subject of tobacco."[32] Whelan, on a campaign to counter the silence, worked with the American Council on Science and Health to ask the ten leading women's magazines to run articles on the growing incidence of smoking-induced disease among women, just as they had done to promote the Equal Rights Amendment. None of the ten magazines—*Cosmopolitan, Harper's Bazaar, Ladies' Home Journal, Mademoiselle, Ms., McCall's, Redbook, Seventeen, Vogue,* or *Working Woman*—would run such an article.

The Seven Oath-Takers

Television, confronted with FCC moves to make it run anti-smoking commercials to counter what the FCC considered misleading cigarette ads, aired a few documentaries, most of them emphasizing the uncertainty of the tobacco link. The best of them was by CBS in 1965. But Howard K. Smith, of ABC, speaking on a public-television panel, expressed what many have seen as the media's treatment of tobacco and disease:

To me that documentary was a casebook example of balance that drained a hot issue of its meaning. On that program there were doctors who had every reason to be objective, who maintained that cigarettes have a causal relation to cancer. On the other side, there were representatives of the tobacco industry, who have no reason to be objective, who state persuasively the opposite. The public was left with a blurred impression that the truth lay between whereas, as far as I am concerned, we have everything but a signed confession from a cigarette that smoking has a causal relation to cancer.[33]

If magazines and broadcasting had been muffled on the national plague, newspapers had been no better. According to medical and other researchers, as well as the editors who produced it, the only lengthy in-depth special feature on tobacco and disease in a standard American daily newspaper was published by the *Charlotte* (North Carolina) *Observer* on March 25, 1979.

The answer lies in a simple statistic: Tobacco was the most heavily advertised product in America, and for a good reason. As the publishing trade journal *Printer's Ink* reported in 1937, "The growth of cigarette consumption has ... been due largely to heavy advertising expenditure. ..." In 1954—the year beyond which any reasonable doubt of the link should have disappeared among the media—the trade journal of newspapers, *Editor & Publisher*, criticizing the American Cancer Society and Surgeon General's reports as "scare news," complained that it had cost newspapers "much lineage and many dollars to some whose business it is to promote the sale of cigarettes through advertising—newspaper and advertising agencies."[34]

It is not surprising that surveys in 1980 by Gallup, Roper, and Chilton found that 30 percent of the public was unaware of the relationship between smoking and heart disease, 50 percent of women did not know that smoking during pregnancy increases the risk of stillbirth and miscarriage, 40 percent of men and women had no idea that smoking causes 80 percent of the 98,000 lung cancer deaths per year, and 50 percent of teenagers did not know that smoking may be addictive.[35]

In 1994 researcher Dr. Stan Glance of the University of California at San Francisco released internal documents from Brown & Williamson on nicotine. Brown & Williamson general counsel Addison Yeaman noted in a confidential memo to his superiors, "Nicotine is addictive. We are then in the business of selling nicotine, an addictive drug."[36]

There was, of course, the famous photograph and television scene of seven leaders of the tobacco industry called before Representative Henry Waxman of California and his committee testifying about the habit-forming character of nicotine. The seven splendidly suited tobacco executives stood behind the witness table, right hands upraised, swearing under oath that they believed that "nicotine is not addictive." They had taken the oath, "so help me God."

They did indeed require the help of the Deity, but He or She must have been listening to a different channel.

PARADISE LOST OR PARADISE REGAINED? SOCIAL JUSTICE IN DEMOCRACY

There was a time when new communications technology promised an era of diverse educational, civic, and entertainment choices beyond anything known before in the United States. Here, at last, would be the most commonly used channels with varieties of entertainment, education, and civic information in the service of a more engaging democracy.

Fiberoptic cable can carry 320 or more video channels in one fiber. Even existing copper wiring to most homes has adopted the technique of multiplexing that permits many channels to travel over one copper wire simultaneously. Ordinary cable to homes in many places offers 91 available channels. Satellite transmission to home rooftop dishes carries more than 120 channels.

All of these could provide not only existing commercial channels now controlled by large corporate conglomerates but also far more channels free of commercials. The multiple public channels could be devoted to all age and taste categories for education, work-related skills, and noncommercialized entertainment. Every city of any size could have clusters of channels strictly for local programming of its choice.

In the 1960s, when these new technologies were in their birth pangs, there was widespread discussion based on the reasonable assumption that in time these new capacities would be used for the public good. Conferences of technologists, social scientists, economists, and journalists considered how best to use them. Major foundations issued highly researched possibilities for a rich spectrum of noncommercial programs. Books were written on the coming bright new world. All assumed that the United States would adapt the new technologies to the special needs of the breadth and variety of the country's geography and population. The country would finally achieve what some other modern democracies already had in operation, and perhaps more.

But it was not to be. There would be no use of these technologies for noncommercial civic programs. Commercial broadcast media corporations rapidly increased their control of every significant medium, including daily newspapers and magazines. The news ideas were reported in news stories and industry publications. But as media conglomerates grew in size and acquired the largest news organizations, the assumption of noncommercial use of the new technologies ceased to appear.

The commercial conglomerates did their political best to elect members of Congress and the White House who then dared not offend them by creating a large public system whose audiences would reduce ratings for the commercialized channels. The big media were loud in the clamor for deregulation of everything possible. Private media power successfully used its political power.

The failure of the vision for enlarged public channels is filled with ironies:

Most new communications technologies were established with taxpayers' money. Like the Internet, satellite transmission, for example, would not exist without its creation of communications satellites by government agencies and subsidies paid for with peoples' taxes. The airwaves, the broadcast frequencies on which most Americans depend, happen to be public property. For all practical purposes these public airwaves have been expropriated by giant media corporations.

When the United States defeated Japan in World War II and established an American administration to reconstruct the old Imperial Government, it mandated that Japan create a noncommercial, unpoliticized broadcast system that would not depend on annual parliamentary appropriations. The Japanese adopted their present broadcasting system because the American occupying forces declared publicly that no modern democracy should be without one. That is why Japan's NHK has the most capacious, diverse, and varied noncommercial broadcasting system in the world, with the British Broadcasting Company second.[1] Both are financed by a fixed tax on broadcast receivers in each home, comparable to annual auto registration fees in the United States. Both the Japanese and the English clearly are sufficiently pleased with the arrangement to have maintained it for more than half a century.

There are now dual systems in Japan with private operation with commercials and pay radio and television. Britain, too, now has commercial channels in ITV, alongside the BBC channels.

The comparatively tiny U.S. public system depends on congressional appropriations. Public broadcasting remains tiny because commercial broadcast conglomerates have the lobbying power and campaign contributions to make certain that Congress will not mandate a system like NHK for the United States, even though it was the United States that demanded that Japan must have one.

Today, the five huge corporate conglomerates are free to behave as though they "own" every major broadcast channel of communication in the country. In addition, they also own most of the production companies that create the programs.

The large media conglomerates do not want greater political and social diversity because it would dilute their audiences and thereby reduce the fees they can demand for the commercials that produce their unprecedented profit levels. They have defeated moves by Congress and federal agencies to alter their restrictive policies. In addition, they have used their power to create new laws that limit even more the entry of new media into the national scene. They have been a most powerful force in shifting the political spectrum of the United States to the right.

The artificial control over the country's political spectrum was demonstrated in 2001 by large-scale protests against the United States' invasion of Iraq. The protests were organized almost entirely via the Internet, the one important medium not yet controlled by the media monopolies. Initially, the standard media owned by conglomerates systematically underreported most of the thousands of protesters who took to the streets across the country and the world. Only after foreign news agencies reported the numbers more accurately—and many Americans used access to these foreign news agencies by Internet—did the American conglomerates alter their earlier inaccurate reporting.

This limitation of the major media extends beyond national policies. The media giants, left largely free to do what they wish, have found ever-lower levels of coarsened culture and models. Prime-time television "reality" programs glorify some of the more revolting emotions in the human psyche—deceit, cynical sexuality, greed, and the desire to exploit, humiliate, and elicit shattering emotional breakdowns on camera. The control of most of what the American public reads, sees, and hears is not a merely technological phenomenon, nor is it just an item in the nation's economy. It is a phenomenon that goes to the heart of the American democracy and the national psyche.

The major media socialize every generation of Americans. Whether the viewers and listeners are conscious of it or not, they are being "educated" in role models, in social behavior, in their early assumptions about the world into which they will venture, and in what to assume about their unseen millions of fellow citizens. One dictionary definition of "socialize" is "To fit for companionship with others; make sociable in attitude or manners." The impact of the mass media on this socialization is not merely a theory that exists in dictionary definitions. The fact that violence on television increases real violence in society has been studied and confirmed for more than thirty years. More than 1,000 studies, including a Surgeon General's special report in 1972 and a National Institute of Mental Health report ten years later, showed television violence is directly related to violence and aggression in children, especially children under age eight. By the time an American child is 18, he or she has seen 16,000 simulated murders and 200,000 acts of violence.[2]

As mentioned earlier, most local television news is a nightly litany of bloody accidents and crimes, known in the television studios as a policy of "if it bleeds, it leads."

Violence on television exists in many foreign countries,

but in few does it equal the extent of its suffusion in American television. TV is the most commonly used baby-sitter in the country. Corporate programming and a heedless Congress have permitted this baby-sitter to be an instructor in mayhem and murder. It is not surprising that studies show that while actual crime has dropped in the United States, public fear of crime and violence has risen. This is not unconnected to an industry that by law is supposed to be regulated and granted broadcast licenses on the basis of "the public interest."

In the 1950s and 1960s, Senator John O. Pastore, Democrat of Rhode Island, as chair of a Senate subcommittee on communications, regularly called leaders of the major broadcast corporations before him to berate them for suffusing the public with gratuitous sex and violence. So did other members of Congress, like Representative Edward Markey of Massachusetts and Senator Fritz Hollins of South Carolina. They did not bring a permanent change, but during their period of leadership they did create a palpable restraint among the major networks, who took pains to skirt what they saw as limits to congressional permissiveness. Once those limits ended with repeal of the Fairness Doctrine in the 1980s, so did any sense of restraint by the major broadcast media.

The damage has gone beyond national cultural values. The power of the conglomerates to sustain myths about national policies has produced growing chaos and crisis in cities and states across the country. The major media for decades have printed and broadcast the mythology that the people of the United States are crushed by the highest taxes among modern democracies. The opposite is true. Of all comparably developed countries, United States citizens pay—in all taxes of every kind—29.7 percent of the country's gross domestic product, while the average for the twenty-four countries of the Organization for Economic Co-operation and Development is 38.7 percent. The United Kingdom, for example, pays 33.6 percent, Canada 35.6 percent, Germany 39 percent, and Sweden 49.9 percent.[3]

To add insult to injury, the country has the lowest income tax among peer nations for its wealthy citizens. The top tax for millionaires used to be 70 percent; in recent years the top rate has been cut to 33 percent.

No one loves to pay taxes. Voters in the countries mentioned could vote against candidates who support the higher taxation, but they seldom do so. They tolerate higher taxes because they value their guaranteed health care, their living wages, their housing for all, and all the other social programs that are either missing in the United States or remain a hodgepodge depending on the city or state in which an American citizen happens to live. Yet the major media in the United States have been the emphatic voice of every politician and corporate chieftain complaining about "confiscatory taxes."

There is, of course, a remedy. It is true that media power is political power. But it is also true that people power is political power. It has prevailed in the past and it can in the present. Our present conglomerated mass media did not come full-blown from some untouchable deity. They came into existence only because of actions of the Congress of the United States and the presidents who appointed the agencies that are commanded by law to regulate the nonprint media, particularly the Federal Communications Commission, under law the shepherds whose duty is to regulate radio and television. In the early years of the century the conservative three-person majority tore down the fences and let the flock do whatever it pleased wherever it pleased. There was much public protest. The two Democratic minority members held hearings in cities that asked for them, and every hearing was filled to overflowing with outraged listeners and viewers.

The printed media are protected by the First Amendment of the U.S. Constitution, but owners of very large numbers of newspapers are not exempt from antitrust law, especially in what is now a widespread collusion among owners of newspapers to buy and swap papers in order to let one owner have papers covering one large regional cluster that overcomes smaller, independent papers competing for readers and advertisers. It is not surprising that the major printed media have been weak or silent on the abuse of "the public interest" by the licensed media corporations of which they are a part. The same five giant conglomerates also own most of the production companies that create the programs that will be transmitted by the same conglomerates' networks. They own 80 percent of cable networks and use each of the properties to promote their other programs.[4]

As the twenty-first century progresses, so do the possibilities of immense growth in media outlets. President Theodore Roosevelt, a Republican, and President Franklin Roosevelt, a Democrat, demonstrated that conglomerates and monopolies harm the common good and are not beyond the reach of law. Nor are they beyond the reach of the American voters, who increasingly sense that something is wrong in unfair distribution of national wealth, in the growing difficulty of securing proper housing for middle- and low-income families, and in a seemingly numb National Labor Relations Board (NLRB) that once blocked punitive treatment of legal union organizing in the attempt to provide a living wage for the country's workers. There are a number of cases in which newspaper reporters have been illegally fired for union activity that did not disrupt work; their appeals to the NLRB will take—they have been told by the agency—from three to six years for final judgment. In the meantime, newspaper managements typically hire expensive law firms whose specialty is union-busting.

It is not too late to mandate use of the enormous capacities of the country's communications technology and the powers of antitrust actions to diminish the domination of the media by a few powerful conglomerates in whose interest it has been to eliminate from the airwaves and often newspaper and major magazine columns those who speak for social justice.

The raw power of major corporations joined with the media conglomerates has aroused increasing protest on the Internet and in the alternative print and broadcast media. More young people—once the age group attributed the lowest percentage of voting among those eligible—have become activists, mobilizing protests, petitions, and votes. The remedy ultimately will rely on the ballot box.

More of the public, young and old, seem to take with growing seriousness their exercise of the American privilege granted by the U.S. Constitution, permitting every citizen eighteen and over, male and female, to vote for president, vice president, and members of Congress.

These have become the voices of hope.

NOTES

Citations to the New York Times *refer to the national edition; citations to the* Wall Street Journal *refer to the western edition.*

Foreword

1. U.S. Census Bureau, Current Population Reports, "Money Income in the United States: 2001," table A-2.

CHAPTER ONE: COMMON MEDIA FOR AN UNCOMMON NATION

1. *New York Times,* 24 March 2003, 15.
2. *Luce and His Empire,* W. A. Swanberg, (Scribner's Sons, New York, 1972); *CNN MONEY,* 10 January 2000; and *Washington Post,* 16 September 2003, A2.
3. http://media.guardian.co.uk/news/story/0,7541,941565,00.html
4. *The New Yorker,* 9 November 1998, 34.
5. Opensecrets.org, Center for Responsive Politics, for 2000.
6. *Fortune 500,* 2002, and *Fortune Global 500,* 2002, www.fortune.com
7. Harvey Swados, ed., *Years of Conscience: The Muckrakers* (Cleveland: Meridian Books, 1962).
8. Mark Hertsgaard, *On Bended Knee* (New York: Farrar Straus Giroux, 1988).
9. *Vanity Fair,* July 2003, 14.
10. *Index of Free Expression,* www.indexonline.org/news/20030319—unitedstates.shtml
11. S. Rendall, J. Naureckas, and J. Cohen, *The Way Things Aren't: Rush Limbaugh's Reign of Error* (New York: New Press, 1995).
12. *New York Times,* 8 December 2002, sec. 4, 7.
13. *National Journal Technology Daily,* 19 September 2002.
14. *Statistical Abstract of the United States, 2001,* 121st ed. (Washington, D.C.: U.S. Census Bureau, 2001), table 1121.
15. Ben H. Bagdikian, *The Media Monopoly,* 1st ed. (Boston: Beacon Press, 1983).
16. www.dsmarketing.com/usgov—ampli.htm

17. www.thisnation.com/question/028.html; www.historylearningsite. co.uk/finance.htm
18. American Enterprise Institute, "Vital Statistics on Congress," 1984–85 ed. (Washington, D.C.: American Enterprise Institute, 1985), 67, 74, tables 3-7 and 3-5.
19. Center for Responsive Politics, http://opensecrets.org/overs/blio .aspCycle=2000
20. *New York Times*, 6 September 2002.
21. Ibid; www.nydailynews.com/news/story/18669p-17595c.html
22. www.forbes.com
23. *Wall Street Journal*, 13 October 2003.
24. Ibid.; www.forbes.com
25. www.forbes.com
26. http://slate.msn.com/id/1862
27. Ibid.

CHAPTER TWO: THE BIG FIVE

1. www.oldtimecooking.com/Fads/stuff__booths.html
2. *Statistical Abstract of the United States, 2001*, tables 1126, 1128, 1131, 1132, 1133, and 1137.
3. Ibid., tables 1121 and 1271.
4. *Plunkett's Entertainment & Media Industry Almanac, 2002–2003* (Houston: Plunkett Research Ltd., 2002), 7.
5. *Columbia Journalism Review*, www.cjr.org/owners/aoltimewarner .asp
6. *New York Times*, 23 January 2003, 1; *New York Times*, 21 April 2003, C1.
7. *Fortune Magazine*, 15 April 2000, www.fortune.com/home__channel/ fortune500
8. http://disney.go.com/vault/read/walt/index.html
9. http://disney.go.com/disneyaloz/head/Walt
10. www.kitzenwadl.com/site/p183.htm
11. http://disney.go.com/disneyatoz/waltdisney/maincollection/ waltstoryepisode15.html
12. www.achievement.org/autodoc/eisObio-1; www.cjr.org/year/95/6/ ovitz.asp
13. www.latimes.com
14. http://archive.salon.com/books/log/1999/08/13/eisner
15. *Wall Street Journal*, 1 December 2003, 1.
16. William Shawcross, *Murdoch* (New York: Simon & Schuster, 1992), 165–67.

17. www.motherjones.com/mother_jones/MJ95/murdoch.html

18. *New York Times,* 8 October 2003, sec. 3, 1.

19. www.cjr.org/owners/newscorp.asp

20. *New York Times,* 12 August 2003, A17.

21. www.iht.com/articles/89505.htm

22. Rod and Alma Holmgren, *Outrageous Fortune* (Carmel, Calif.: Jackson Press, 2001), 39.

23. *The Nation,* 7–14 January 2002.

24. Erik Barnouw, *The Golden Web* (New York: Oxford University Press, 1968), 2:56–57.

25. A. M. Sperber, *Murrow and His Life and Times* (New York: Bantam Books, 1986).

26. *Executive Enterprise Briefing Book,* October 1986, 20–21; http://ccs.mit.edu/ebb/prs/iokey.html

27. http://www.museum.tv/archives/etv/M/htmlM/mergersanda/mergersanda.htm; *Business Week Online,* 8 May 1989, 119

28. www.ketupa.net/viacom2.htm

29. www.businessweek.com/1999/99_14/b3623001.htm?scriptFramed

30. www.cjr.org/owners/bertelsmann.asp

31. www.thenation.com/issue/981228fisch.htm

32. *Wall Street Journal,* 1 December 2003, 1.

33. *King Henry IV, Part II,* act III.

34. *Broadcasting & Cable,* 13 May 2002, 42.

35. http://media.guardian.co.uk

36. http://archives.cjr.org/year/03/2/lists.asp

37. Ibid.

38. Ibid.

39. Ibid.

40. *Encyclopedia Britannica,* 14th ed., 20: 826.

41. *Encyclopedia Britannica,* 11th ed., 14: 996.

CHAPTER THREE: THE INTERNET

1. http://ei.cs.vt.edu/~history/Internet.History.2.html

2. http://ftp.arl.army.mil/~mike/comphist/eniac-story.html

3. Ibid.

4. http://ftp.arl.net/2/mike/comphistory/eniac-stor7.html

5. http://cyberatlas.internet.com/big_picture/geographics/print/0,,5911_969541,00.html

6. *San Francisco Chronicle,* 21 April 2003, E3.

7. *Webster's New World Dictionary of Computer Terms,* 6th ed. (New York: Simon & Schuster, 1997).

8. www.tu-chemnitz.de/phil/english/chairs/linguist/real/independent/llc/Conference1998/Papers/Nesi.htm
9. *Statistical Abstract of the United States, 2001,* table 1118.
10. *New York Times,* 6 January 2003, 1.
11. *New York Times,* 17 April 2003, F1.
12. Ibid.
13. *Columbia Journalism Review,* November/December 2002, 33.
14. *New York Times,* 4 April 2003, E7.
15. www.uta.edu/english/V/students/collab4/lori.htm
16. www.alternet.org/story.html?StoryID=11854
17. *New York Times,* 20 July 2003, WK3.
18. *New York Times,* 13 March 2003, C1.
19. *New York Times,* 23 April 2003, A10.
20. *San Francisco Chronicle,* 28 April 2002, E1.
21. *New York Times,* 22 April 2003, C1.
22. *Wall Street Journal,* 7 May 2003, 1.
23. *New York Times,* 18 June 2003, C1.
24. U.S. Constitution, article 1, section 8, provision 8.
25. www.clwbar.org/resipsa/jan99/copyright.html
26. www.cnn.com

CHAPTER FOUR: (NOT) ALL THE NEWS THAT'S FIT TO PRINT

1. www.newline.com/sites/wagthedog/Story/index.html
2. Details from U.S. Department of Labor, Bureau of Labor Statistics, 30 January 2001, as reported in "Nation's Unemployment Rises," *New York Times,* 5 January 2002, C1.
3. *San Francisco Chronicle,* 13 April 2001.
4. *New York Times,* 14 April 2001, 1.
5. www.wsws.org/articles/2002/dec2002/lott-d24.shtml
6. State of the Union Speech, 28 January 2003, as released by White House on 28 January 2003.
7. *New York Times,* 10 July 2003, A10.
8. www.waxman.house.gov/news__files/news__articles__jackpot__cabinet__2__24__01.htm
9. *National Journal,* 15 April 2003, 1.
10. http://byrd.senate.gov/byrd__newsoct2002/rls__oct2002/rls__oct2002__2.html
11. *New York Times,* 7 September 2002, 1.
12. Sam Tanenhaus, "Bush's Brain Trust," *Vanity Fair,* July 2003, 114.
13. Senator Hiram Johnson arguing against U.S. entry into World War I,

Speech to U.S. Senate, 1917, in *MacMillan Dictionary of Quotations,* Congressional Record, 1918. 59.

14. A. M. Sperber, *Murrow: His Life and Times* (New York: Bantam Books, 1986), 418.
15. Personal interview with William Shawn, editor of *The New Yorker,* 14 May 1981.
16. Leo Nikolaevich Tolstoy, *War and Peace,* trans. Rosemary Edmonds (London: Penguin Books, 1978).
17. Page Smith, *A New Age Begins: A People's History of the American Revolution* (New York: McGraw-Hill, 1976), vol. 2.
18. *The Oxford History of the American People,* ed. Samuel Eliot Morrison (New York: Oxford University Press, 1965).
19. W. A. Swanberg, *Citizen Hearst* (New York: Charles Scribner's Sons, 1961).

CHAPTER FIVE: ALL THE NEWS THAT FITS?

1. Henry Treece, *The Crusades* (New York: New American Library, 1962).
2. http://archive.salon.com/tech/feature/2001/09/25/arabs_media/print.html
3. Abraham Lincoln, State of the Union Speech to Congress, 1 December 1862.
4. *World News, Inter Press Service,* www.oneworld.net/external/?url=http%3A%2F%2Fwww.oneworld.org%2Fips2%2Fjul98%2F23_13_097.html
5. *The Nation,* 1 July 1989, 4.
6. M. Moscowitz, M. Katz, and R. Levering, *Everybody's Business,* (San Francisco: Harper & Row, 1980), 78 *et seq.*
7. *The Columbia Encyclopedia,* 5th ed. (New York: Columbia University Press and Boston: Houghton Mifflin, 1993).
8. Ibid.
9. Ibid.
10. *New York Times,* 8 June 1951, 1.
11. *New York Times,* 6 December 1975, 12.
12. *New York Times,* 13 September 1973, 1.
13. *New York Times,* 30 August 2002, A4.
14. www.fair.org/articles/suharto-itt.html
15. *San Francisco Chronicle,* 24 April 2003, B5.
16. Charles Rappleye, "Cracking the Church-State Wall," *Columbia*

Journalism Review, January/February 1998, 20; *American Journalism Review,* October 1997, 13.

17. Ibid., 20–24.
18. www.google.com/search?hl=en&ie=ISO-8859-1&q=Jay+Harris%2C +former+publisher+San+Jose+Mercury&btnG=Google+Search
19. www.alternet.org.by Jeff@democraticmedia.org
20. Charles Layton, "Ignoring the Alarm," *American Journalism Review,* March 2003, 21.
21. *Statistical Abstract of the United States, 2002,* table 947; Housing Related Expenditures, National Low-Income Housing Coalition, August 2002, 2.
22. *Business Week,* 5 October 1998.
23. *Statistical Abstract of the United States, 2001,* table 54; market study by Investment Company Institute, www.ici/org/ici__frameset.html.
24. Report 149, 2001 report of Americans for Democratic Action, "The Housing Crisis," Washington, D.C., www.adaction.org/pubs/ 149housingcrisis.html.
22. www.americanfreepress.net/RFA__Articles/Tax__Expert__Says __Sleeping__IRS__G/tax__expert__says__sleeping__irs__g.html
26. Trudy Lieberman, "Lifting the Veil," *Columbia Journalism Review,* January/February 2001, 57.

CHAPTER SIX: PAPER IN THE DIGITAL AGE

1. *Spiritual Media,* Roy Kurzweil, (Viking, New York, 1999); www.planetebook.com/mainpage.asp?webpageid=110
2. www.time.com/time/time100/artists/profile/lucy.html
3. "Circulation of U.S. Daily Newspapers by Population Group," in *Editor & Publisher Yearbook International, 2002,* 82nd ed. (New York: Editor & Publisher, 2002), vii.
4. Ibid., ix.
5. Ben H. Bagdikian, *Reports of an Exaggerated Death* (Berkeley, Calif.: Markle Foundation, 1970).
6. *Plunkett's Entertainment & Media Industry Almanac, 2002–2003* (Houston: Plunket Research, 2002), 33.
7. Ben H. Bagdikian, *The Information Machines* (New York: Harper & Row, 1971), 8.
8. "Newspapers Published in Foreign Countries," *Editor & Publisher Yearbook International, 2002,* sect. 3, 4, 16, 77.
9. "U.S. and Canadian Daily Newspapers," Newspaper Association of

America and Audit Bureau of Circulation, 2001; *Editor & Publisher Yearbook International, 2002,* sect. 1, 5, 6, 9, 3, 7.

10. *Plunkett's Entertainment & Media Industry Almanac, 2002–2003,* 27.
11. Audit Bureau of Circulation; *Plunkett's Entertainment & Media Industry Almanac, 2002–2003.*
12. *Plunkett's Entertainment & Media Industry Almanac, 2002–2003,* 27.
13. Ibid.
14. *Statistical Abstract of the United States, 2001,* table 1134.
15. *The Nation,* 17 February 2003, 7.
16. *Wall Street Journal Online,* 24 January 2003.
17. www.hmco.com/news/release_123102.html
18. *New York Times,* 27 January 2003, A6.
19. Bagdikian, *The Information Machines,* xx.
20. *New York Times,* 1 March 2003, A19.
21. www.hoovers.com/ndustry/snapshot/10,2204, 3400.html
22. *Statistical Abstract of the United States, 2001,* table 852.

CHAPTER SEVEN: REBELLION AND REMEDIES

1. *The Media Monopoly,* 1st ed. (Boston: Beacon Press, 1983), 38.
2. http://talkshows.about.com/library/weekly/aso12902.htm; S. Rendall, J. Naureckas, and J. Cohen, *The Way Things Aren't: Rush Limbaugh's Reign of Error* (New York: New Press, 1995).
3. http://www.tvrundown.com/views/talkrad2.html
4. www.usdoj.gov/atr/public/guidelines/12576.htm
5. *Les Brown's Encyclopedia of Television,* 3rd ed. (Detroit: Gale Research, 1992), 180.
6. *Journalism Quarterly,* Fall 1985, 497.
7. *American Journalism Review,* June 1998, 46.
8. www.requestline.com/archives/May 96/ pirate
9. Terrence Smith, *The Lehrer News Hour,* 8 January 2003.
10. *Washington Post,* 2 July 2002, A13.
11. Giorgio de Santillana, *The Crime of Galileo* (Chicago: University of Chicago Press, 1955).
12. www.ketupa.net/elsevier2.htm
13. *Publishers Weekly Online,* 3/16/98.
14. www.wiley.com/WileyCDA/Section/id-146.html
15. www.earlham.edu/~peters/writing/acrl.htm
16. www.arl.org/sparc; Scholarly Publishing & Academic Resources Coalition, Washington, D.C.
17. *New York Times,* 8 December 1998, D2.

18. www.arl.org/scomm/mergers/MergerRelease-530.pdf
19. Ibid.
20. http://creativecommons.org/faq
21. http://en.wikipedia.org/
22. *New York Times,* 19 May 2003, C4.
23. *New York Times.* 13 January 2003, C4.
24. www.youthvote2000.org/info/factsheet.htm
25. www.freespeech.org
26. *Zine Yearbook, Vol #6,* www.bookfinder.com/. . ./0966482948/-6k
27. Edmund Morris, *Theodore Rex* (New York: Modern Library, 2001), 73.
28. Letter to W.T. Berry, 4 August 1822, quoted in *Letters and Other Writings of James Madison,* published by Order of Congress, 4 vols., R. Fendell, ed. (Philadelphia: Lippincott, 1865), 3:276.

CHAPTER EIGHT: "WON'T THEY EVER LEARN?"

1. Kenneth A. Randall, president of the Conference Board, quoted in the *Los Angeles Times,* 3 December 1980, 1. The Conference Board, a policy study group, is supported by major industries.
2. Don Carlos Seitz, *Joseph Pulitzer* (New York: Simon & Schuster, 1924), 35. Pulitzer's trustee device did not save the *New York World.* The paper continued to enjoy prestige and influence because of its writers, among them Walter Lippmann, Heywood Broun, Alexander Woollcott, Frank Cobb, Herbert Bayard Swope, and Franklin P. Adams. But Pulitzer's will of 1904 and codicil permitted relatives to succeed original trustees, and family heirs had different ideas for the paper. After years of high profits and a few years of reduced ones, the heirs killed the most famous paper, the morning *World,* then they killed the *Sunday World,* and sold the evening *World* to its New York competitor, the Scripps-Howard *Telegram,* where it became the *World-Telegram.*
3. Oliver S. Owen, *Natural Resource Conservation,* 2nd ed. (New York: Macmillan, 1975); hazardous waste data from *Time,* 22 September 1980, 58.
4. Grant McConnell, *Private Power and American Democracy* (New York: Knopf, 1966).
5. *Harvard Business Review,* January/February 1977, 57.
6. *Business Week,* 31 January 1977, 107.
7. *San Francisco Chronicle,* 17 July 1979, 40.
8. Department of Justice, Law Enforcement Assistance Administration, *Illegal Corporate Behavior,* October 1979.

9. Gregory C. Staple, "Free-Market Cram Course for Judges," *The Nation*, 26 January 1980, 78–81.

10. Ovid Demaris, *Dirty Business* (New York: Harper's Magazine Press, 1974), 10.

11. *New York Times*, 15 July 1979, 1.

12. Data provided to author by IRS.

13. *The Nation*, 11–18 August 1979, 101.

14. G. William Domhoff, *The Powers That Be* (New York: Random House, 1978), 44.

15. Senate Committee on Government Operations, *Advisory Committees*, 1970.

16. Mark Green and Andrew Buchsbaum, *The Corporate Lobbies* (Washington, D.C.: Public Citizen, February 1980).

17. Sheila Harty, *Hucksters in the Classroom* (Washington, D.C.: Center for the Study of Responsive Law, 1979).

18. Each year a national panel is asked to select the most important developments untouched or deemphasized by the major media. The panel is directed by the Department of Sociology, Sonoma State University, California.

19. James North, "The Effect: The Growth of the Special Interests," *Washington Monthly*, October 1978.

20. *Wall Street Journal*, 27 July 1977, 1.

21. *Dun's Review*, May 1977, 76.

22. *Broadcasting*, 27 April 1981, 76.

23. Senate Subcommittee on Administrative Practices and Procedures, *Sourcebook on Corporate Image and Corporate Advocacy Advertising*, 1978, 882.

24. *Editor & Publisher*, 8 December 1979, 10.

25. *Editor & Publisher*, 24 November 1979, 15.

26. Stephen Hess, *The Washington Reporters* (Washington, D.C.: Brookings Institution, 1981).

27. *Wall Street Journal*, 4 August 1976, 32.

28. John Brooks, "Profile," *The New Yorker*, 5 January 1981, 41.

29. Bureau of the Census, *Statistical Abstract of the United States, 1980* (Washington, D.C., 1981), 487, 481.

30. David Finn, *The Business-Media Relationship* (New York: American Management Association, 1981), 50.

31. *Dun's Review*, May 1977, 81.

32. Quoted in *Mother Jones*, February/March 1980, 32.

33. Senate Subcommittee on Administrative Practices and Procedures, *Sourcebook on Corporate Image and Corporate Advocacy Advertising*, 1978, 78.

34. Senate Committee on the Judiciary, *Sourcebook*, 581.

35. Michael Gerrard, "This Man Was Made Possible by a Grant from Mobil Oil," *Esquire*, January 1979, 62.

36. *Broadcasting*, 29 September 1980, 46.

37. *The Nation*, 24 May 1980, 609.

38. *Broadcasting*, 12 May 1980, 30.

39. *Columbia Journalism Review*, September/October 1981, 26. The Mobil ad described an energy-saving project of the Benedictine Sisters in Erie, Pennsylvania. Mobil had asked the sisters to grant it permission to use them and their project in its ads. The Benedictine Sisters refused. Mobil nevertheless did use the sisters and their project in the Mobil ad that ran in ten major newspapers. When the prioress wrote to each paper, disassociating the sisters from the ad, only the *Los Angeles Times* printed her letter. The papers that refused were the *Wall Street Journal*, the *Denver Post*, the *Chicago Tribune*, the *Washington Post*, the *New York Times*, the *Boston Globe*, the *Dallas Times Herald*, the *Houston Post*, and the *Christian Science Monitor*.

40. Gerrard, "This Man Was Made Possible . . ."

41. "The Big Oil Shuffle," *New West*, 16 July 1979, 24.

42. Ibid.

43. Gerrard, "This Man Was Made Possible . . ."; Milton Moskowitz, Michael Katz, and Robert Levering, eds., *Everybody's Business Almanac* (New York: Harper & Row, 1980), 513–17.

44. Department of Energy, Financial Reporting System, *Performance Profiles of Major Energy Producers, 1979*, July 1981.

45. Edward F. Roby, UPI Story A262, 5 June 1981.

46. The ad ran in eleven major newspapers, including the *New York Times*, on June 18, 1981.

47. House Committee on Ways and Means, *Recommendations of the Task Force on Foreign Source Income*, 8 March 1977; House Committee on Government Operations, *Foreign Tax Credits Claimed by the U.S. Petroleum Companies*, 24th report, 1978; *The Foreign Tax Credit and U.S. Energy Policy: Report to the United States Congress by the Comptroller General* (Washington, D.C.: 10 September 1980), particularly i and ii.

48. Testimony of Jack A. Blum, Counsel, Independent Gasoline Marketers Council, before the House Committee on Government Operations, 13 March 1979. Also Hobart Rowen, "Chinese Shuffle Trade Policy to Accommodate U.S.," *Washington Post*, 24 December 1978.

49. Edward F. Roby, UPI Story A221, 6 July 1981; UPI Story A271, transmitted 7 July 1981 for use 11 July 1981. The story that some major oil companies had written Secretary Watt to request reduction in acreage open for bids also appeared in major newspapers in stories written by other reporters: Andy Pasztor, "Offshore Energy

Leasing Plans Trimmed as Interior's Watt Retreats Amid Criticism," *Wall Street Journal*, 6 July 1981; Charles R. Babcock, "Watt Defies Critics of Oil Plan for Oil Leases," *Washington Post*, 7 July 1981. Similar stories also appeared in trade papers, including *Oil Daily*, 9 June 1981. But only Roby and UPI were mentioned in the counterattack by Exxon and petroleum public relations agencies.

50. Teletype on Exxon's national public relations wire: "To Business Desks, PRW3/Press Relations Wire Wash 347-5155. For Immediate Release 07/10/81. EXXON USA SUPPORTS CHANGES IN OFFSHORE LEASING PROGRAM. Several news reports recently have misrepresented Exxon's position on the Department of Interior's proposed changes in the offshore leasing program.... FYI, UPI moved a story 8 July 81 for weekend use ... by Edward Roby." The same message was sent by printed press release to editors around the country: "News, Exxon Company, U.S.A.... July 10, 1981. EXXON USA SUPPORTS CHANGES IN OFFSHORE LEASING PROGRAM. Houston—Several news reports ..." Roby was similarly named.

51. Press release of American Petroleum Institute, Washington, D.C., 28 July 1981: "NOTE TO EDITORS: The attached statement by Charles J. DiBona, president of the American Petroleum Institute, is provided in response to inquiries from the news media about offshore leasing proposals of Interior Secretary James G. Watt."

52. Quoted in *Editor & Publisher*, 4 July 1981.

CHAPTER NINE: FROM MYTHOLOGY TO THEOLOGY

1. Neuharth, "Newspapers: Dominating Their Markets; Gannett: Never a Down Quarter," address to the New York Society of Security Analysts, 11 March 1976.

2. Frank Luther Mott, *American Journalism: A History, 1690–1960* (New York: Macmillan, 1972), 649; Carl Lindstrom, *The Fading American Newspaper* (New York: Doubleday, 1960).

3. Lindstrom, *The Fading American Newspaper*, 90.

4. Alfred McClung Lee, *The Daily Newspaper in America* (New York: Macmillan, 1937), 196.

5. *The First Freedom* (Carbondale: Southern Illinois University Press, 1968), 21–22.

6. Lee, *Daily Newspaper in America*, 112.

7. *Editor & Publisher*, 16 February 1963.

8. White, quoted in George Seldes, *Lords of the Press* (New York: Julian Messner, 1938), 274.

9. William Allen White, *The Autobiography of William Allen White* (New York: Macmillan, 1964), 629.

10. Personal observations and the *Los Angeles Times*, 7 September 1978, 1.

11. *Broadcasting*, 25 May 1981, 65; *Editor & Publisher*, 8 August 1981, 10, and 19 September 1981, 27.

12. Ben H. Bagdikian, *Reports of an Exaggerated Death* (Berkeley, Calif.: Markle Foundation, 1970).

13. "Notice of Special Meeting and Joint Proxy Statement," Gannett Co., Inc., Rochester, N.Y., 25 January 1979.

14. From memorandums to Gannett local publishers made available to the author.

15. Lee, *Daily Newspaper in America*; Federal Trade Commission, Bureau of Competition, *Proceedings of the Symposium on Media Concentration*, vol. 1, 14–15 December 1978; *Editor & Publisher Yearbooks*; *Yale Law Journal*, vol. 74 (1965), 1339.

16. Otis Chandler, quoted in *Business Week*, 21 February 1977, 59.

17. *Editor & Publisher*, 10 March 1979, 16.

18. *Circulation 80/81*, 19th ed. (Malibu, Calif.: American Newspaper Markets, 1980).

19. *Value Line Investment Advisory Service*, 22 September 1979.

20. From *Washington Journalism Review*, October 1980.

21. National Black Media Coalition, "Gannett-Combined Communications Merger: Background and Policy Implications" (Washington, D.C., 7 June 1978).

22. *John Morton Newspaper Research Letter*, 30 June 1979, 2.

23. Neuharth, speech to 93rd Annual Convention of American Newspaper Publishers Association, 23 April 1979, reported in *Editor & Publisher*, 18 October 1980, 16.

24. From Gannett memorandums made available to the author.

25. Cassandra Tate, *Columbia Journalism Review*, July/August 1981, 51–56.

26. Tate, *Columbia Journalism Review*.

27. *Rochester Patriot*, 23 October–5 November 1974, 1

28. Jon O. Newman, U.S. District Circuit Judge, "Memorandum of Decision," *Gannett Co. Inc. v. The Register Publishing Co.*, Civil No. B-74-123, 10 April 1980.

29. *Editor & Publisher*, 23 June 1979, 14.

30. *New York Times*, 6 March 1979.

31. *Los Angeles Times*, 7 September 1978, 1.

32. *John Morton Newspaper Research Letter*, 31 January 1979, 8.

33. *Editor & Publisher Yearbook*, 1974 and 1978, citing circulation data for previous years from Audit Bureau of Circulation.

34. Neuharth, address to American Society of Newspaper Editors, 2 May 1977, published by Gannett Company.
35. Calculations by the author.
36. *Emporia Gazette,* 2 October 1979, 4.
37. *Emporia Gazette,* 30 September 1979, 4.
38. *Publishers Auxiliary,* 5 November 1979, 1, 3.
39. *Parsons Sun,* 1 October 1979, 6.
40. *Emporia Gazette,* 30 September 1979, 4.
41. Pam Eversole, "Consolidation of Newspapers: What Happens to the Consumer?" *Journalism Quarterly,* Summer 1971, 245.
42. *Straus Editor's Report,* 13 December 1969, 1.
43. *Help: The Useful Almanac, 1978–1979* (Washington, D.C.: Consumer News, 1978), 398.
44. "Quantity of News in Group-Owned and Independent Papers: Independent Papers Have More," master's thesis, Graduate School of Journalism, University of California, Berkeley, 15 June 1978.
45. Annual summaries of *Editor & Publisher* and *John Morton Newspaper Research Letter.* Employment figures for Gannett newspaper employees from John C. Quinn, senior vice president for news for Gannett Company. In 1966 Gannett had 6,500 employees of all kinds in its newspapers. In 1980 it had 15,755, of whom 4,122 were engaged in news operations (as opposed to production, sales, and the like). Quinn stated that the company had no record of 1966 figures for newsroom employees but did have such records for 1974. I applied the 1974 percentage of newsroom employees, as given to the company, to the 1966 figure for all newspaper workers in the chain and obtained the estimate of 1,430 newsroom workers in 1966. This is probably slightly in error, though not substantially, because the 1966 total had not yet been reduced by automation in nonnews functions, as the total of workers was by 1974. My calculation is that the 1966 estimate could vary by as much as 57 newsroom workers for the entire chain, a maximum variation that would not affect the basic conclusion. Despite the addition of many papers and new editions, the average size of Gannett papers remained remarkably close from 1966 to 1980. In 1966 the average Gannett daily paper had a circulation of 44,539; in 1980 circulation was 43,988.
46. Scripps-Howard. Daniel B. Wackman, Donald M. Gillmor, Cecile Gaziano, and Everett E. Dennis, "Chain Newspaper Autonomy as Reflected in Presidential Campaign Endorsements," *Journalism Quarterly,* Autumn 1975, 411–20; *Editor & Publisher,* 4 November 1972, 9–11; *New York Times,* 29 October 1972, 21; *Wall Street Journal,* 26 September 1980, 1.

47. CBS-TV, "The Business of Newspapers," 14 July 1978.

48. *Editor & Publisher*, 20 April 1968.

49. Lloyd Gray, "From 'Moderately Liberal' to 'Doctrinaire Libertarian,'" *Bulletin of the American Society of Newspaper Editors*, February 1981.

50. Ralph R. Thrift Jr., "How Chain Ownership Affects Editorial Vigor of Newspapers," *Journalism Quarterly*, Summer 1967, 329.

51. Stephen Hess, *The Washington Reporters* (Washington, D.C.: Brookings Institution, 1981), 136–66.

52. "New Cash System Gives Gannett Extra Funds," *Editor & Publisher*, 1 December 1979, 13.

53. *Editor & Publisher*, 10 January 1981, 55.

54. *Editor & Publisher*, 4 December 1976, 10.

55. *Editor & Publisher*, 25 December 1976, 8.

56. *Editor & Publisher*, 14 July 1979, 9.

57. *Los Angeles Times*, 7 September 1978, 1.

58. *Santa Fe New Mexican*, 27 February 1976, 1.

59. Peter Katel, "When the Takeover Doesn't Take," *Bulletin of the American Society of Newspaper Editors*, February 1981, 23.

60. Ibid.

61. Judge Santiago E. Campos, "Memorandum Opinion," *Robert M. McKinney v. Gannett Co., Inc., and* The New Mexican, Civil No. 78-630 C, 17 March 1981, 19–20.

62. Campos, "Memorandum Opinion."

63. Supplied to author by Gannett Company.

CHAPTER TEN: "DEAR MR. PRESIDENT..."

1. Jonathan Daniels, "An Editor's Diagnosis," *Saturday Review of Literature*, 30 April 1955, 11.

2. Berlin correspondence obtained by the author through Freedom of Information Act.

3. From annual editions of *Editor & Publisher Yearbook*; Christopher H. Sterling and Timothy R. Haight, *The Mass Media: Aspen Institute Guide to Industry Trends* (New York: Praeger, 1978); Federal Trade Commission, *Proceedings on the Symposium on Media Control*, vols. 1 and 2, 1978.

4. *Progressive*, July 1979, 39.

5. Frank Leeming, Katharine Graham, Joseph Costello, and the National Association of Broadcasters, *Congressional Quarterly*, 2 August 1980, 2179.

6. Nick Kotz, *Progressive*, July 1979, 40.

7. Senate Subcommittee on Antitrust and Monopoly, *Hearings*, pt. 6, in consideration of Newspaper Preservation Act.
8. *Editor & Publisher*, 18 April 1981, 222.
9. Senate Subcommittee on Antitrust and Monopoly, *Hearings*, 1967–69.
10. Christopher Lydon, "Aide Says Nixon Opposes Easing of Trust Laws for Weak Papers," *New York Times*, 21 June 1969, 30. Weeks later, the Department of Commerce, taking a position on the Newspaper Preservation Act for the first time in the three-year history of the proposal, issued a statement for the Nixon administration in favor of the bill. Eileen Shanahan, "Nixon Supports Newspaper Bill," *New York Times*, 26 September 1969, 94.
11. Dirks Brothers, *Newspaper Newsletter*, 31 October 1972, 1.
12. Ben H. Bagdikian, "The Fruits of Agnewism," *Columbia Journalism Review*, January/February 1973.
13. Paul Delaney, "Cox Tells Papers to Endorse Nixon," *New York Times*, 23 October 1972.

CHAPTER ELEVEN: ONLY THE AFFLUENT NEED APPLY

1. Nizen, quoted in *Editor & Publisher*, 3 January 1981, 15.
2. Number of ad pages, revenues, and dividends from annual reports of F-R Corporation.
3. Origins of the Schell article, its consequences, and statements of William Shawn from personal interview with Shawn, editor of *The New Yorker*, 14 May 1981.
4. From periodic readership studies by *The New Yorker* and from Simmons Surveys.
5. *Wall Street Journal*, 4 June 1981, 14.
6. *FOLIO: 400*, September 1981, 32.
7. Paul Klein, quoted in *Broadcasting*, 9 January 1978, 32.
8. *Broadcasting*, 9 January 1978, 32.
9. *Broadcasting*, 10 November 1980.
10. *Public Relations Journal*, November 1978.
11. From Bureau of the Census, *Historical Statistics of the United States* (Washington, D.C., 1975); Bureau of the Census, *Statistical Abstract of the United States, 1981* (Washington, D.C., 1981).
12. John C. Ginn, speech before Newspaper Forum, reported in *John Morton Newspaper Research Letter*, 9 April 1980.
13. Monograph by William B. Blankenburg, "Newspaper Ownership

and Circulation Behavior," University of Wisconsin, Madison, 3 August 1981.

14. Transcript of interview with Chandler by KABC-TV, Los Angeles, 18–29 October 1979.
15. *Washington Post,* 24 July 1977.
16. *Profiles of The New Yorker Subscribers and Their Households* (New York: *The New Yorker,* n.d.). Though undated, the book reports a 1980 survey.
17. *The New Yorker,* 5 October 1981.

CHAPTER TWELVE: DR. BRANDRETH HAS GONE TO HARVARD

1. *American Journalism* (New York: Macmillan, 1972), 231.
2. Alfred McClung Lee, *The Daily Newspaper in America* (New York: Macmillan, 1937), 317.
3. *San Francisco Chronicle,* 3 January 2003, C3.
4. Frank Presbery, *The History and Development of Advertising* (New York: Doubleday, Doran, 1929), 396.
5. Erik Barnouw, *Tube of Plenty* (New York: Oxford University Press, 1975), 170.
6. Federal Communications Commission, *Second Interim Report by the Office of Network Study, Television Network Program Procurement* (Washington, D.C., 1965).
7. Senate Committee on Interstate and Foreign Commerce, *Report* (Washington, D.C., 1963), 446–53.
8. Individual verbatim testimony in FCC hearing is from *New York Times,* 27 September 1961, 28 September 1961, 29 September 1961, 30 September 1961, 3 October 1961, 4 October 1961, 5 October 1961, 7 October 1961, 8 October 1961.
9. *Fortune,* 31 December 1979, 70.
10. *New York Times,* 28 September 1961, 163.
11. Barnouw, *Tube of Plenty,* 163.
12. Theodore Peterson, *Magazines in the Twentieth Century* (Urbana: University of Illinois Press, 1975), 5.
13. *Time,* 28 September 1942, 51–52.
14. Peterson, *Magazines in the Twentieth Century,* 279.
15. "Look, Reader's Digest." *Advertising Age,* 19 November 1962, 1.
16. *Advertising Age,* 17 April 1972, 85.
17. Ben H. Bagdikian, "Newspaper Mergers," *Columbia Journalism Review,* March/April 1977, 19–20.

18. *Publishers Weekly,* 17 June 1968, 49.
19. Housing Research Group, *For Sale or for Rent* (Washington, D.C.: Center for Responsive Law, 1978).
20. *Editor & Publisher,* 18 October 1980, 20.
21. "Food Section Survey," Food Editors Conference, Chicago, October 1977.
22. *Editor & Publisher,* 31 March 1979, 11.
23. *Editor & Publisher,* 29 March 1980, 15. Joseph N. Uhl, director of the project, said that papers stopped carrying the reports after complaints from grocers.
24. *Washington Journalism Review,* October 1980, 46–47.
25. *Editor & Publisher,* 31 January 1981, 7, 44
26. http://users.erols.com/mwhite28/waisat 8.atm#smokers.
27. Moskowitz et al., *Everybody's Business Almanac.*
28. *Frontline,* www.pbs.org/wgbh/pages/frontline/shows/settlement/timelines/criminal.html
29. *New York Times,* 22 July 1963, 35.
30. R. C. Smith, "The Magazines' Smoking Habit," *Columbia Journalism Review,* January/February 1978, 29–31.
31. *Mother Jones* carried articles on smoking hazards in its issues of April 1979 and January 1980, after which all its advertisements from tobacco companies were canceled. From interviews with publisher of *Mother Jones.*
32. Press release of American Council on Science and Health, San Francisco, 29 January 1980.
33. "The Deadly Balance," *Columbia Journalism Review,* Fall 1965, 13.
34. *Editor & Publisher,* 24 July 1954.
35. Meyers, Iscoe, Jennings, Lenox, Minsky, and Sacks, *Staff Report of the Cigarette Advertising Investigation* (Washington, D.C.: Federal Trade Commission, May 1981), 5.
36. *Frontline,* www.pbs.org/wgbh/pages/frontline/shows/settlement/timelines/criminal.html

AFTERWORD: PARADISE LOST OR PARADISE REGAINED? SOCIAL JUSTICE IN DEMOCRACY

1. *World Press Encyclopedia ,* vol. 1, 559.
2. www.parentstv.org/ptc/facts/mediafacts.asp
3. www.tcf.org/Publications/Tax/History.html
4. www.creativecommunity.us

ACKNOWLEDGMENTS

Many years ago a fellowship from the John Simon Guggenheim Foundation permitted me to suspend news reporting for a year in order to study the history of newspapers and the evolution of their individual, family, and corporate ownership. I spent months in the stacks of the Library of Congress, receiving the benefit of its helpful staff. May that institution be forever protected from enemies, domestic and foreign. Later, the John and Mary Markle Foundation supported extensive research on factors that make for failure and success in newspapers and for travel to all parts of the country to interview publishers on why their papers had failed or, with others, why they thought their papers had succeeded. These grants led to my belief that there was a process emerging that would bring fundamental change in all mass media industries. Annual grants from the Committee on Research of the Academic Senate of the University of California at Berkeley and sabbatical leaves from the Graduate School of Journalism were indispensable.

Many research assistants helped along the way: Marian Bryant, Amy Troubh, Suzanne Donovan, Alysson Pytte, Dan Wohlfeiler, Fred Goff, Zoia Horn, Lyn Heffernan, Gail Nichols, and the Data Center of Oakland with its unparalleled corporate files of world newspapers.

Thanks to my son, Chris Bagdikian, and to Patti Keller, Roger Rosenblum, Jonathan Coppersthwaite, and especially Joshua Waggy, a magician who saved innumerable lost documents in Microsoft's purgatory and provided therapy for my various computers. For work on this major revision of the entire book, Michael Levy, a professional research librarian, displayed a wizardry for locating arcane information that convinces me that if he and computers had been around in 1930, he would have found Judge Crater. Bart Harloe, librarian at St. Lawrence University, provided crucial guidance to people and organizations who contributed to the section on the impact of monopoly on scientific and scholarly research.

My gratitude to the editors of Beacon Press, who have had faith in this work over the years, from the first edition twenty years ago, before critiques of the mass media had become a cottage industry, to this basically new book, the seventh edition, that deals with new media in a new world. Special thanks to my editor on this new edition, Christopher Vyce.

My everlasting thanks to my wife, Marlene Griffith, who interrupted her own editing in order to give warm support and frequent rescue to a husband with a receding hairline and deadline in order to apply her penetrating eye and incorruptible logic.

I recite the cliché of acknowledgments in order to protect the innocent: many helped but I alone am responsible for the final results.

BEN H. BAGDIKIAN

INDEX